CONTEXTS
WRITING and READING

CONTEXTS

WRITING and READING

Second Edition

Jeanette Harris
TEXAS TECH UNIVERSITY

Ann Moseley
EAST TEXAS STATE UNIVERSITY

HOUGHTON MIFFLIN COMPANY • BOSTON

Dallas • Geneva, Illinois • Palo Alto • Princeton, New Jersey

To Paul W. Barrus, who taught us the value of reading
and writing.

Acknowledgments

The authors are grateful to the following for granting permission to reprint excerpts from their work:

Mortimer J. Adler, "How to Mark a Book," *Saturday Review of Literature,* July 6, 1940. Copyright © 1940 by Mortimer J. Adler; copyright © renewed 1967 by Mortimer J. Adler. Reprinted by permission of the author.

From *I Know Why the Caged Bird Sings* by Maya Angelou. Copyright © 1969 by Maya Angelou. Reprinted by permission of Random House, Inc.

From *Please Explain* by Isaac Asimov. Copyright © 1973 by Isaac Asimov. Reprinted by permission of Houghton Mifflin Company.

Peggy Charren and Martin W. Sandler, *Changing Channels: Living (Sensibly) with Television,* © 1983, Addison-Wesley Publishing Co., Reading, Massachusetts. Pages 45–46, 61–63. Reprinted with permission.

From *The Water is Wide* by Pat Conroy. Copyright © 1972 by Pat Conroy. Reprinted with permission of Houghton Mifflin Company.

From *I Heard the Owl Call My Name* by Margaret Craven. Reprinted by permission of Doubleday, a division of Bantam, Doubleday, Dell Publishing Group, Inc.

From *Nobody Ever Died of Old Age* by Sharon R. Curtin. Copyright © 1972 by Sharon R. Curtin. Parts of this excerpt appeared as "Aging in the Land of the Young" in *The Atlantic Monthly,* July 1972. By permission of Little, Brown and Company in association with the Atlantic Monthly Press.

From "Just Enough for the City" by Robert Murray Davis as originally appeared in *North Dakota Quarterly,* Vol. 54, pp. 240–247. Reprinted by permission.

From *Writing With Power* by Peter Elbow, pp. 13, 14–15. Copyright © 1981 by Oxford University Press, Inc. Reprinted by permission.

From *Invisible Man* by Ralph Ellison. Reprinted by permission of Random House, Inc.

From *College is Only the Beginning* by John N. Gardner and A. Jerome Jewler. © 1985 by Wadsworth, Inc. Reprinted by permission of the publisher.

From *Between Parent and Teenager* by Haim G. Ginott. Reprinted by permission of Dr. Alice Ginott.

Nathan Glazer, "Some Very Modest Proposals for the Improvement of American Education" is reprinted by permission of *Daedalus,* Journal of the American Academy of Arts and Sciences, Values, Resources, and Politics in America's Schools, Vol. 113, No. 4, Fall 1984, Cambridge, MA.

From *Elvis Is Dead and I Don't Feel So Good Myself* by Lewis Grizzard is reprinted by permission of Grizzard Enterprises, Inc.

From *All Creatures Great and Small* by James Herriot. Copyright © 1972 by James Herriot. Reprinted by permission of St. Martin's Press, Inc., New York, and Harold Ober Associates Incorporated.

From *Something in Common* by Langston Hughes. Reprinted by permission of Harold Ober Associates Incorporated. Copyright 1952 by Langston Hughes. Copyright renewed 1980 by George Houston Bass.

Acknowledgments are continued on page 392.

Cover photograph by R. Terry Walker/The Picture Cube.

Library of Congress Catalog Card Number: 88-81334

Student Edition ISBN: 0-395-38006-5

Instructor's Annotated Edition ISBN: 0-395-48854-0

BCDEFGHIJ-S-9543210-89

CONTENTS

PREFACE

Contexts, Second Edition, like the first edition, reflects our conviction that writing and reading skills are most effectively developed when they provide a learning context for each other. *Contexts* teaches writing and reading as an integrated process and provides numerous examples and exercises to help students learn the concepts and develop the skills that are essential to both disciplines.

NEW TO THIS EDITION

We have made several important changes that make the integration of instruction in writing and reading even more effective in this Second Edition.

- **Increased variety of reading selections.** We have selected all of the readings carefully so that they will challenge but not overwhelm students, varying the length so that students can have experience with both long and short passages. Many readings are familiar literary selections; others are taken from textbooks representing different academic disciplines or from current periodicals. The reading selections within the chapters also include student writing and our own model paragraphs and essays.
- **Additional instruction on summarizing, outlining, critical reading, and essay examinations.** We have emphasized outlining throughout the text instead of isolating it in one chapter. We have expanded the section on summarizing and added a new section on critical reading and on writing essay examinations.
- **New chapter on methods of development.** We have completely rewritten this chapter to reflect current theory on this topic more accurately.
- **Two featured Reading/Writing Assignments at the end of each chapter.** We have added an additional Reading/Writing Assignment to each chapter. Emphasizing reading and writing as recursive processes, the exercises that accompany the reading selections emphasize the concept of process—preparation, drafting, and review. Also, we have included additional instruction on prewriting and prereading and checklists for editing and revising.
- **Revised Appendixes.** We have added an appendix on punctuation and an appendix on irregular verb forms.

ORGANIZATION

As before, Part One begins with reading and writing paragraphs and moves to essays; Part Two covers sentence structure, usage, and punctuation. This organization reflects our belief that students need a language context in which to develop reading and writing skills and that the paragraph is the most effective context for learning these skills initially. All of the concepts that the students learn in studying the paragraph can be applied later to the essay and the sentence. We encourage teachers to intersperse instruction on the sentence with instruction on the paragraph and essay, but we believe that instruction on the sentence, and the corresponding emphasis on editing skills, can also be covered in the latter half of the course.

Part One leads students step by step through the process of reading and writing effective paragraphs and essays. Chapter One provides students with an overview of the reading and writing processes. Chapter 2 introduces students to the important concept of general and specific words and sentences and to simple outlining. In Chapter 3, "Main Ideas," students begin an intensive study of the paragraph. Chapter 4, "Supporting Main Ideas," continues the study of the paragraph by providing practice with factual and sensory details, explaining the concepts of coordination and subordination, and introducing planning outlines. Chapter 5, "Developing Main Ideas," focuses on the familiar methods of development—narration, description, illustration, comparison/contrast, classification, cause and effect, and definition. Chapter 6, "Arranging and Connecting Ideas," discusses first the most common patterns of arrangement—chronological order, space order, and order of importance—and then the use of transitions to reinforce these patterns. With Chapter 7, "Reading and Writing Essays," students begin to read and write essays as well as paragraphs. Chapter 8, "Summarizing and Reacting to Ideas," concludes the first part with instruction on study outlines, summarizing, drawing conclusions, and critical reading and writing.

Part Two emphasizes the sentence but also continues instruction on reading and writing paragraphs and essays in the two Reading/Writing Assignments at the end of each chapter. Chapter 9, "The Simple Sentence," focuses on the essential elements and the basic patterns of the sentence. Chapter 10 illustrates how the simple sentence can be expanded through modification. Chapter 11, "Coordination: The Compound Sentence," and Chapter 12, "Subordination: The Complex Sentence," continue the instruction on coordination and subordination, this time at the sentence level. The editing sections included at the end of each chapter focus on writing correct sentences, with particular attention to punctuation, misplaced and dangling modifiers, fragments, and common run-on sentence errors.

The four appendixes, "Capitalization," "Spelling," "Forms of Irregular Verbs," and "Punctuation," offer additional instruction that can be used by individual students or by the class as a whole.

The exercises in the text focus consistently on the important role of *context* in both reading and writing. Sentence composition, sentence combining, and cloze passages promote reading comprehension as well as writing fluency. Various exercises allow students to develop their abilities to use effective transitions, establish paragraph coherence and unity, and write different types of sentences. Most exercises emphasize correctness rather than errors, providing models but also pointing out options; however, practice in editing and proofreading for specific types of errors is also included.

ACKNOWLEDGMENTS

Although at the beginning of this project we naively believed that the Second Edition would be much easier to write than the first, we discovered that revising *Contexts* was much like writing the original book and that our indebtedness to those who helped us was even greater this time around. We were especially fortunate in having the following thoughtful, articulate reviewers evaluate the manuscript at various stages: Hilda Attride, Riverside City College, CA; Shirley Biggs, University of Pittsburgh; Carolyn M. Birden, Community College of Philadelphia; George R. Bodmer, Indiana University Northwest; Baji Majette Daniels, Contra Costa College, CA; Jan Delasara, Metropolitan State University, CO; Karen Nelson Gleeman, Normandale Community College, MN; Karen Hattaway, San Jacinto College, TX; Diane A. Henningfeld, Adrian College, MI; Patricia Hinchey, Pennsylvania State University; Susan Huard, Community College of the Finger Lakes, NY; David B. Jacobson, Contra Costa College, CA; Paul J. Kameen, University of Pittsburgh; Larry G. Mapp, Middle Tennessee State University; Karen Quinn, University of Illinois at Chicago; John Roggenbeck, Henry Ford Community College, MI; Deborah Smith, Southern University, LA; Doris Snyder, Northeastern Oklahoma A & M.

We would also like to thank the students who contributed paragraphs and essays and Susan Mitchell and Phillip Ballard, who shared with us the essays their students had written based on the assignments in the first edition. Finally, we would like to thank our families and friends, whose support was as essential to this second edition as it was to the first.

J. H.
A. M.

CONTEXTS
WRITING and READING

Part One

THE PARAGRAPH

Context can be defined as the immediate surroundings of a person or thing. Your home, work, and school are the contexts in which you operate in your daily life. But language also has context. Words and sentences usually exist within a larger language context, and, to a great extent, it is this context that determines their meaning. For example, the word *ring* can refer to a piece of jewelry or the sound that a bell makes. Almost every word has different meanings or shades of meaning. You can *make* a bed, a decision, an error, a pie, a new start, or a mess.

In order to understand words, you must see or hear them in context—in a sentence with other words that give you clues to their meaning. Even sentences are more easily understood in context. The meaning of a given sentence frequently depends on the sentences that come before and after it. For example, read the following sentences to decide what each one "means."

1. The wind and hail damaged the new plant.
2. The young woman made the basket easily.
3. His chest was badly damaged.

The first sentence could be a report of weather damage to a recently planted bush or to a newly built factory. The second sentence could describe a basketball player or a weaver of baskets. And the third sentence could be a medical report or a description of a piece of broken furniture. Without the sentences that come before and after, you cannot be sure what these sentences mean. In order to communicate clearly, a writer must provide a context for the reader, who then uses that context to determine the writer's meaning.

The need for context is only one of many concerns that readers and writers share. Reading and writing are related processes that require many of the same skills. Furthermore, reading often provides you with information and ideas that you can use when you write. And writing about what you read helps you understand and remember what you have read.

This book reflects our conviction that reading and writing skills are more effectively developed when they create a context for each other. Some lessons may seem more like reading lessons to you, and others may seem more like writing lessons (old habits of thinking of the two separately are hard to break). But many of the lessons will be so integrated that you will not really be sure whether to think of them as reading lessons or writing lessons. We hope, in fact, that by the end of the book you will not even be concerned about making a distinction because you will have accepted the idea that a reading lesson is also a writing lesson and that a writing lesson is also a reading lesson. When you reach that point, you will have become a better reader and a more effective writer.

Chapter 1

THE READING/WRITING PROCESS

Asked to describe what happens when she writes, one student responded, "My writing is a process of thinking, writing, thinking, scratching out, thinking, writing again, and sometimes starting the whole process over." This same student also commented that, for her, "Writing is a struggle with the pen to sort out a complex bundle of words." It is not easy to step back and view yourself as a reader or a writer. By the time you are an adult, these processes have become so familiar that you seldom think about what you do when you read or write. But one of the most important steps in improving your writing and reading skills is becoming aware of what happens as you read and write.

First, good readers and writers realize that both processes consist of three broad stages:

1. Preparation (prereading and prewriting)
2. Reading/writing (processing of information)
3. Review (rereading and rewriting)

Effective readers and writers usually go through all three stages when they read or write, most often in the order in which they are listed here. However, each stage merges with the others; that is, one stage does not have to end completely before another stage begins. Writers and readers may therefore move back and forth between the stages, proceeding to one before completing another or returning to an earlier one before moving forward again. Or they may engage in two stages at the same time. For example, a writer may discover new ideas while rewriting or discard an idea (thus "rewriting") before beginning to write. In addition, readers and writers may go through each step repeatedly. A reader may go over a reading selection several times before understanding it, and a writer may write several drafts before producing one that is satisfactory.

Following are four drafts of a student paragraph on the general topic of "animals." Notice how the writer gradually limits, develops, and focuses the subject. In the first version, or "freewriting," he writes whatever comes to mind, merely exploring the idea of animals in general and how they relate to humans.

FREEWRITING

There are many different types of animals. They live all over the world. Many animals can live in areas that people have not been able to. Animals come in many different sizes and shapes. Their are thousands of different kind of species. A good place to study the life style of animals is the zoo. Many of them help humans, some are harmful to humans. Humans have killed off some species of animals by changing the geological aspects of the land. One thing that people and animals have in common is that they have to share the land.

At this point, the writer is merely recording his random thoughts on the general subject of animals. The writer hasn't decided on a particular subject, and he hasn't considered correct spelling and punctuation. Notice in the next version, the first draft, that the writer focuses on a single idea from his freewriting—the idea that some animals are "harmful to humans"—and narrows his subject to a particular animal, the brown bear. The writer uses only this one idea from his freewriting; however, this idea becomes the focus of his developing paragraph.

FIRST DRAFT

The brown bear is an animal that makes it's home in the wilderness. They are travelers and cover considerable amount of territory in search of food. When a cub grows tired it will ride on the mother's back. The brown bear is normally a peaceful creature but when wounded it becomes very dangerous. An intruder caught between a cub and its mother may be seriously injured or killed. Unlike other animals the brown bear attacks without warning. Its great strength, long claws, and sharp teeth makes it a defensive animal. The brown bear is a wild animal, therefore it should be observed with a great amount of caution.

Although the writer has found his subject—the brown bear—he has not found a specific focus; that is, he does not yet know what he wants to say about the brown bear—what the main point of his paragraph is going to be. But in the next version, his second draft, the writer narrows his subject still further, focusing specifically on the idea that the brown bear is a dangerous animal. Notice that he uses an idea from the last sentence of the first draft to begin his second draft.

SECOND DRAFT

The brown bear is an animal that should be observed with a great amount of caution. It is a wild animal that makes its home in the wilderness. The brown bear is normally a peaceful creature but when wounded it becomes very dangerous. The female bear is very protective of its cub. An intruder caught between a cub and its mother may be seriously injured or killed. Unlike other animals the brown bear attacks without warning. It's great strength, long claws, and sharp teeth makes it very dangerous. The bear is also a meat eating animal and therefor must sometimes kill for its food. A human killing bear is rare, but there are cases of such animals. Every precaution should be taken if one is caught in the surroundings of a brown bear.

The writer is now sure of what he wants to say. He has included the information that his readers need and has arranged the information so that a reader can move easily from one idea to the next. In the final draft, the writer corrects several errors in spelling and punctuation.

FINAL DRAFT

The brown bear is an animal that should be observed with a great amount of caution. It is a wild animal that makes its home in the wilderness. The brown bear is normally a peaceful creature, but when wounded it becomes very dangerous. The female bear is very protective of its cub. An intruder, caught between a cub and its mother, may be seriously injured or killed. Unlike other animals, the brown bear attacks without warning. Its great strength, long claws, and sharp teeth make it very dangerous. The bear is also a meat-eating animal and therefore must sometimes kill for its food. A human-killing bear is rare, but there are cases of such animals. Every precaution available should be taken if one is caught in the surroundings of a brown bear.

Donald Kelly

The information and ideas presented in this final version are much more easily understood than are the unrelated sentences of the freewriting and first draft. As the writer rewrote this paragraph, his own understanding of what he wanted to say obviously grew. Finally, he edited and proofread his paragraph for errors in spelling and punctuation. Thus, in the final version, he communicates more clearly with his reader because he has learned, in the process of writing and rewriting, what he wants to say.

Readers as well as writers struggle with the process of making meaning. As writers, we write and rewrite, trying to understand our own ideas and communicate them clearly to our readers. As readers, we read and reread, trying to understand the ideas and information provided by the writer. Thus, readers and writers do not always move quickly and directly from preparation to final review. Many rewritings and rereadings may be necessary. The following diagram emphasizes that the various stages do not always follow each other in a neat, orderly fashion:

FIGURE 1

Even though these stages vary each time you read or write, you need to understand them and the ways they relate to one another.

PREPARATION

Your preparation for both reading and writing is of two types: long-term and short-term. Long-term preparation consists of everything you have done and learned in your life. Thus, in one sense, you have been preparing all your life for each reading and writing assignment that you do, because your ability to read and write depends on your prior knowledge and experience. You are able to communicate with others because you have shared similar, though not identical, experiences and backgrounds. For example, when a writer describes feelings of pride or guilt or anger, you understand those feelings because you have also experienced them. And when you write about an awkward or embarrassing incident, you know that most of your readers will understand because they have had similar experiences.

Thus, your previous reading, ideas, feelings, and experiences make you your own best source of information for reading and writing. However, to use your long-term preparation effectively, you must learn how to make this resource available through short-term preparation; that is, you must learn how to tap your memory by using prereading and prewriting strategies.

PREREADING STRATEGIES

To prepare to read, you should first *survey* the selection to be read in order to gain a general understanding of the subject and main ideas. To survey a reading selection efficiently, look briefly at the title, introduction, main headings, first sentences in paragraphs, and conclusion. This quick preview should give you a fairly accurate idea of the author's subject, purpose, and main ideas. Then, as you begin to read, you will already know something about what the writer is going to say and will be recalling from your own experiences and background the information and ideas that you need to comprehend what you are reading.

A second strategy that will help you prepare to read effectively is to ask yourself questions about what you are going to read. After you have surveyed the material to be read, establish a definite purpose for reading by turning the title and main headings into questions. For example, if you are reading a chapter in your biology book entitled "The Effect of Photosynthesis on Plant Life," rephrase the title as a question: What is the effect of photosynthesis on plant life? Then read to find the answer. As you encounter different headings in the chapter, rephrase them as questions also. Asking specific questions about a passage before reading it gives you a definite purpose for reading and improves your concentration and comprehension.

PREWRITING STRATEGIES

You also need to prepare for writing by using specific strategies. In each of the Reading/Writing Assignments, we suggest one or two prewriting activities that will help you discover ideas about what you are writing and help you plan and organize those ideas. Each of these prewriting strategies gives you the opportunity to think about your subject—to "mull it over"—from various points of view.

As you write your paragraph or essay, you will continue to think about your subject, perhaps changing your mind or modifying your ideas as you write. Sometimes, even when you are not thinking directly about a writing assignment, an idea will come to you. This conscious and unconscious "thinking time" is also part of your preparation for writing.

READING/WRITING

The central part of the reading/writing process is the processing of information and ideas.

READING

After you have surveyed the reading selection and established a purpose for reading by asking questions about it, read to answer those questions. If the writer has provided accurate clues to the content of the selection and if you have predicted that content successfully, you will find the answers to your questions as you read.

Do not be afraid to reread sentences or paragraphs that you do not understand. Even the best readers must occasionally reread in order to comprehend if the material is difficult or if their minds have wandered.

Also, do not hesitate to vary your rate of reading. Good readers have flexible reading rates that vary, depending on the material being read and their purpose for reading it. For example, if you are reading a mystery novel, you will usually read rapidly. If you are skimming the want ads in the newspaper to locate a job or an apartment, you will probably read even more rapidly. However, if you are reading a textbook to learn complex material or understand difficult ideas, you will need to read more slowly and carefully.

When you are reading material that you need to learn, you may want to underline significant passages or main ideas. Or you may want to take notes or outline the material as you read. Some readers find that underlining or taking notes as they read helps them understand what they are reading. Other readers find that reading a selection through initially without writing anything works best for them. They go back and take notes or underline later when they review. You will have to experiment to find the strategies that work best for you, but writing nearly always reinforces reading comprehension and retention.

WRITING

Writing, like reading, is an act of discovery. Do not hesitate to make changes as new ideas or discoveries come to you. A good writer, like a good reader, is flexible. Do not limit yourself to the ideas you have before you begin to write. Even in the final review stage, you may have new insights that will strengthen your writing, making it more vivid, more interesting, or more readable.

The number of drafts you write depends on how many discoveries you make as you write. The writer who requires several drafts is often a better writer than the one who "gets it right" the first time. Just as an artist shapes and reshapes, colors and recolors, so a writer writes and rewrites until the finished product achieves the purpose for which it is intended.

REVIEW

The final stage of the reading/writing process is *review*. Review involves rereading and rewriting. Readers reread to be sure they comprehend what they have read. Writers rewrite to be sure their readers comprehend what they have written. As you have already learned, however, the rereading and rewriting stages are not limited to the final part of the process. Readers reread when a passage goes in a direction that they have not expected or when relationships among ideas are not clear—in other words, anytime they fail to comprehend what they are reading. Writers rewrite when they realize that a draft is not accomplishing its purpose—sometimes even starting over in the middle of a draft—or when they get fresh ideas or new insights.

REREADING

To review a reading selection, you may repeat your previewing procedure, focusing again on the title, introduction, main headings, and conclusion; you may review your questions to see if you can answer them fully and correctly; or you may review your notes. Occasionally, you may want to reread the entire selection. Or you may choose to take notes on what you have read during the review stage rather than during the initial reading. Remember that the reviewing, whatever form it takes, is as important to comprehension and retention as is the actual reading, so do not omit this important stage of the process. You may, however, want to delay it until a later time or to review quickly when you have finished reading and then to review more carefully just before a class discussion or an exam.

REWRITING

In rewriting, you assume the difficult role of being a reader of your own writing. In order to rewrite effectively, you must learn to look at your writing objectively—to resee it as your reader will.

Rewriting, like rereading, may occur at any point during the process and may involve a single word or the entire composition. As illustrated in the diagram below, rewriting is itself a process that exists within the larger process of writing:

FIGURE 2

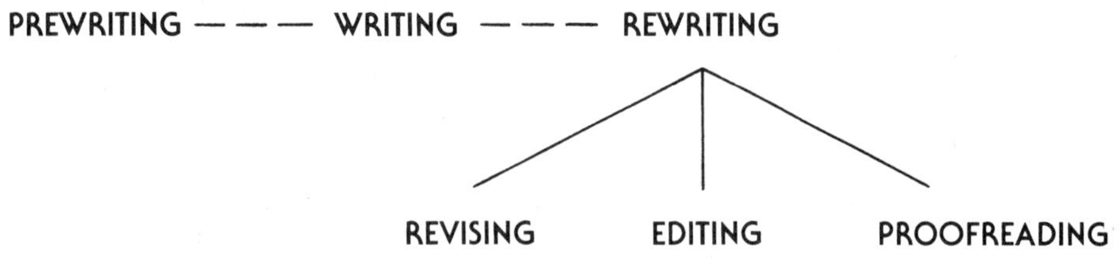

PREWRITING — — — WRITING — — — REWRITING

REVISING   EDITING   PROOFREADING

Thus, we use the word *rewrite* to include three different functions: revising, editing, and proofreading. To *revise* means to make important changes in the content, focus, or organization of a draft; to *edit* means to make changes or corrections in sentence structure, usage, and word choice; and to *proofread* means to make minor corrections in the final copy. If you become too concerned with correctness (editing and proofreading) during your early drafts, you may inhibit your writing process. Get your ideas down on paper and organized before you worry about spelling errors and punctuation. Knowing that you can attend to matters of style and correctness on later drafts can free you to think more clearly and creatively on early drafts. Save editing and proofreading primarily for the final stages.

READING/WRITING ASSIGNMENT 1A

HOW TO MARK A BOOK
Mortimer J. Adler

Each chapter in *Contexts* contains two Reading/Writing Assignments. As you work through the book, these assignments will gradually become more challenging. In these first Reading/Writing Assignments, you will not be asked to write a complete paragraph or essay, but you will be asked to respond to your *reading* by *writing*. Assignment 1A explains reading strategies that will be helpful to you as a college student; Assignment 1B gives you practice in the important prewriting strategy of freewriting.

Pre-Reading/Writing Exercise

How do you read the assignments that your instructor gives you in your textbook? Are you a conscientious student who begins with the first sentence of each chapter or essay and reads through to the very last sentence without a pause or a break? If so, you are undoubtedly a very dedicated student, but you are probably not nearly as effective a reader as you can be. You may even sometimes find yourself nodding off or daydreaming, and you may often reach the end of the chapter without understanding or remembering much of what you have read. In order to become a more effective reader, you need to learn to read *actively* rather than passively. That is, you need to learn to *participate* in the reading process by recreating the writer's meaning in your own mind.

If your reading is not as effective as it should be, you need a strategy for reading that helps you organize the ideas and details that you read. A sensible and proven method of reading, understanding, and remembering information is shown below:

Prereading Phase	*S* urvey
	Q uestion
Reading Phase	*R* ead
	R espond
Reviewing Phase	*R* ecite
	R eview

The prereading phase of *surveying* and *questioning* will help you comprehend and remember what you have read. First, look carefully at the chapter or essay title and fix in your mind the general topic of the reading. For example, the title of this chapter, "The Reading/Writing Process," should give you a focus for reading. Next, read the chapter introduction. Then survey the chapter, looking at headings and subheadings (such as "Prewriting Strategies" on p. 7). Note any numbered points or any charts or graphs (such as the one on p. 9). Visuals like these often compress information into a form that is easy to understand and remember. Finally, read the conclusion and any questions that appear at the end of the reading. Your survey should take only a few minutes, but it should give you a fairly good idea of the subject or subjects to be discussed, of the general organization of the material, and of the amount of information to be covered. (If the reading is too long for one sitting—20 pages or more—you should mark a place to stop and take a break.)

As you survey, you should also think of questions to keep in mind while you read. Rephrasing titles, headings, and subheadings as questions is often helpful. For example, you can rephrase the subheading "Review" on p. 8 as the question, "What is the review process?" and then read to answer your question. In addition, you can increase your interest and therefore your comprehension by asking yourself how the material to be read is related to your own experiences. Thus, you could ask yourself, "How can the review stage help me become a better reader or writer?"

To apply this active method of reading, look at Mortimer J. Adler's "How to Mark a Book" on page 11. Survey the selection by reading the introductory paragraph, the main headings, the first sentence of each paragraph, the headings in the numbered lists, and the concluding paragraph. As you survey, turn the title and major headings into questions that you can expect the selection to answer. Since the title suggests a question, rephrase it as "How should *I* mark a book or chapter?" In the space that follows, write the questions you posed for the two major headings:

1. _____

   _____

2. _____

   _____

Reading Exercise

As you *read* the following essay, search actively for the answers to your questions. If necessary, rephrase your questions in your mind as you read to help you focus on Adler's most important points. Remember, too, that in reading actively you *respond* to what you are reading; that is, sometimes you may agree with Adler, and sometimes you may disagree with him. Occasionally, you may be confused by one of his statements, but more often you will think, "That's really a good idea!" As you read, then, feel free to indicate in the margins your responses to specific statements. Use the symbols "yes," "no," "?," and "!" to show your responses.

1   You know you have to read "between the lines" to get the most out of anything. I want to persuade you to do something equally important in the course of your reading. I want to persuade you to "write between the lines." Unless you do, you are not likely to do the most efficient kind of reading.

Reasons for Marking

2   Why is marking up a book indispensable to reading? First, it keeps you awake. (And I don't mean merely conscious; I mean wide awake.) In the second place, reading, if it is active, is thinking, and thinking tends to express itself in words, spoken or written. The marked book is usually the thought-through book. Finally, writing helps you remember the thoughts you had, or the thoughts the author expressed. Let me develop these three points.

3   If reading is to accomplish anything more than passing time, it must be active. You can't let your eyes glide across the lines of a book and come up with an understanding of what you have read. Now an ordinary piece of light fiction, like, say, "Gone with the Wind," doesn't require the most active kind of reading. The books you read for pleasure can be read in a state of relaxation, and nothing is lost. But a great book, rich in ideas and beauty, a book that raises and tries to answer great fundamental questions, demands the most active reading of which you are capable. . . .

4   If, when you've finished reading a book, the pages are filled with your notes, you know that you read actively. The most famous *active* reader of great books I know is President Hutchins, of the University of Chicago. He also has the hardest schedule of business activities of any man I know. He invariably reads with a pencil, and sometimes, when he picks up a book and pencil in the evening, he finds himself, instead of making intelligent notes, drawing what he calls "caviar factories" on the margins. When that happens,

he puts the book down. He knows he's too tired to read, and he's just wasting time.

5   But, you may ask, why is writing necessary? Well, the physical act of writing, with your own hand, brings words and sentences more sharply before your mind and preserves them better in your memory. To set down your reaction to important words and sentences you have read, and the questions they have raised in your mind, is to preserve those reactions and sharpen those questions.

6   Even if you wrote on a scratch pad, and threw the paper away when you had finished writing, your grasp of the book would be surer. But you don't have to throw the paper away. The margins (top and bottom, as well as side), the end-papers, the very space between the lines, are all available. They aren't sacred. And, best of all, your marks and notes become an integral part of the book and stay there forever. You can pick up the book the following week or year, and there are all your points of agreement, disagreement, doubt, and inquiry. It's like resuming an interrupted conversation with the advantage of being able to pick up where you left off.

7   And that is exactly what reading a book should be: a conversation between you and the author. Presumably he knows more about the subject than you do; naturally, you'll have the proper humility as you approach him. But don't let anybody tell you that a reader is supposed to be solely on the receiving end. Understanding is a two-way operation; learning doesn't consist in being an empty receptacle. The learner has to question himself and question the teacher. He even has to argue with the teacher, once he understands what the teacher is saying. And marking a book is literally an expression of your differences, or agreements of opinion, with the author.

Ways of Marking

8   There are all kinds of devices for marking a book intelligently and fruitfully. Here's the way I do it:

1. *Underlining*: of major points, of important or forceful statements.

2. *Vertical lines at the margin*: to emphasize a statement already underlined.

3. *Star, asterisk, or other doo-dad at the margin*: to be used sparingly, to emphasize the ten or twenty most important statements in the book. (You may want to fold the bottom corner of each page on which you use such marks. It won't hurt the sturdy paper on which most modern books are printed, and you will be able to take the book off the shelf at any time and, by opening it at the folded-corner page, refresh your recollection of the book.)

4. *Numbers in the margin*: to indicate the sequence of points the author makes in developing a single argument.

5. *Numbers of other pages in the margin*: to indicate where else in the book the author made points relevant to the point marked; to tie up the ideas in a book, which, though they may be separated by many pages, belong together.

6. *Circling of key words or phrases.*

7. *Writing in the margin, or at the top or bottom of the page, for the sake of*: recording questions (and perhaps answers) which a passage raised

in your mind; reducing a complicated discussion to a simple statement; recording the sequence of major points right through the books. I use the end-papers at the back of the book to make a personal index of the author's points in the order of their appearance.

9   The front end-papers are, to me, the most important. Some people reserve them for a fancy bookplate. I reserve them for fancy thinking. After I have finished reading the book and making my personal index on the back end-papers, I turn to the front and try to outline the book, not page by page, or point by point (I've already done that at the back), but as an integrated structure, with a basic unity and an order of parts. This outline is, to me, the measure of my understanding of the work.

Adapted from Mortimer J. Adler, "How to Mark a Book"

1. Adler's main point, or main idea, is that to read efficiently you must not only read "between the lines" but also

_____

2. What three reasons for marking a book does Adler introduce in his second paragraph?

a. _____

_____

b. _____

_____

c. _____

_____

3. What questions can you ask to guide you as you read the third paragraph?

_____

_____

4. Write below any words from Adler's essay that are unfamiliar to you:

_____

_____

As you encounter unfamiliar words in your college classes, record in a journal or a personal vocabulary list (1) the unfamiliar word, (2) the context in which the word was used, and (3) the appropriate definition.

Example: Word—*fundamental*

Context—"fundamental questions"

Definition—basic, important, essential

Discussion Questions

1. With which of Adler's statements do you agree?

2. Do you disagree with any of Adler's statements or find any of his suggestions confusing?

3. Which of his suggestions will be the most helpful to you in your reading and studying?

Reviewing Exercise

Now, look back at Adler's essay and apply to it at least three of his own suggestions for marking your reading. Think also about the questions you asked yourself before you began to read. Does the text you have marked answer your questions? For most of you, the answer will be "Yes." To help you remember the important points you have marked, we suggest that you recite and review what you have read.

You may *recite* by answering your questions in your mind, thinking of examples if possible. An even more effective method, however, is to recite on paper by taking notes on important ideas. If you are reading a short essay such as Adler's, you may be able to combine recitation with review, but in reading longer works, you will want to recite after each section or subsection. Avoid taking too many notes as you read; because each sentence will seem important as you are reading it, you may underline too much or take too many notes. If you take notes in outline form (see Chapters 2, 4, and 8 for help with outlining), you will have an excellent summary of your reading for later review and study. You may even want to keep a reading journal for each class in which you record your questions and reactions as well as your notes.

Finally, after you finish reading and taking notes on a chapter or essay such as "How to Mark a Book," *review* by looking over your underlining, your marginal comments, and your notes. Check your memory on the content by reviewing the main ideas and supporting points. (Cover up your supporting points or "answers" and use questions or main headings as memory cues.) Save these notes for later use in reviewing for examinations.

If you have not taken notes on your reading, or if your notes are not complete enough to help you remember the major points, repeat the survey phase with which you started. This prereading technique can be as helpful in reviewing a chapter as in preparing you to read it. You may want to apply this reading strategy to further chapters in *Contexts*—especially those in Part One—and to your other college textbooks.

READING/WRITING ASSIGNMENT 1B

THE BENEFITS OF FREEWRITING
Peter Elbow

Pre-Reading/Writing Exercise

A *process,* as defined by the *American Heritage Dictionary of the English Language,* is a "series of actions, changes, or functions that bring about an end or result," an "ongoing movement," or a "progression." As this definition suggests, neither reading nor writing is the one-step process that we often try to make it. Both processes require preparation and review.

By this time in your life, you have had at least seventeen or eighteen years of experience, observations, and reading to use as the raw materials of your reading and writing. For a specific assignment, you may want to do additional outside reading, but you should realize that you are your own best source of information and that you already have the information you will need for most of the writing assignments in this book. However, you need to learn about specific prewriting strategies so that you can bring information from deep within your memory to the surface.

To prepare for this reading/writing assignment, write three words that describe how you *feel* about writing:

_____

_____

_____

After you finish, compare your feelings with those of your instructor and your classmates.

Reading Exercise

When you write, do you sometimes have trouble "getting started"? Even famous writers admit that they are frightened by the blank page; for example, Ernest Hemingway reported that he always continued a sentence or a thought to the top of the next page so that he wouldn't have to face that blankness. One technique for combatting this fear is *freewriting.* Peter Elbow, who first introduced freewriting, explains the process. As you read Elbow's essay, underline seven ways that freewriting can help you become a better writer.

1   Freewriting is the easiest way to get words on paper and the best all-around practice in writing that I know. To do a freewriting exercise, simply force yourself to write without stopping for ten minutes. Sometimes you will produce good writing, but that's not the goal. Sometimes you will produce garbage, but that's not the goal either. You may stay on one topic, you may flip repeatedly from one to another: it doesn't matter. Sometimes you will produce a good record of your stream of consciousness, but often you can't keep up. Speed is not the goal, though sometimes the process revs you up. If you can't think of anything to write, write about how that feels or repeat over and over "I have nothing to write" or "Nonsense" or "No." If you get stuck in the middle of a sentence or thought, just repeat the last word or phrase till something comes along. The only point is to keep writing.

* * *

2   Thus, freewriting is the best way to learn—in practice, not just in theory—to separate the producing process from the revising process. Freewriting exercises are push-ups in withholding judgment as you produce so that afterwards you can judge better.

3   Freewriting for ten minutes is a good way to warm up when you sit down to write something. You won't waste so much time getting started when you turn to your real writing task and you won't have to struggle so hard to find words. Writing almost always goes better when you are already started: now you'll be able to start off already started.

4   Freewriting helps you learn to write when you don't feel like writing. It is practice in setting deadlines for yourself, taking charge of yourself, and learning gradually how to get that special energy that sometimes comes when you work fast under pressure.

5   Freewriting teaches you to write without thinking about writing. We can usually speak without thinking about speech—without thinking about how to form words in the mouth and pronounce them and the rules of syntax we unconsciously obey—and as a result we can give undivided attention to what we say. Not so writing. Or at least most people are considerably distracted from their meaning by considerations of spelling, grammar, rules, errors. Most people experience an awkward and sometimes paralyzing *translating* process in writing: "Let's see, how shall I say this." Freewriting helps you learn to *just say* it. Regular freewriting helps make the writing process *transparent*.

6   Freewriting is a useful outlet. We have lots in our heads that makes it hard to think straight and write clearly: we are mad at someone, sad about something, depressed about everything. Perhaps even inconveniently happy. "How can I think about this report when I'm so in love?" Freewriting is a quick outlet for these feelings so they don't get so much in your way when you are trying to write about something else. Sometimes your mind is marvelously clear after ten minutes of telling someone on paper everything you need to tell him. (In fact, if your feelings often keep you from functioning well in other areas of your life frequent freewriting can help: not only by providing a good arena for those feelings, but also by helping you understand them better and see them in perspective by seeing them on paper.)

7   Freewriting helps you to think of topics to write about. Just keep writing, follow threads where they lead and you will get to ideas, experiences, feelings, or people that are just asking to be written about.

8   Finally, and perhaps most important, freewriting improves your writing. It doesn't always produce powerful writing itself, but it leads to powerful writing.

Peter Elbow, *Writing with Power*

1. Write below the seven ways that freewriting can improve your writing.

a. _____

_____

b. _____

_____

c. _____

_____

d. _____

_____

e. _____

_____

f. _____

_____

g. _____

_____

2. Many words have three main parts: a prefix, a root, and a suffix. In the word *freewriting* itself, *write* is the base, or root, word; *-ing* is a suffix; and *free-* functions as a prefix. A prefix occurs at the beginning of a word and alters its meaning. Thus, the prefix *re-* added to *writing* would form the word *rewriting,* meaning "to write again." Here are the meanings of five common prefixes: *syn-* means "together," *dis-* means "apart, away, or aside," *trans-* means "across, beyond, or through," *de-* means "down or away, and *per-* means "through or by." Use the meanings of these prefixes to help you define the following words:

a. syntax _____

_____

b. distracted _____

_____

c. transparent _____

_____

d. depressed _____

_____

e. perspective _____

_____

Writing Exercise

As you learned in the passage by Elbow, to freewrite you simply write rapidly for several minutes without stopping and without worrying about form or correctness. You can freewrite about a particular subject, such as animals, school, or crime. Or you can simply write about whatever comes to mind, repeating words or phrases if you cannot think of something else to write. Usually, this free flow of words loosens up your thoughts, and one idea leads you to another. At the end of five or ten minutes, you may be writing about something entirely different from what you started writing about. Often, writers discover a topic as they write.

Now, freewrite for five or ten minutes about how writing makes you feel. Do not stop to think as you write, and if you cannot think of anything to write, simply write, "I cannot think of anything to write" until an idea comes to you. The most important thing is to keep your pen or pencil moving across the page. When your teacher says, "Begin," start your writing with the sentence "Writing makes me feel . . ."

Reviewing Exercise

Now look back at your freewriting and write below the most interesting phrase, sentence, or idea—an idea that you might like to talk about or write more about.

_____

_____

Group Reviewing Exercise

Exchange freewritings with one or two classmates. Underline the most interesting idea or sentence in one another's freewritings and then compare your choices with those of your classmates. Did you underline the same ideas or different ideas?

Chapter 2

GENERAL and SPECIFIC

The ability to distinguish between general and specific terms is a skill that is basic to both reading and writing. A *general* term can be defined as one that is broad, that encompasses more than one of a kind; a *specific* term is more limited, less broad in scope. Consider the word *child.* Can you think of a word that refers to a concept that is more general than *child?* For example, which of the following terms is more general than *child?*

infant

girl

boy

person

adult

teenager

Did you select the word *person? Person* is a more general concept than *child* because a child is just one type of person. The words *infant, girl, boy, adult,* and *teenager* refer to other types of persons. Like the word *child,* these words are less general than the word *person.*

Now let's think about concepts that are *more specific* than the word *child.* Which of the following terms is more specific than the term *child?*

human being

adult

youth

Charlie Brown

baby

Did you select the term *Charlie Brown?* The term *human being,* like the word *person,* is more general than the word *child.* And the terms *adult, youth,* and *baby* are all equal to the word *child* in that they all refer to concepts that are equally general. Children, youths, adults, and babies are all types of human beings, but the term *Charlie Brown* refers to a specific child.

GENERAL AND SPECIFIC WORDS

A word, or term, can be categorized as general or specific only when it is compared with another word or words. For example, the word *vegetable* is more specific than *plant* but more general than *zucchini.* And the word *car* is more specific than *vehicle* but more general than *sedan.*

You see examples of general and specific relationships every day. For example, a restaurant menu usually classifies specific food choices under general headings.

EXAMPLE

Meats	Vegetables	Desserts
Baked ham	Green beans	Cheesecake
Broiled salmon	Scalloped potatoes	Apple pie
Roast beef	Corn	Chocolate cake
Fried chicken	Sautéed mushrooms	Ice cream

This detailed menu provides you with both general and specific information, including in several instances how the particular types of food are prepared.

Whether you are reading a menu, a newspaper, or a textbook, you will find that you need both general and specific terms. When you write, you should use both general and specific terms to make your meaning as clear as possible. Being able to distinguish between general and specific words can therefore help you be a better reader and writer. The activities that follow will help you reach this goal.

EXAMPLE

The following list includes one general and three specific terms:

> flower (general)
>
> rose (specific)
>
> carnation (specific)
>
> tulip (specific)

In this group, *flower* is the most general word. *Carnation, rose,* and *tulip* are more specific words because they are types of flowers. The relationship of the general word *flower* to the specific kinds of flowers is diagrammed in Figure 3.

FIGURE 3

General: flower		
	Specific: carnation	
	Specific: rose	
	Specific: tulip	

EXERCISE 2.1

For practice in identifying general and specific words, study the following word groups and circle the most general word in each group.

1. poodle
   (dog)
   collie
   dachshund

2. Bill Cosby
   Alan Alda
   (actor)
   Burt Reynolds

3. cheddar
   Swiss
   mozzarella
   (cheese)

4. (furniture)
   couch
   table
   chair

5. situation comedies
   (television shows)
   soap operas
   game shows

6. bridge
   poker
   (card games)
   gin rummy

EXERCISE 2.2

The following list contains three specific words and a blank space for the general word that describes them. Study the specific words in the example below and then write an appropriate general word in the blank space.

EXAMPLE

General: _Snake_

  Specific: cobra

  Specific: rattlesnake

  Specific: copperhead

You might have written *reptile* in the blank because cobras, rattlesnakes, and copperheads are all reptiles. However, *reptile* is actually a broader word than you need because it describes not only cobras, rattlesnakes, and copperheads—all of which are snakes—but also turtles, lizards, and other reptiles besides snakes. The best answer is the word *snake,* which is general enough to include each of the words listed but not so general that it includes other types of reptiles.

Now study each of the following lists of specific words and write an appropriate general word in the blank provided.

1. General: _Color_
     Specific: red
     Specific: blue
     Specific: yellow

2. General: _President_
     Specific: John Kennedy
     Specific: Harry Truman
     Specific: Ronald Reagan

3. General: _Jewelry_
   Specific: diamond
   Specific: emerald
   Specific: ruby

4. General: _Cloth_
   Specific: linen
   Specific: silk
   Specific: cotton

5. General: _Wood_
   Specific: oak
   Specific: maple
   Specific: pine

6. General: _Fish_
   Specific: trout
   Specific: bass
   Specific: salmon

The word groups that you have studied thus far in this chapter have contained words on two levels of generality. That is, each group has contained one general word and three words that are equally specific. The following group of words also contains one term that is more general than the others, but the remaining words express different levels of specificity.

EXAMPLE

lawyer (general)

criminal lawyer (specific)

defense lawyer (more specific)

F. Lee Bailey (most specific)

In this example, *lawyer* is the most general word. *Criminal lawyer* is more specific than *lawyer,* but since criminal lawyers can be either prosecutors or defenders, *defense lawyer* is even more specific than *criminal lawyer.* Most specific is *F. Lee Bailey,* a well-known defense lawyer. Thus, no two terms in this group are equally specific. The diagram in Figure 4 illustrates the general/specific relationships among these terms.

FIGURE 4

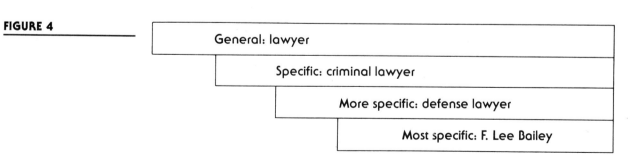

EXERCISE 2.3

Study the following group of words to determine the general/specific relationships: America, United States, California, North America. Then write these words in the appropriate spaces below:

EXAMPLE

General: _America_

Specific: _North America_

More specific: _United States_

Most specific: _California_

Did you decide that *America* is the most general word, *North America* more specific, *United States* even more specific, and *California* the most specific word? Now, arrange in order from general to specific the words in each of the following groups.

1. math, Algebra II, subject, algebra

   General: _subject_

   Specific: _math_

   More specific: _Algebra_

   Most specific: _Algebra II_

2. car, two-door sedan, vehicle, sedan

   General: _vehicle_

   Specific: _Car_

   More specific: _Sedan_

   Most specific: _two-door sedan_

3. dog, collie, animal, mammal /mammal/

   General: _Animal_

   Specific: _mammal_

   More specific: _dog_

   Most specific: _collie_

4. sport, football, team sport, professional football

General: _Soort_

Specific: _Team sport_

More specific: _Football_

Most specific: _Professional football_

5. nonfiction, book, *The Life of Abraham Lincoln,* biography

General: _Book_

Specific: _nonfiction_

More specific: _biography_

Most specific: _The life of Abraham Lincohn_

6. Jefferson High School, school, high school, public school

General: _School_

Specific: _Public school_

More specific: _High school_

Most specific: _Jefferson High School_

GENERAL AND SPECIFIC STATEMENTS

Thus far in this chapter, you have been learning to distinguish between general and specific words. However, statements as well as words can be classified as general or specific. In order to be an effective reader and writer, you must be able to distinguish between general and specific statements.

Like a word, a statement can be viewed as general or specific only in relation to other statements. For example, read the sentences below. Can you determine which one of them is the most general?

1. Luke Skywalker, the hero of *Star Wars* and its sequels, became the hero of many young fans a few years ago.

2. In recent years, young people have admired violent movie heroes such as Dirty Harry and Rambo.

3. Each generation of young people seems to elevate certain movie characters to the status of folk heroes.

4. In past generations, the Lone Ranger and Superman had their loyal followings.

Did you select sentence number 3 as the most general statement? Can you see that the other three sentences about specific heroes support this general statement with several specific statements? The combination of a general statement and specific statements is an important characteristic of paragraphs. The following exercises will give you practice in combining general and specific statements.

EXERCISE 2.4

The sample exercise below contains three fairly specific statements. In the space provided, write a general statement that expresses the idea supported by the specific statements.

EXAMPLE

General statement: _____

_____

Specific statement: Craig has made 90s on all of his English quizzes.

Specific statement: He received an A on his major English theme.

Specific statement: He also earned such a good grade on his mid-term exam that he was exempt from the English final.

Your statement should be general enough to include each of the specific statements but not more general than the specific statements suggest. For example, the statement "Craig made good grades on his English tests" is too specific because it doesn't include the statement about his English theme; the statement that "Craig earned good grades in all his classes" is too general because the specific statements refer only to his English class. An appropriate general statement for the sentence group is "Craig has made excellent grades in his English class." Now, write an appropriate general statement for each of the following groups of sentences.

1. General statement: _The utility cost is increased this_

yearly

Specific statement: The cost of gasoline has increased 40¢ per gallon in the last year.

Specific statement: A quart of oil costs more than it did six months ago.

Specific statement: My electric bill was $30 higher this December than it was last December.

2. General statement: _____

_____

Specific statement: In the 1950s crew cuts gave way to ducktails as Elvis Presley's influence began to grow.

Specific statement: Long hair was the style adopted by most men in the 1960s.

Specific statement: During the 1970s most males gradually started wearing their hair shorter, and by the 1980s a neatly trimmed look was preferred by most men.

3. General statement: _Smoking is not good for your health_

_____

Specific statement: Smoking can cause permanent stains on teeth.
Specific statement: Smoking contributes to heart disease.
Specific statement: Smoking can cause lung cancer.

EXERCISE 2.5

The example below contains one fairly general statement and spaces for three more specific statements. Write an appropriate specific statement in each of these spaces.

EXAMPLE

General statement: Yesterday's weather was unpleasant.

Specific statement: _It was rain in the evening._

_____

Specific statement: _It was cold in the morning_

_____

Specific statement: _It was windy at noon_

_____

You might have written in these spaces such statements as "The temperature was 10°," "Snow fell all day," and "The wind blew at thirty miles per hour." Many other specific statements are possible for this exercise, but you should be sure that your statements are more specific than the general statement and that they directly support it.

Now, apply what you have learned in this example to each of the sentence groups that follow. For each group, write three specific statements to support the general statement.

1. General statement: A fast-food restaurant offers certain advantages.

Specific statement: _Customers could save more time than the regular restaurant._

Specific statement: _Fast food restaurants give customer_

Specific statement: _____

2. General statement: Even in our modern society, many superstitions exist.

Specific statement: _____

Specific statement: _____

Specific statement: _____

3. General statement: I wear different clothes for different occasions.

Specific statement: _____

Specific statement: _____

Specific statement: _____

INTRODUCTION TO OUTLINING

Outlining is a method of organizing ideas by indicating their relationship to one other. Like a diagram, an outline is a blueprint or plan of a completed work. It is a skeleton that allows you to see the essential framework of a piece of writing.

Since an outline visually represents general and specific relationships, in order to outline you must understand how to distinguish between general and specific concepts. For example, *tree, grass,* and *flower* are three general categories. Thus, on an outline, you would arrange them as three equal headings:

EXAMPLE

tree

grass

flower

Then, if you wanted to include some specific examples of each of these three general categories, you could place them under the appropriate headings. For example, if you wanted to list *oak, elm, pine,* and *fir* under *tree,* you would list these four specific types of trees under the general heading *tree.*

EXAMPLE

Tree

    oak

    elm

    pine

    fir

You could also add letters or numbers to your outline to make the relationships clearer.

EXAMPLE

1. Tree

    a. oak

    b. elm

    c. pine

    d. fir

Or you could use a different system of representation, as long as you continued to indicate that *tree* is the most general term and that *oak, elm, pine,* and *fir* are specific examples or types of trees.

FIGURE 5

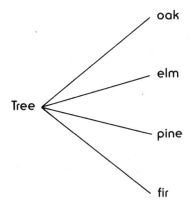

EXERCISE 2.6

On a separate sheet of paper, continue the outline started above by identifying in the following list two other main headings to add to the main heading of *tree*. Then organize the plants under these three headings. Use any format you like for your outline, but be sure that you represent accurately the relationships between the general headings and the more specific types and examples of each.

rose	fir	*Grass*
pine	tulip	*Flower*
elm	tree	*Tree*
daisy	flower	
grass	maple	
spruce	orchid	
rye grass	bluegrass	
Bermuda grass	oak	
violet	carnation	
pecan	St. Augustine grass	

Formal and Informal Outlines

Both formal and informal outlines indicate what is important and what is less important and how the various ideas relate to one another. But the purposes of formal and informal outlines differ. An informal outline, such as a planning or study outline, is written for the benefit of the writer himself or herself. Therefore, the forms of informal outlines vary widely. Some are little more than well-organized lists; others are diagrams consisting of circles and arrows or boxes inside boxes. As long as it communicates to the one who wrote it, an informal outline serves its purpose.

Formal outlines, in contrast, are written by a writer for a reader other than himself or herself. The purpose of a formal outline is to provide the reader with information about what has been outlined. Formal outlines are most appropriately used as tables of content. They are frequently included with long reports, research papers, and proposals as a guide to the contents. Since formal outlines must communicate clearly to a reader, the writer must use a traditional form that is familiar to everyone. Look at the following example of a formal outline:

Main idea: Literature has traditionally been divided into three categories.

I. Fiction
   A. Novel
   B. Short story

II. Drama
    A. Tragedy
    B. Comedy
       1. Low comedy
       2. High comedy
III. Poetry

You should be able to determine from this formal outline that the three main types of literature are fiction, drama, and poetry. You should also be able to see that fiction can be divided into the subcategories of novel and short story and that drama can be divided into tragedy and comedy. Further, you can see from this outline that low comedy and high comedy are types of comedy. The numbers and letters assigned to the different entries on the outline and the system of indentation indicate the relative importance of the entries and their relationship to one another.

In an informal outline this same information might be shown as follows:

Main idea: Literature can be divided into three types.

1. Fiction
    Novel
    Short story
2. Drama
    Tragedy
    Comedy (high and low)
3. Poetry

In this informal outline, numbers, indentation, and parentheses are used to communicate the same information about relative importance and relationships that was given in the formal outline. Any number of variations of this type of listing could be used to create an effective informal outline.

Now look at the following example of still another type of informal outline:

Main idea: Literature can be divided into three types.

FIGURE 6

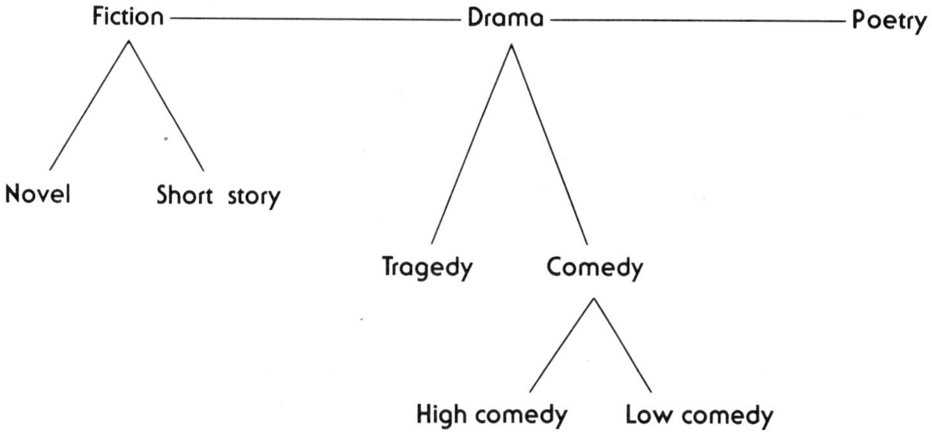

Sentence Outlines

In an outline, either formal or informal, you can use sentences rather than words or phrases. Using what you have learned about general and specific, you can easily construct a simple sentence outline. As an example, let's use the second general statement given in the exercise on page 28:

Even in our modern society, many superstitions exist.

To use this sentence in a formal outline, you could identify it with a Roman numeral and place it at the left margin of the page:

EXAMPLE

I. Even in our modern society, many superstitions exist.

Under this general statement, you could list several specific statements. You could identify these with capital letters. You could also indent them to indicate that they are more specific than the general statement:

EXAMPLE

I. Even in our modern society, many superstitions exist.
   A. Many people believe that certain actions bring good or bad luck.
   B. Others faithfully read horoscopes.
   C. Still others stay home on Friday the 13th.

If you want to include in your outline even more specific details, you could add these details under the appropriate statement.

EXAMPLE

I. Even in our modern society, many superstitions exist.
   A. Many people believe that certain actions bring good or bad luck.
      1. They often avoid walking under ladders to ward off bad luck.
      2. They cross their fingers for good luck.
   B. Others faithfully read horoscopes.
   C. Still others stay home on Friday the 13th.

EXERCISE 2.7

In the following exercise, construct a simple outline by writing specific examples and details under the general statement that is given.

I. Americans are becoming increasingly health conscious.

   A. _____

1. _____

2. _____

B. _____

    1. _____

    2. _____

C. _____

    1. _____

    2. _____

_____

READING/WRITING ASSIGNMENT 2A

GRADUATION DAY
Maya Angelou

Pre-Reading/Writing Exercise

Writing outlines, paragraphs, and essays requires you to make clear distinctions between general and specific ideas. Before you can clarify these relationships, however, you must know what you want to write about. Freewriting is one helpful prewriting method; another excellent strategy is *journal writing.*

A journal records and communicates your thoughts, ideas, reactions, and observations. It is not the same as a diary, which is usually a record of daily events. In both a diary and a journal, you are writing primarily to yourself; that is, you are your own audience. However, in a journal you write not just about what you do but also about what you think, see, and feel. The purpose of a journal is to allow you to discover—to question and explore, to think critically, and to write freely about your thoughts.

Although most instructors react to journal entries with written comments, they usually do not evaluate them in the same way as they do other written assignments. Thus, you should not be overly concerned with correctness but should feel free to experiment with your journal writing, trying not only new ideas but also new words and new styles of writing.

You may write in your journal as often as you wish. However, writing in your journal will be easier and more enjoyable if you make at least one entry a week, and you may want to write daily entries. You may be able to use the ideas that you record in your journal in your writing assignments.

For your first journal entry, write about a significant event that you remember from your youth or childhood. Before writing, spend a few minutes thinking about this time of your life. Was it happy or unhappy? What incidents and feelings do you remember most? Why were these incidents and feelings important? Now, write about one of these events in your journal.

Reading Exercise

In the story below, Angelou tells about a special event that she remembers from her youth. As you read this story, or narrative, think about your own graduation from junior high or high school or about another important event in your life—perhaps a birthday, a contest, or a sports event.

1   The weeks until graduation were filled with heady activities. A group of small children were to be presented in a play about buttercups and daisies and bunny rabbits. They could be heard throughout the building practicing their hops and their little songs that sounded like silver bells. The older girls (nongraduates, of course) were assigned the task of making refreshments for the night's festivities. A tangy scent of ginger, cinnamon, nutmeg and chocolate wafted around the home economics building as the budding cooks made samples for themselves and their teachers.

2   In every corner of the workshop, axes and saws split fresh timber as the woodshop boys made sets and stage scenery. Only the graduates were left out of the general bustle. We were free to sit in the library at the back of the building or look in quite detachedly, naturally, on the measures being taken for our event.

3   Even the minister preached on graduation the Sunday before. His subject was, "Let your light so shine that men will see your good works and praise your Father, Who is in Heaven." Although the sermon was purported to be addressed to us, he used the occasion to speak to backsliders, gamblers and general ne'er-do-wells. But since he had called our names at the beginning of the service we were mollified.

4   Among Negroes the tradition was to give presents to children going only from one grade to another. How much more important this was when the person was graduating at the top of the class. Uncle Willie and Momma had sent away for a Mickey Mouse watch like Bailey's. Louise gave me four embroidered handkerchiefs. (I gave her three crocheted doilies.) Mrs. Sneed, the minister's wife, made me an underskirt to wear for graduation, and nearly every customer gave me a nickel or maybe even a dime with the instruction "Keep on moving to higher ground," or some such encouragement.

5   Amazingly the great day finally dawned and I was out of bed before I knew it. I threw open the back door to see it more clearly, but Momma said, "Sister, come away from that door and put your robe on."

6   I hoped the memory of that morning would never leave me. Sunlight was itself still young, and the day had none of the insistence maturity would bring it in a few hours. In my robe and barefoot in the backyard, under cover of going to see about my new beans, I gave myself up to the gentle warmth and thanked God that no matter what evil I had done in my life He had allowed me to live to see this day. Somewhere in my fatalism I had expected to die, accidentally, and never have the chance to walk up the stairs in the auditorium and gracefully receive my hard-earned diploma. Out of God's merciful bosom I had won reprieve.

Maya Angelou, *I Know Why the Caged Bird Sings*

1. What is the most general statement in the first paragraph of this story?

_____

2. What is the most general statement in the last paragraph?

_____

3. In the first two paragraphs, Angelou writes about several specific activities that occurred before her graduation. Write three specific statements about these activities.

a. _____

_____

b. _____

_____

c. _____

_____

4. Explain what Angelou means by the phrase "the day had none of the insistence maturity would bring it in a few hours."

_____

_____

_____

5. What does the maturity of the day suggest about Angelou's experience?

_____

6. What had frightened Angelou before her graduation day?

_____

7. Some of the words in this story may be unfamiliar to you. For example, in the last sentence of the second paragraph, Angelou uses the word *detachedly* to describe the graduates as they watched the preparations for their graduation. You might look this word up in a dictionary, but you might also be able to discover its meaning by taking the word apart to see if it contains any familiar words or word parts. If you remove the suffix *-ly,* you have the word *detached,* which is easier to understand. And if you remove the second suffix, *-ed,* you have an even simpler word—*detach.* You might at this point remember that the prefix *de-* often means "from" or "away from," and you might also now be able to see that *detach* is similar to *attach,* a word you probably already know well. So even without a dictionary you might be able to figure out that *detachedly* means "separately" or "standing apart from."

The two words below contain word parts that should be familiar to you. Draw a slash between the two main parts of each word and then, in the spaces provided, define each word.

a. nongraduates _____

_____

b. backsliders _____

_____

8. Another word that might be unfamiliar to you is *reprieve,* in the last sentence of the final paragraph. This word cannot be taken apart and analyzed as easily as the word *detachedly.* But there is another way to discover the meaning of unfamiliar words. One can often define a word by looking closely at its context—the sentence or paragraph in which it appears. Look carefully at the paragraph in which the word *reprieve* appears. Notice that Angelou says that she had expected to die before graduation and that she was grateful that she had been allowed to "live to see this day." And in the sentence in which *reprieve* appears, she mentions God's mercy. You might guess from these context clues that the word *reprieve* means a "postponement or delay of punishment."

Use the context to help you define each of the words below. You may wish to check your definitions with a dictionary.

a. wafted _____

_____

b. ginger _____

_____

c. purported _____

_____

d. mollified _____

_____

e. fatalism _____

_____

Writing Exercise

Reread your journal entry about an important event that you remember from your childhood or youth. What made you remember this event, and why is it important to you? Was the event pleasant or sad, exciting or frightening? (Perhaps after reading and discussing Angelou's narrative, you have thought of another event you would prefer to write about. If you wish, you may write another journal entry before proceeding with this exercise.) The exercises below will help you narrow and focus your journal entry so that it can evolve into an effective paragraph.

1. Write below one *general* statement about this event and why it was important to you.

_____

_____

2. Write three *specific* statements about this event.

a. _____

_____

b. _____

_____

c. _____

_____

Reviewing Exercise

Working in small groups of three or four, read your general and specific statements aloud to the members of your group. Then, using suggestions from your group as well as your own ideas, revise your general and specific statements.

1. Revised general statement:

    _____

    _____

2. Revised specific statements:

    a. _____

    _____

    b. _____

    _____

    c. _____

    _____

Optional Writing/Rewriting Exercise

Use your general and specific statements as the basis of a paragraph. Support each specific statement with additional specific details.

READING/WRITING ASSIGNMENT 2B

COLLEGE—A NEW BEGINNING
John N. Gardner and A. Jerome Jewler

Pre-Reading/Writing Exercise

Whether you are returning to school after an absence of several years or have just graduated from high school, you will find college an exciting experience—sometimes rewarding, sometimes frustrating. Think about the experiences you have already had in college—perhaps your first campus visit, registration, or the first class day—and then write below the one word that best describes these experiences:

_____

Reading Exercise

As you read the following passage, identify Professor Patterson's attitude toward entering freshmen.

1   "You won't want to come into the office today anyway," [a colleague] tells me. "The freshmen are arriving, and it's a mess over here. . . ."

2   It certainly is a mess. Hundreds of station wagons packed with steaming students, their families, and their endless belongings seek nonexistent parking spots along a few feet of curb. Irritable mothers and fathers bicker about when, where, and whether to park. Campus police do what they can to direct traffic, but they know it is beyond their control; the rules will have to bend a little more than usual today. . . . It *is* the messiest day of the year, no doubt about it. It is also my favorite.

3   So begins Charlotte J. Patterson's tribute to arriving freshmen. A psychology professor at the University of Virginia, Patterson feels a great deal of empathy with new students—with their hopes, dreams, and fears. What does it mean to be a freshman in a new setting on the first days of a fall semester? Professor Patterson views it as a new beginning:

> It makes me think of those slushy days in early spring when the snow is melting and one cannot step down anywhere without splashing. Even when I am cold and wet, I cannot hate those days; they presage too much. Freshman arrival is also a mess, but I cannot hate it either. They appear in town like young green shoots, sprouting up everywhere, looking for light. Their faces hang out the windows of dorms like tiny new buds on an old, old tree. Someone else may worry about the sun and the soil and the possibility of frost; for them, it is enough just to *be*.
>
> Yes, today is the beginning of a new life. One day you're Mama's child, living at home; the next day, you're a freshman and on your own. The end of childhood. Instant adulthood. Or is it? *Freshman!* I like the word. The very label itself suggests the dilemma. Should it be pronounced with emphasis on the *fresh* or on the *man?* It points both ways. It doesn't matter whether you think of adulthood as a journey or as an arrival; today it is clearly a step on the path. Freshman fantasies and freshman fears can be seen on every young face.

4   Even if you are returning to college after several years' absence or are entering for the first time after working or raising a family, attending college in the 1980s will be an adjustment for you. College is an exciting time, perhaps the most exciting time in your life. But it's also a time of major adjustments and some disappointments. Most fields of study have become quite competitive, and the information explosion has lead to greater demands on those attempting to absorb all that information. There is a growing need for a more structured and formalized introduction to college, and freshman orientation/freshman seminar courses have become popular on campuses from Maine to California.

John N. Gardner and A. Jerome Jewler, *College Is Only the Beginning: A Student Guide to Higher Education*

1. Professor Patterson writes that the arrival of the freshmen is the "messiest day of the year." What are three specific details that she uses to support her general observation?

a. _____

_____

b. _____

_____

c. _____

_____

2. Professor Patterson and her colleague, another professor at her university, have quite different attitudes toward the arrival of the freshmen. What are their attitudes?

_____

_____

3. How is Professor Patterson's comparison of the arrival of the freshmen to a slushy spring day appropriate?

_____

_____

_____

_____

_____

4. The prefix *pre-* means "before"; the root, or base, *-sage* means "to perceive or know." What does *presage* mean in this passage?

_____

5. Patterson explains what it means to be a freshman by dividing the word *freshman* into its two parts—*fresh* and *man.* What does *fresh* suggest about being a freshman?

_____

_____

What does *man* suggest?

_____

_____

Writing Exercise

Write a journal entry about your current impression of college. In your opening sentence include the word you wrote in the Pre-Reading/Writing Exercise to describe your feelings about college life. Then add one or more experiences to support this impression. Be sure to use specific details and examples to support your general impression.

Rewriting Exercise

After you have written your journal entry, observe campus life closely to see if your first impression changes or remains the same. Try to determine whether the people you meet are new students, advanced students, or faculty members. How can you tell? How do students and faculty members spend their time? What seems important to most students? What seems important to most faculty members? What impression do you have of certain places on campus, such as the library, bookstore, learning center, cafeteria, and gym? How is campus life similar to or different from life in the "real world"?

You may want to discuss your observations and reactions with other class members. If your observations have changed your general impression of your campus or of campus life, write a new journal entry or paragraph showing how your feelings have changed. If your impression has remained much the same, select an aspect of campus life other than the one you wrote about earlier. Then, focusing on this element of campus life, write another journal entry or paragraph. Begin your journal entry or paragraph with a general statement. Then support your general statement with several specific statements.

Chapter 3

MAIN IDEAS

Now that you have learned to distinguish general words from specific words and general statements from specific statements, you are ready for a more complete explanation of paragraphs and of how good writers use both general and specific statements to write effective paragraphs. As you read the following student paragraph, notice the combination of general and specific statements.

My room indicates the disorganized way I run my life. My bed is very seldom made and is usually quite a mess. The closet is a storehouse for old books, boxes of junk, and tools which are not arranged in any order at all. My drawers are full of old papers, checks, and other items that should be in some order but aren't. Clothes are usually strung out all over the room, and my book shelf is a mass of confusion with my record albums and tapes mixed with my books and drawing utensils. My room reflects my lifestyle, which is usually disorderly.

Bill McRee

1. Write below the general statement that begins this paragraph:

_____

2. Notice that most of the other sentences in the paragraph are specific details that describe the room's appearance. All of the sentences support the general idea that the student's lifestyle is disorderly. List below three of these specific details.

a. _____

b. _____

c. _____

3. Based on the observations you have made about this paragraph, write below your own definition of a paragraph.

_____

_____

4. Did you include in your definition the following characteristics?
    a. The paragraph begins with a general statement.
    b. The paragraph consists of a series of sentences that are all related to the general statement.
    c. The sentences that follow the general statement give specific details about it.

You might define a paragraph as a group of sentences that develops one main idea. The main idea of a paragraph is the general statement that the other sentences support or explain. It is usually stated and often occurs at the very beginning of the paragraph. In the paragraph about the disorganized student, the main idea statement is the first sentence. Another term for main idea statement is *topic sentence.*

A paragraph may be a complete composition in itself, or it may be part of a longer composition. In either case, a well-developed paragraph usually consists of the same three parts that make up any composition: an introduction, a body, and a conclusion. In fact, a well-developed paragraph is a composition in miniature. The introduction to the paragraph is often the topic sentence, which includes the *subject* (what the paragraph is about) and the *focus* (what the paragraph is going to say about the subject). In the paragraph about the disorganized student, the room is the subject and the fact that it reflects the student's disorganized life is the focus. The body of the paragraph consists of several sentences that discuss and develop the topic sentence. The supporting statements are specific rather than general and develop the main idea by examining it in more detail. The conclusion of a paragraph is often a general statement that reemphasizes the main idea expressed in the topic sentence.

The diagram in Figure 7 shows the form and proportions of a model paragraph. Notice that the first word in the paragraph is indented several spaces (usually five to eight) from the margin. Notice too that the introduction is brief, consisting only of the topic sentence. The body of the paragraph is much longer than either the introduction or the conclusion. The conclusion, like the introduction, is brief, usually only one or two sentences.

FIGURE 7

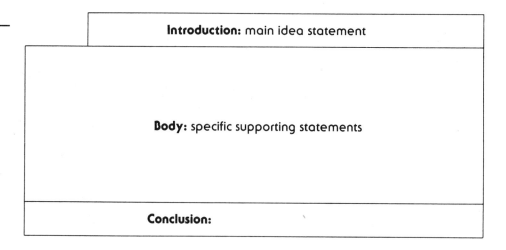

Introduction: main idea statement

Body: specific supporting statements

Conclusion:

This paragraph model is just that—a model, or pattern, to help you in reading and writing paragraphs. Later, in this and future chapters, you will learn about other paragraph patterns. If you observe paragraphs in books, magazines, and newspapers, you will notice that professional writers often write paragraphs that do not follow set patterns. Experienced writers may omit topic sentences, combine patterns, and vary methods of organization to suit subject and purpose. In learning to write, however, you will find that you can develop your writing—and reading—ability more quickly and easily if you start with a simple and specific model such as this one.

Note: Many magazines and books show paragraphing with spacing instead of indentation. Often, as in this textbook, the first paragraph in an essay or section begins at the margin, but additional paragraphs are indented. In writing your own paragraphs and essays, however, you should always indent the first line to show the beginning of a paragraph.

EXERCISE 3.1

The following student paragraphs follow the pattern of the model paragraph. That is, they begin with a topic sentence, are developed by specific supporting statements, and end with a concluding statement. Read each of the paragraphs, carefully examining the details. Then select—from each group of three sentences—the topic sentence that best expresses the main idea supported by the details; write the sentence in the space provided.

PARAGRAPH A

1. My grandfather gives me money whenever I need it.
2. My grandfather is an interesting person.
3. Since my father died, my grandfather and I have become very close.

_____

(Topic sentence)

_____

He always gives me helpful advice. Whenever I have a problem that I can't talk over with my mother, I go to my grandfather. And when I need financial help, my grandfather is always willing to help. For example, when I am sick and need medication, my grandfather tells me to get the medication on his drugstore account. My grandfather is always there to give a helping hand. I look upon him as the father that I lost.

Ray C. Walker

PARAGRAPH B

1. France has one of the world's best programs for taking care of the elderly.

2. Old people in our society are not cared for as well as they are in other countries.

3. Old people should be cared for by their children.

_____

(Topic sentence)

_____

Here in America, elderly people are usually put into old folks' homes, left by themselves, and forced to live on a fixed income. They are not given a tax break or exempted from taxes. When they get sick, they either pay for treatment themselves, or the bills are paid by their families if the costs exceed what is allowed by Medicare. In other countries, however, the situation is much different. In France, for example, elderly people are given free medical services. In Italy, they are exempted from certain taxes. And in the Far East, old people are considered very knowledgeable. This knowledge is put to good use for the benefit of the entire family. The old people are made to feel that they continue to contribute to the family's well being. Americans might learn from other countries how to improve the lives of their old people.

Robert Stidham

PARAGRAPH C

1. An ivy consists of three useful parts: the leaves, the stem, and the roots.

2. The ivy is the most popular house plant because it is easy to grow.

3. Florists usually stock several different kinds of ivy.

_____

(Topic sentence)

_____

The broad, green leaves are not only decorative but also functional. The leaves take in energy from the sunlight; this energy is necessary for the growth of the plant. Attached to the leaves, the stems also serve an important purpose. They carry food from the roots to the leaves. The roots get the food from the water, fertilizer, and nutrients in the soil. All three of these parts are essential for the continued life and health of the ivy.

Phyllis Onley

PARAGRAPH D

1. It is difficult to speak on an unfamiliar subject.

2. The ability to speak in public is an asset.

3. Public speaking really makes me nervous.

_____

(Topic sentence)

_____

The thought of having to speak to a large audience makes me sick. I hate having more than two people looking at me at the same time. I also dislike being given a specific subject on which to speak, such as the Equal Rights Amendment or some aspect of foreign relations with a strange country. These topics make me nervous because I don't know a lot about them. Another thing that makes me nervous is the thought that I might bore my listeners. When it comes to public speaking, I would rather do something else.

Jim R. Sprague

EXPRESSING MAIN IDEAS AS TOPIC SENTENCES

A topic sentence is the general statement that expresses the main idea of a paragraph. In very simple terms, it tells the reader what the paragraph will be about. As illustrated in the model paragraph, the topic sentence usually, but not always, comes at the beginning of the paragraph. The other sentences in the paragraph relate directly to the topic sentence, explaining, expanding, developing, and supporting it.

Subject and Focus

An effective topic sentence has two basic parts: *subject* and *focus*. The subject is what the paragraph is about, and the focus is what is said about the subject. In Paragraph D above, for example, the subject is "public speaking" and the focus is "nervous." The focus may express an attitude or opinion ("My roommate is annoying.") or it may simply indicate what is to follow ("My roommate has three annoying habits."). In other words, the focus is the idea you will develop in your paragraph.

Note: The topic sentence should not be a statement of fact, such as "My roommate is from Ohio" or "My roommate is five feet and ten inches tall," because such statements need no further development or support.

In each of the three topic sentences given as examples below, the subject has been underlined once, and the focus has been underlined twice.

Computers have changed the way we write.

College students study in different ways.

In his report, the researcher identified three new types of tumors.

In most topic sentences the grammatical subject of the sentence is the same as the subject of the topic sentence, and the predicate of the sentence is the same as the focus. In order to express both subject and focus, a topic sentence must be a complete sentence. Most topic sentences are in the form of a statement and should not be confused with titles or subjects, which are usually expressed as phrases. Compare the examples below:

Subject or title: My Favorite Class

Topic sentence: My favorite class this semester is a speech class that is teaching me the art of persuasion.

Subject or title: Going to the Dentist

Topic sentence: A visit to the dentist terrifies me.

Subject or title: How to Give a Great Party

Topic sentence: In order to give a successful party, you must plan in advance.

Notice that the titles (or subjects) tell what the paragraph is about but not what you are going to say about your subject. In other words, the title expresses the subject but not the focus.

EXERCISE 3.2

In each of the topic sentences given below, underline the subject once and the focus twice.

1. Most adults find learning a foreign language difficult.

2. Telephones intrude into the privacy of our daily lives.

3. Music relaxes as well as entertains.

4. Some students experience a great deal of financial stress.

5. Many gun-related accidents involve children.

6. Television commercials communicate forcefully and clearly.

7. Parents of teenage children often feel unappreciated.

8. Not all students like living in a college dorm.

9. Driving in a large city requires nerves of steel.

10. Committees often create more problems than they solve.

Narrowing the Topic Sentence

Notice that the topic sentences in the exercise above are general statements that can be developed by specific details and examples. Since a paragraph is usually less than one page in length, an extremely broad and vague topic sentence is inappropriate. Thus, in deciding on a topic sentence for your paragraph, choose an idea that is general but not *too* general—an idea that you can explain fully in less than a page.

Often a statement that is too general to serve as a topic sentence can be narrowed by the addition of a specific time, place, or person. For example, look at the following sentence:

Sports are exciting.

This statement is so broad that it cannot possibly be developed adequately in a single paragraph. If you narrow the statement by specifying a particular type of sporting event or activity, you will have a workable topic sentence:

Watching a football game keeps me involved.

If you narrow further, you will have an even more effective topic sentence:

Watching the 1988 Super Bowl game between the Washington Redskins and the Denver Broncos kept me on the edge of my chair.

Notice that as you narrow your topic sentence by adding more specific details, it becomes a longer sentence. In general, the more words you use, the more specific your statement will be. Notice also that in the examples above, we have made both the subject and the focus of the topic sentence more specific:

Subject	**Focus**
1. Sports	are exciting.
2. Watching a football game	keeps me involved.
3. Watching the 1988 Super Bowl game between the Washington Redskins and the Denver Broncos	kept me on the edge of my seat.

The exercise below will provide you with practice in narrowing statements so that they will be effective topic sentences. As you revise these sentences, keep in mind the following guidelines:

1. A topic sentence should always be a complete sentence.
2. A topic sentence should not merely state a single fact.
3. A topic sentence should be a general statement but not too broad or vague.

EXERCISE 3.3   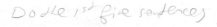 Do the 1st five sentences

Rewrite each broad statement below, narrowing both subject and focus. You will need to change words and add new words.

1. Education is necessary.

_____

_____

2. My friends are very important to me.

_____

_____

3. Exercise improves health.

_____

_____

4. Prices have risen.

_____

_____

5. Pollution causes serious problems.

_____

_____

6. Television is boring.

_____

_____

7. Teachers require too much homework.

_____

_____

8. Modern medicine improves our lives.

_____

_____

9. Movies are better (or worse) than ever.

_____

_____

10. Fashions change quickly.

_____

_____

EXERCISE 3.4

Choose one of your narrowed topic sentences in the exercise above and write a paragraph developing it. In writing your paragraph, follow the model on page 43. Begin with your narrowed topic sentence, add specific supportive details, and end with a conclusion that restates the topic sentence.

IDENTIFYING THE MAIN IDEA IN A PARAGRAPH

Before you can understand what you read, you must be able to identify main ideas and separate them from supporting details. In other words, you must be able to distinguish between the general statements that state the main idea of the paragraph and the specific statements that support the main idea. In most paragraphs the main idea is stated in a topic sentence, or main idea statement. Although this sentence occurs most often at the beginning of the paragraph, it may occur at various other places within the paragraph.

Main Idea as First Sentence

Often, the main idea appears only once in a paragraph. Most frequently, the main idea statement occurs at or near the beginning of the paragraph, usually as the first sentence. Remaining sentences, then, give explanations, examples, and details. This pattern (general to specific) is illustrated below in Figure 8 and the sample paragraph. Underline the main idea statement in the paragraph.

FIGURE 8

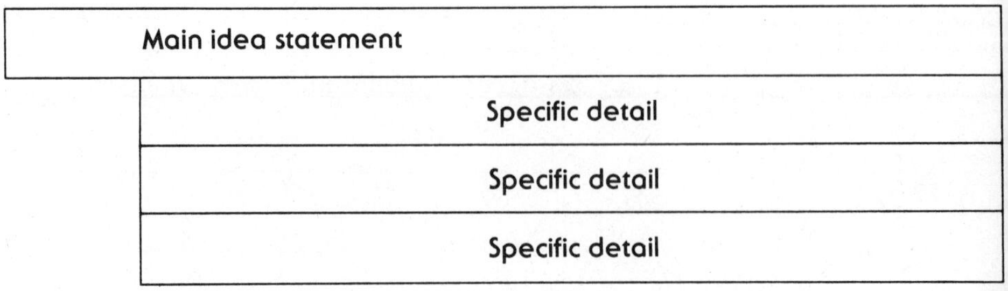

Main idea statement		
	Specific detail	
	Specific detail	
	Specific detail	

The frail-looking woman who opened the door was very old. She wore her silvery white hair in a neat bun on top of her head. Her face rippled with wrinkles, and her eyes were sunken into her skull. She extended to me a thin, gnarled hand, covered by almost transparent, bluish skin. When she asked me to come in, her voice quavered slightly. But her clear blue eyes studied me closely as I entered her house.

Main Idea as Last Sentence

The main idea also occurs frequently as the last sentence of a paragraph. In this case, the paragraph starts with details or examples and concludes with the main idea. This paragraph pattern (specific to general) is illustrated in Figure 9 and the sample paragraph. Underline the main idea statement in the paragraph.

FIGURE 9

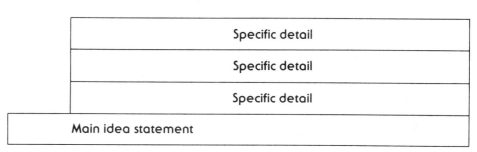

A few years ago only travelers and truck drivers ate breakfast in a restaurant. Today certain restaurants actually specialize in serving breakfast. Pancake houses, omelette shops, and croissant bars compete with cafeterias, truck stops, and coffee shops for the breakfast trade. This change in an established eating pattern—eating bacon and eggs in the privacy of our own homes—is the result of several factors. First, women's liberation and our current economic situation have combined to put women in the work force. A woman who must be at the office or the plant by 8:00 A.M. doesn't have time to prepare a hearty breakfast of biscuits, bacon, and eggs each morning. Second, Americans' tastes are becoming more sophisticated. Traditional breakfast fare seems rather dull compared to Belgian waffles, French omelettes, or huevos rancheros (Mexican eggs with hot sauce). Third, restaurants now offer a wide variety of breakfast items, many of which appeal to those of us who gave up Wheaties when we realized that we were not going to be champions. Increasingly, the American breakfast is moving out of the home and into the marketplace.

Main Idea as First and Last Sentence

The main idea is often stated at both the beginning and the end of a paragraph. However, the final statement of the main idea is not merely a restatement of the topic sentence. The last sentence reinforces the main idea, but it also reflects the conclusions that the writer has reached. This pattern (general to specific to general) is illustrated in Figure 10 and the sample paragraph that follows it. Underline the main idea statements in the sample paragraph.

FIGURE 10

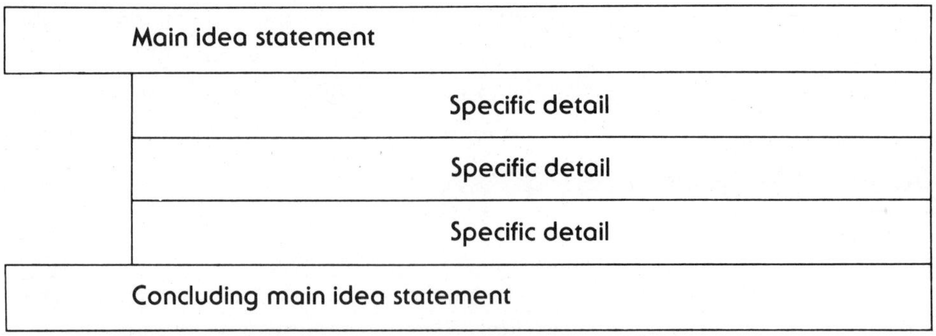

Main idea statement		
	Specific detail	
	Specific detail	
	Specific detail	
Concluding main idea statement		

The weather in West Texas is completely unpredictable. Winter often brings warm, sunny days while summer and spring may surprise residents with periods of cool, cloudy weather. The wind may blow fiercely one day and be completely calm the next. Drought may plague the region at times, only to be followed by heavy rainfall and even flooding. At one time or another, and in no particular order, West Texans experience blinding dust storms, record-breaking heat waves, tornadoes, hail, thunderstorms, and "blue northers"—those sudden cold spells that sweep across the Panhandle and into the state from the north. The climate throughout West Texas is often dramatic, sometimes disagreeable, but seldom dull.

Main Idea as Second Sentence

The main idea may also be stated in the second (or even the third or fourth) sentence of a paragraph. In this pattern, the first sentence or sentences serve as an introduction to the main idea, which restricts or narrows the focus expressed in the first sentence(s). Or the first sentence(s) may function as a transition, linking the paragraph to the preceding one. This paragraph pattern (introduction/transition to general to specific) is illustrated below in Figure 11 and the sample paragraph that follows it. Underline the main idea statement in the paragraph.

FIGURE 11

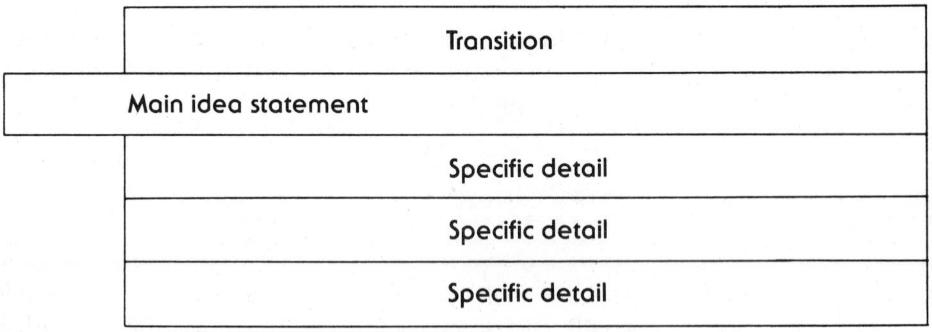

	Transition	
Main idea statement		
	Specific detail	
	Specific detail	
	Specific detail	

In the past few years, millions of Americans have begun to exercise. Unfortunately, many of these energetic but amateur athletes have sustained serious injuries. Tennis players have ruined their elbows, joggers their knees, and aerobic dancers their ankles. More serious injuries are often sustained by those who play competitive sports such as basketball or football. Even lifting weights involves certain risks to muscle tissue and bones. Although some athletic injuries require only time and rest in order to heal, others result in permanent damage.

EXERCISE 3.5

The students who wrote the following paragraphs placed their main idea statements in various positions. Read each paragraph carefully and underline its main idea statement. Indicate in the space provided which paragraph pattern each student used:

> Main idea as first sentence
>
> Main idea as last sentence
>
> Main idea as first and last sentence
>
> Main idea as second sentence

PARAGRAPH A

Football season is the beginning of a confusing and hectic time for me. Having all the children and grandchildren, a group of fourteen people, home for Sunday dinner when the Cowboys are playing is a trying situation. The real fans sit with eyes glued on the television and expect everyone else to watch the game or shut up. The others, who are not as interested in football, laugh and talk even though these activities disturb the hollering, screaming fans. The grandchildren running in and out of the house cause more confusion. As I cook dinner, serve everyone, and referee the children, I begin to feel like the battered football that has been thrown all over the field.

Doris Osborn

Paragraph pattern: _____ 1st sentence _____

PARAGRAPH B

The rain drenched my clothes, teardrops my cheeks, and puddles my shoes and socks. Passing motorists slowed to make sure someone was attending me. My classmates walked cautiously, hesitantly by me—some pitying, some stifling nervous titters, and others horrified at what all of them saw. I watched my little sister come out of her kindergarten class, and I began crying even more. My second-grade teacher, Miss Brown, had rushed outside as soon as the other children told her I'd had an accident; she was holding me tightly, her raincoat dripping more water on my already soaked pants. She "cooed" and "aahed" and told me everything was going to be okay. I knew she was lying. Nothing, *nothing* was ever going to be okay again. . . . I had wet my pants while waiting to be picked up from school, and everyone in the world knew it! This was the most embarrassing moment in my life.

Paragraph pattern: _____

PARAGRAPH C

The basic shots in basketball are the set shot, the lay-up, and the jump shot. The set shot is about the easiest to learn in the game of basketball. To perform the set shot, the player stands in one position and shoots the ball into the basket. The lay-up is a fairly easy shot also. In this shot, the player dribbles the ball up to the goal, jumps, and lays the ball off the backboard into the basket. The last, the jump shot, is the most difficult shot. When shooting the jump shot, a player has to dribble, jump, and shoot all in one motion. Basketball is more fun to play after a player has mastered each of these shots.

Kevin Pannell

Paragraph pattern: _____

PARAGRAPH D

stop at p.59

James Bond is a character with a style of his own. He is an expert at everything he does. When it comes to a car race, he is A. J. Foyt. When it comes to skiing, there is no one on the slopes who can keep up with him. There is nothing he can't do. When an actor can do all this, the final test is women. Believe it or not, Bond is an expert on that subject too. All he has to do is make eye contact with a woman, and she is his for the night. While all this is taking place, he is constantly being shot at. The funny part about it is that he never gets hit. If I could become Bond for one day, I would fulfill my wildest dreams.

Robert Story

Paragraph pattern: _____

PARAGRAPH E

The self-paced earth science lab in Henderson Hall is a practical room designed for learning. On exhibit in three separate locations are glass-enclosed display cases which are filled with shiny minerals and layered rocks and even some oddly shaped fossils. Lining the room are twelve learning tables, each equipped with a tape player and a slide projection screen. Dotting the walls are bunches of colored photographs with an occasional map sprinkled here and there. Three display tables showing various charts and globes are located for easy access in the center of the room. The room is respectfully quiet. A graduate assistant meanders through the room, providing help whenever it is needed. All in all, the Henderson lab is set up to make learning easier.

Paul Clubine

Paragraph pattern: _____

54   THE PARAGRAPH ▪ PART ONE

The following paragraphs have all been taken from college textbooks. Read each paragraph carefully and then underline the main idea. In the space provided indicate the paragraph pattern.

PARAGRAPH A

The assassination of John Kennedy had a profound impact on American society and culture. Because of its suddenness, news of the killing wrenched the American people from the routines of their daily lives. People would later remember exactly what they were doing when they first heard the news. As word of the shooting spread from Dallas, people everywhere crowded around televisions and radios seeking further information. The sophistication of the public media made the assassination a national event, an experience that was shared simultaneously throughout the country and the world. Surveys later revealed that 92 percent of all Americans learned of the assassination within two hours and that more than half of all Americans watched the same television coverage of the event. Millions of citizens were glued to their television sets on November 24 and watched Jack Ruby murder the suspected assassin. As Pearl Harbor had shocked an earlier generation of Americans, the assassination of Kennedy and its aftermath touched the lives of the entire nation.

David W. Noble et al., *Twentieth Century Limited*

Paragraph pattern: _____

PARAGRAPH B

Geography comes from a Greek word whose literal meaning is "description of the earth." But modern geography is concerned with people as well as with the earth, and with relationships and analysis as well as with description. Geographers analyze the physical world and examine relations between places in order to throw light on the patterns and nature of human society. They investigate the interrelationship that exists between people and their physical environment. They examine regional differences, and attempt to account for them. Geographers pick out regional patterns, and try to draw regional lines and identify regional relationships. The earth and its spatial framework, and the pattern of distribution of people and elements on the earth's surface, are studied by geographers to develop a better understanding of the human world. They set people in the framework of the earth they inhabit.

Rhoads Murphey, *Patterns of the Earth*

Paragraph pattern: _____

PARAGRAPH C

One of the tools a wise customer uses is knowing the right time to buy. For instance, you should get linen products, sheets, towels, and blankets during the January White Sale. Each January, merchants reduce the prices of all kinds of household goods, including those made of cotton, wool, or other fabrics. Smart consumers wait until January to buy such products. Shop for winter clothes in the spring, tennis rackets in the fall, and skis in the summer. A good time to shop for Christmas cards and wrapping is a week or two after Christmas.

John S. Morton and Ronald R. Rezny, *Consumer Action*

Paragraph pattern: _____

PARAGRAPH D

Home information networks will make it possible to receive news from computer terminals in the home. The information will be received when the household wants it and at a reasonable price. Any Touch-Tone telephone now used in homes can, with a minor change, also be used as a computer input terminal. The telephone buttons become the keys of a terminal input device. By keying in a code number, an individual will be able to request from an outside computer storage unit the particular news that he or she is interested in. International events, sports results, business news, and home-making news will all be available. The computer will respond with the requested information in seconds. The news material will be printed on a home printer device. Pictures will be displayed either on a TV set equipped with special devices or on a Picture-phone device.

Beryl Robichaud et al., *Introduction to Data Processing*

Paragraph pattern: _____

PARAGRAPH E

Scientists are no exception, but they are devoted to a very specialized cause: the discovery of the nature of nature through basic research. No one else will find the cures for cancers or concern themselves with black holes in space. Cancer research is understandable in the eyes of the general public. It is obviously practical, but black holes may seem to be silly things on which to spend money. The same thing might have been said about the researches of Copernicus. All he did was discover that the earth is not the center of the universe. Although everyone may not consider this fact important, it does have a profound effect on some religious views. Scientists are devoted to the discovery of truth and to expressing it openly for anyone to use.

John W. Harrington, *Discovering Science*

Paragraph pattern: _____

PARAGRAPH F

Soap opera was another legacy from radio to television. The soaps in those early days began with some basic dilemma, then spun fantastic plots and subplots around it. Sometimes it took years to work out the details. One of the original stories, "Our Gal Sunday," wandered on through years of elaborate plots based on the theme expressed in every episode: "Can a girl from a little mining town in the West find happiness as the wife of a wealthy and titled Englishman?" The same basic set of characters carried through the months and years, with new ones disappearing as emphasis shifted.

Robert D. Murphy, Mass Communication and Human Interaction

Paragraph pattern: _____

Implied Main Idea

In some paragraphs the main idea or topic sentence is not stated. Rather, it is suggested or *implied* throughout the paragraph. In the sample paragraph below, the main idea is implied rather than stated. Read the paragraph carefully and then state the main idea in your own words. Key words that provide you with clues to the main idea of the paragraph have been italicized.

On his *inauguration day, Andrew Jackson* mounted his horse and rode to the White House, followed by *a crowd of* 10,000 visitors. The people *pushed* into the White House, climbing on delicate furniture to see the new President. *Excited* supporters trod on valuable rugs with muddy boots, *turned over* pieces of furniture, and *broke* expensive glassware. They *pushed* and *shoved* to get next to the new President, who, after being backed helplessly against a wall, climbed out a back window.

Main idea: _____

_____

_____

Although this paragraph does not have a stated main idea or topic sentence, each sentence is an important detail that suggests or implies the main idea. One way that you could have stated the main idea is that "On Andrew Jackson's inauguration day, his excited supporters destroyed valuable White House property and even endangered the president."

In your reading you will sometimes find paragraphs in which the main idea is implied rather than stated. When you read a paragraph with an implied main idea, you must use the supporting details to help you determine—or infer—the main idea. The main idea you formulate from these details is an *inference.* The process of inferring a main idea from the details within a paragraph is similar to the process of inferring the meaning of an unfamiliar word from its context. In both situations, you use the information given to help you infer what the writer implies.

As a writer, you may occasionally write a paragraph with an implied main idea. If you choose not to include a topic sentence, however, you should keep your main idea clearly in mind, being sure that each detail develops the main idea so clearly that your reader will have no difficulty understanding it.

EXERCISE 3.7

In the three paragraphs below, the main idea is implied rather than stated. Read each paragraph carefully and then state in your own words its main idea:

PARAGRAPH A

He was the only non-American student in the history class. Since most of the discussions focused on American history and culture, he had little to contribute. He was also very shy, especially when he was called on to answer a question. To make matters even worse, he had to work on a group project with three girls, a situation that only increased his normal shyness.

Main idea: _____

_____

PARAGRAPH B

In the distant past, writers labored with quill pens and ink, carefully forming each letter by hand. The fountain pen, when it appeared on the writing scene, was viewed as a marvelous convenience. Then the typewriter provided writers with a much more efficient method of writing, a method that for many years was viewed as the ultimate in writing convenience. When the correcting typewriter came along, writers thought they had died and gone to heaven. Today, however, writers who use computers and word processing programs to write scorn "old-fashioned" typewriters.

Main idea: _____

_____

PARAGRAPH C

Daytime television is dominated by soap operas and quiz shows. Newscasts are brief, sports events are rare, and first-run sit-coms are nonexistent. After the morning shows, which end about the time people's workdays begin, the tube emits the shrieks of quiz show contestants. These inane, materialistic orgies are followed by the high, but seldom serious, drama of the soap operas with their endless crises and passionate sex. Weekly dramatic shows are in some instances clearly related to daytime soap operas but more frequently focus on crime, mystery, or professions such as law, medicine, journalism, and teaching. In the late afternoon, the quiz shows return briefly to spur once more the materialistic cravings of viewers. But, as the workday ends, television provides viewers with newscasts, sports events, situation comedies, serious dramas, and documentaries. Nighttime viewers can choose from movies, comedies, news stories, musical variety shows, and numerous "specials."

Main idea: _____

_____

EXERCISE 3.8

The following paragraphs have been taken from college textbooks. Read each paragraph carefully. The main idea is stated in some of these paragraphs; in others it is implied. In each paragraph underline the main idea statement or words that give clues to the main idea. Then, in the space provided, write the main idea in your own words.

PARAGRAPH A

Some of the resources you have read about—air, water, soil, plants—have been important to people for thousands of years. Some mineral resources have also been important for a long time. For example, early hunters used a certain kind of rock (flint) to make their spearpoints and arrowheads. And people have long valued gold for its beauty. But many other minerals were not resources for early people. They did not know how to use coal or oil. They did not know how to process iron to make tools from it. Therefore none of these minerals were resources for them. Many of the minerals people use today have only become important resources in the past century or two.

Arthur Getis and Judith M. Getis, *Geography*

Main idea: _____

_____

Is the main idea stated or implied? _____

PARAGRAPH B

As we read a work of literature, at some point we develop a sense of its quality. In the case of fiction, we may decide that the story it tells is "great," "good," or just "so-so," and thus we begin to evaluate. Often our initial response is subjective, based largely on personal tastes and prejudices. Such a reaction is natural; after all, we must start somewhere. No doubt many professional critics first come to an assessment of an author's work by way of preference and bias. But sheer curiosity might get the better of us and make us ask: Why? Why is this story so enjoyable or moving, and that one not quite satisfying? To find out, we need to probe the elements of fiction and study its techniques. We need to examine the parts so that we might gain a fuller understanding and appreciation of the whole.

Anthony Dubé et al., Structure and Meaning: An Introduction to Literature

Main idea: _____

_____

_____

Is the main idea stated or implied? _____

PARAGRAPH C

Obviously, beyond the very necessities for life itself, the distinction between needs and wants is not clear, at least not for society as a whole. . . . If you live in the suburbs or in a rural area where there is no public transportation, you may believe that you need a car. Others might need only a bicycle and occasional taxi fares. You may also believe that you need a college education in order "to succeed." Again, others may well reject this idea. Likewise, some families need a washer and dryer, some don't. Most profess the need for a refrigerator and a stove; others need only a cafeteria meal ticket or a hot plate and a cold cellar. The point is that most things an individual or family considers to be needs are not really vital to life but are simply higher-order wants.

Daniel McGowan, Contemporary Personal Finance

Main idea: _____

_____

Is the main idea stated or implied? _____

PARAGRAPH D

The Court is neither free to rule on all controversies in American society nor capable of correcting all injustices. Not only do institutional obstacles prevent the Court from considering certain major questions, but even when it has the authority, the Court exercises considerable self-restraint. Judicial restraint can be based on philosophical as well as on practical considerations. Many justices believe certain types of questions should not be considered by the Court. Furthermore, the court often evades those issues on which it can expect little political or public support. John P. Roche states that the Court's power "has been maintained by a wise refusal to employ it in unequal combat."

Robert S. Ross, American National Government

Main idea: _____

_____

Is the main idea stated or implied? _____

PARAGRAPH E

A woman from another culture, after having an American male shake her hand, remarked that she was glad he decided to shake her hand and not her head. The normative behavior for greeting varies from culture to culture. Among some Eskimos, you lick your hands and then draw them first over your own face and then over the face of the stranger whom you are greeting. The Burmese and Mongols greet one another by smelling each other's cheeks. Polynesians embrace and rub each other's back, and in some places they greet by placing one arm around the neck of the other person and tickling him or her under the chin.

Diana K. Harris and William E. Cole, *Sociology of Aging*

Main idea: _____

_____

Is the main idea stated or implied? _____

PARAGRAPH F

In early days the settlers had little opportunity to manufacture goods. As the colonies became larger and more settled, some manufacturing began. Goods were not made in factories, as they would be today, but by people in their homes. In time, colonial manufacturing grew until it threatened to hurt the sale of goods made in England. So Parliament passed other acts to make sure that articles made in the colonies would not interfere with the sale of English goods. Colonists might make their own clothes or hats, for example, but they could not manufacture clothes or hats to sell in other colonies or in other countries. Colonists might also manufacture iron, but were not allowed to make it into finished articles.

Howard B. Wilder et al., *This Is America's Story*

Main idea: _____

_____

Is the main idea stated or implied? _____

THE LANGUAGE OF CLOTHES
Alison Lurie

Pre-Reading/Writing Exercise

You have already learned that certain prewriting strategies such as freewriting and journal writing can help you find and limit a subject. Another excellent technique for focusing a subject and generating ideas for reading and writing is *brainstorming*. To brainstorm, you simply list ideas randomly as you think of them. As in freewriting, you do not worry about spelling or arrangement; you just write the ideas down before they slip from your memory. For example, a brainstorming session about the topic "computers" might produce the following list:

Apple	interface
IBM	cursor
monitor	delete
bytes	disk
word processing	printer
WordStar	budget
boot	memory
disk drive	create files
DOS	lose files

After you have produced a list of ideas for writing, you can select the most promising possibilities for further consideration. From the above list, for example, you might want to do another brainstorming or freewriting about the topic "word processing." This brainstorming might produce the following list:

revising	WordStar
English class	WordPerfect
composition	hard disk
report	floppy disk
editing	block
spelling check	delete
easy	move
better grade	insert

From this list, you might write a paragraph about how word processing can help you make a better grade on your English composition.

To prepare for the following reading and writing exercises, brainstorm for a few minutes about the subject "clothes." Then *observe* closely the clothes worn on campus by students, faculty members, secretaries, administrators, maintenance workers, etc. If you wish, brainstorm again or freewrite about clothes. Underline the details in your prewriting that interest you the most—perhaps those that focus on a particular article, type, or style of clothing. Do these details focus on a particular article, kind, or style of clothing? Do they focus on the clothing worn by a particular group of people such as students or faculty members? Do these details reflect the personality, interests, values, or occupational needs of the wearer? Write below a general statement that summarizes these details:

_____

_____

_____

Reading Exercise

In the following paragraph Alison Lurie discusses clothes as a "language." Read the paragraph to discover some of the ways clothes help us to communicate with others.

For thousands of years human beings have communicated with one another first in the language of dress. Long before I am near enough to talk to you on the street, in a meeting, or at a party, you announce your sex, age and class to me through what you are wearing—and very possibly give me important information (or misinformation) as to your occupation, origin, personality, opinions, tastes, sexual desires and current mood. I may not be able to put what I observe into words, but I register the information unconsciously; and you simultaneously do the same for me. By the time we meet and converse we have already spoken to each other in an older and more universal tongue.

Alison Lurie, *The Language of Clothes*

1. Is Lurie's main idea stated or implied? _____

What is her main idea?

_____

_____

_____

2. An *analogy* is a detailed comparison in which concrete images are used to explain abstract ideas. For example, a game such as chess (concrete image) is often used as an analogy for life (abstract idea). In "The Language

of Clothes," however, Lurie creates an effective analogy by reversing this pattern. That is, she uses an abstract idea to explain a more concrete subject. What is Lurie's analogy?

_____

_____

_____

3. Clothing communicates many different kinds of information. Write below six specific types of information identified by Lurie:

_____

_____

_____

4. The adverb suffix -*ly* usually means "in a specified manner or way." Using your dictionary if necessary, define the following -*ly* words from the paragraph by Lurie.

a. possibly _____

b. unconsciously _____

c. simultaneously _____

5. To avoid the unnecessary repetition of words in her paragraph, Lurie uses several synonyms, or words with similar meanings. For example, she uses *tongue* as a synonym for *language*. What are three synonyms that she uses for the verb *talk?*

_____

_____

6. What does Lurie mean when she says that clothing is a "universal tongue"?

_____

_____

Discussion Questions

1. How does clothing reveal "sex, age, and class"?

2. Relying on personal experiences and observations, discuss how clothing reflects occupation, origin, personality, or mood.

Writing Exercise

Write a paragraph for your classmates about some aspect of the topic "clothing." You might decide to write about a particular garment, such as a T-shirt, about an ornament, such as a piece of jewelry, or about a particular kind of clothes, such as jeans or uniforms. You might write about a particular style of clothing, such as "preppie," "yuppie," "punk," or "cowboy"; you might focus on the clothing worn by a particular group of people, such as faculty members or students in a particular fraternity or sorority; or you might show how one person's clothing reveals personality or mood.

Before you begin writing, look back at your brainstorming and at the general statement you wrote earlier. You might be able to use this general statement as your topic sentence. Does it include a clear subject and a clear focus? If necessary, revise until you have a satisfactory topic sentence and then write the rough draft of your paragraph.

Rewriting Exercise

Rewriting, like writing, is a process rather than a one-step operation. In fact, you can divide the rewriting process into three stages—revising, editing, and proofreading.

The first and most important part of the rewriting process is *revising.* When you revise a paper, you *resee* or *rethink* what you have written. In other words, when you revise, you make significant changes in the meaning and organization of a piece of writing. Here are some examples of revision:

1. You realize that your topic sentence does not accurately reflect your main idea, so you write a new topic sentence that expresses the idea developed by your supporting details.

2. You decide that one of your details does not relate directly to your main idea, so you change it or delete it.

3. You realize that your paragraph does not have enough support, so you add more details.

4. You notice that the order of your details is confusing, so you rearrange them.

Any of these major changes are revisions. All writers need to make such revisions because they seldom say exactly what they want to say in exactly the right way the first time. Good writing, like good art, requires reshaping. The first draft is only that—a *draft* for the writer to rework.

After you have revised what you have written, you need to edit your paper. *Editing,* the second part of the rewriting process, involves changes in words and sentences. When you edit, you make your writing more readable, more graceful, and more correct. For example, you correct spelling and punctuation, substitute more effective words for your original choices, and vary your sentence structure. Editing will be discussed further in Part Two, but at this point you need to be aware that your responsibility to your reader includes making your writing as easy to read and as free of distracting errors as possible.

Finally, after you have revised and edited what you have written, you are ready for *proofreading*—the third and final stage in the rewriting process. The purpose of proofreading is to correct minor errors in the final draft of your paper. Often these errors are very difficult to see because writers usually anticipate what is on the page—seeing what they *think* they have written rather than what is actually there. In order to counteract this tendency, deliberately look at each word and sentence to see what you have written or typed. In addition, these suggestions can help you proofread more effectively:

1. Read your paper aloud.
2. Type your paper.
3. Read your sentences backward, one at a time, beginning with the last and working forward.
4. If you are using a word processor, begin reading at the end of your document and scroll backwards.
5. Use a pointer (finger, pen, pencil, or cursor) to force yourself to look at each word on the page.

The rewriting process is never really as simple as this discussion suggests. For example, you may discover while you are editing your paper that you also need to revise part of it, or you may decide as you are proofreading that you need to do more editing. However, you should include each of these stages—revising, editing, and proofreading—each time you rewrite.

Now, answer the questions below before revising your paragraph on clothes.

1. What is your topic sentence?
   a. What is its subject? Is your subject sufficiently limited? If not, limit it further.
   b. What is its focus? Is the focus adequately narrowed? If not, narrow it further.
2. What are your supporting details? What other details could you add? Should you omit any details because they do not support your topic sentence? If so, which one(s)?

Once you are satisfied with the content, organization, and development of your paragraph, you should edit it. Are your sentences clear? Have you chosen the best words to express your meaning? Do you see any errors in spelling or punctuation that might distract your reader? When you have edited your paragraph so that it is as clear and readable as possible, proofread your final copy to see if you have written exactly what you intended to write. Read the sentences backward, beginning with the final one and ending with the first one. Look carefully at each word—not just reading but proofreading.

BAD STUDENTS
Jack W. Meiland

Pre-Reading/Writing Exercise

Throughout Chapter 3 you have been writing and identifying main ideas in paragraphs. You have learned that a paragraph has a *subject* (what the paragraph is about) and a *focus* (the point the writer is making about the subject). As you read passages in *Contexts* and your other college textbooks, you will continue to read for the main idea. However, you need to consider not only subject but also *purpose* and *audience*. The relationship among these three elements is illustrated below:

FIGURE 12

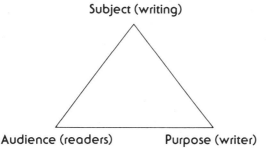

The elements of subject, purpose, and audience are so closely related that no one of them can be changed without affecting the other two.

You will be able to understand many paragraphs and essays better if you think about the writer's purpose, or what the writer wants to accomplish. For example, writers of college textbooks usually want to inform their readers—to present ideas clearly and with convincing support. Other writers may want to entertain or amuse, to stimulate thought or feeling, to explain or make a point, or to persuade their readers to act or think in a certain way. As you read, try to identify the writer's major purpose and decide if it has been achieved.

Readers also need to realize that authors write to meet the specific needs of their audiences, choosing words and examples that are appropriate for the age, sex, occupation, and interests of their readers. Whenever possible, then, you will want to choose articles and books written with an audience like you in mind. For example, if you are doing research for a history report, you would choose articles or books written for students or the general public rather than for scholars or government officials.

The writing situation usually determines a writer's general subject, purpose, and audience. For example, we wrote *Contexts* to help college freshmen understand and improve their reading and writing processes. A technical writer for a large corporation might write a report to explain a particular piece of equipment to new employees, or a realtor might write a description of a house to persuade prospective buyers to purchase it. Writing for a particular audience is like dressing for a specific occasion; you would not wear jeans to a formal wedding reception, nor would you wear a tuxedo or high heels to a picnic. In like manner, writers choose their words and supporting examples to suit their audiences and their purposes.

In your college classes—whether English, history, or psychology—you are often asked to write to show your instructor that you have mastered the required skills or content. Within this learning context, your instructor or text usually provides general topics, purposes, and even audiences. However, the task of determining specific subjects, purposes, and audiences is usually yours.

To help you determine your subject for this Reading/Writing Assignment, think for a minute about what it means to be a "good" student or a "bad" student. Is success as a student measured only in terms of grades? How do you rate yourself as a student? Have you changed as a student since you were young? Are there certain students you admire? Why? How could you improve as a student? What role does a teacher play in determining a student's success?

Brainstorm about this subject, making two lists. In the first column, list some of the qualities that characterize good students. In the second column, list some of the qualities that you associate with bad students.

Reading Exercise

Read the selection below. As you read, compare your ideas about good and bad students with those of the author.

Let me put this in another way. It is true that there are bad teachers—teachers who do not prepare for class, who are arbitrary, who subject their students to sarcasm, who won't tolerate (let alone encourage) questions and criticism, or who have thought little about education. But there are also bad students. By "bad students" I do not mean students who get low grades. Instead, I mean students who do not participate sufficiently in their own education and who do not actively demand enough from their teachers. They do not ask questions in class or after class. They do not discuss the purposes of assignments with their teachers. They do not make the teacher explain the importance and significance of the subject being studied. They do not go to office hours. They do not make the teacher explain comments on papers handed back to the student. They do not take notes on the readings. They just sit in class, letting the teacher do all the work. Education can only be a cooperative effort between student and teacher. By actively participating in these and other ways, you play your proper and necessary part in this cooperative process.

Jack W. Meiland, *College Thinking: How to Get the Best Out of College*

1. Is Meiland's main idea stated in one sentence, stated in more than one sentence, or implied?

_____

Write the main idea in your own words. _____

_____

_____

2. According to Meiland, what are three characteristics of "bad" students?

a. _____

_____

b. _____

_____

c. _____

_____

_____

3. In the second sentence, Meiland uses the word *arbitrary* to describe a bad teacher. Related forms of this word are *arbitrate, arbitrator,* and *arbitration.* The meanings of these words are similar, but the function of each has been changed by a suffix added to the end of the word. The affix *-ary* is an adjective suffix, as in *arbitrary,* or a noun suffix, as in *library; -ate* is a verb suffix, as in *marinate; -or* is a noun suffix meaning "one who"; and *-tion* is a noun suffix meaning "the act of." Use the meanings of these suffixes to help you define these words:

a. arbitrary _____

_____

b. arbitrate _____

_____

c. arbitrator _____

_____

d. arbitration _____

_____

Although these words have similar *denotations* (or dictionary definitions), they have different *connotations* (associations or attitudes). Which of these words has a negative connotation?

_____

Discussion Questions

1. Do you agree with the author that there are bad students as well as bad teachers? Is your idea of a bad student the same as Meiland's? Explain.

2. What are the characteristics of a good student? How can a good student become an even better student?

3. Do you think the author is unfair to students? Why or why not?

4. Discuss how a good teacher can make good students or a bad teacher make bad students.

Writing Exercise

Choose one idea (or a group of related ideas) from your brainstorming and class discussion and develop it into a paragraph for prospective college students planning to enroll at your school (you might even write to particular students you know). Your general purpose will be to help these students make an effective transition into college life. Your specific purpose might be to describe the characteristics of either a good student or a bad student. Or you might discuss how good teachers can make good students or how bad teachers can make bad students. Or you might discuss the qualities needed to succeed in a particular college class such as math or history.

Your paragraph should be informative, including a topic sentence and adequate details to support the point you are making. You may use personal experiences and observations to support your main idea. As you write, keep your readers in mind and try to provide them with helpful information.

Rewriting Exercise

Reread and revise your paragraph, trying to put yourself in the place of your readers. Have you included material that new students would not understand? Have you assumed more knowledge on the part of your readers than you should have? Or, on the other hand, have you talked down to them, giving information that they already have?

As you revise your paragraph, consider also the following questions:

1. What is the purpose of your paragraph?
2. What is your topic sentence?

a. What is its subject? Is the subject sufficiently limited? If not, limit it further.
b. What is its focus? Is the focus adequately narrowed? If not, narrow it further.
3. What are your supporting details. What other details could you add? Should you omit any details because they do not support your topic sentence? If so, which one(s)?
4. Does your paragraph achieve its purpose and communicate to your audience?

After you have revised your paragraph, edit it for problems in sentence structure, punctuation, spelling, and word choice. Then proofread your paragraph for minor errors and omissions.

Chapter 4

SUPPORTING MAIN IDEAS

Well-written paragraphs have a main idea that is either stated in a topic sentence or clearly implied. To communicate convincingly, however, writers must also use facts and details that support the main idea. Read the following paragraph carefully, noticing the details that are used to support the main idea.

> It was a land tortured by weather. There were wet springs when days of pouring rain put creeks out of banks and washed away cotton and corn. At times, before the water could drain off, dust storms blew down from the western plains, clouding the sky and making mouths gritty. Summers were long, hot, dry—worst in the dog days of August, when creeks ran low and scummy and the earth cracked in the sun. The people learned to be grateful for the first cool days of fall, and to bundle up in hard winters when blue northers swept down across Kansas and Oklahoma. They shivered in their shacks and said there was "nothing between them and the North Pole but a bobbed-wire fence."
>
> William Owens, *This Stubborn Soil*

Identify three specific details from this paragraph that support the main idea that the land was tortured by weather.

1. _____

2. _____

3. _____

These specific details about the weather make the main idea vivid and meaningful. The details tell us *how* the land was tortured by the weather. We learn that it was not floods, hurricanes, or earthquakes that the people feared but heat, dust storms, rain, and "blue northers."

FACTUAL AND SENSORY DETAILS

Notice in the reading above the types of details that are included. All of the details are much more specific than is the general statement that expresses the main idea (the topic sentence). However, different types of specific details are used. Some are *factual* (dust storms came from the western plains and northers from Kansas and Oklahoma), but others are descriptive (gritty mouths, scummy creeks, cracked earth). Notice that the descriptive details are all *sensory,* appealing to sight, hearing, smell, taste, or touch. These details help the reader not only to visualize but also to hear, feel, smell, and taste what the writer is expressing. Poetry is full of these sensory details, but good prose is also enriched by their use.

Factual details also help the reader by giving him or her explicit, exact information. Factual details answer such questions as who, what, when, where, why, how, and how many. Often these details provide names, dates, places, numbers, measurements, or statistics.

A good paragraph has an effective balance of the two types of details—sensory and factual. Readers need both types to comprehend fully the main idea. If we read only the general statement that expresses the main idea ("It was a land tortured by weather."), we know very little about the land or what kind of weather the people who lived there endured. The details that support the main idea, however, give us a vivid image of the effects the weather had on the people and land. If we had only the details, on the other hand, we would not be sure exactly what the author was saying about the land. The details without the main idea may leave us wondering what the point of the paragraph is. Thus, good writers and good readers are always concerned about the important relationship between general (main) ideas and specific (supporting) details. Look at the examples below:

EXAMPLES

A. General statement—The clerk looked tired and irritable.
   Factual detail—She had been working behind the busy perfume counter for ten hours.
   Sensory detail—Her feet ached, her voice was almost gone, and she thought that she could not stand another indecisive Christmas shopper.

B. General statement—The fight left the boxer badly injured.
   Factual detail—Four of his front teeth were missing.
   Sensory detail—Purple bruises marked his face, and his eyes were swollen shut.

C. General statement—It was a hot night.
   Factual detail—The temperature never dropped below 90°.
   Sensory detail—The slight breeze that stirred the curtains felt warm on my sweaty skin.

In the examples given above, the general statements are all rather vague and abstract. A tired clerk may be any number of different people in a variety of situations, a boxer may be injured in several different ways, and a hot night in Florida is not the same as a hot night in Maine. The details that support these general statements communicate to the reader specifically what the writer means. The factual details help the reader *understand* the writer's meaning; the sensory details help the reader *experience* the writer's meaning. Working together, the two types of details enable the writer to communicate more exactly and effectively.

EXERCISE 4.1

First, write a sentence using factual details to develop the general statement. Then, write a second sentence that develops the same general statement using sensory details.

EXAMPLE

The sidewalk was hot. (general)

The temperature of the sidewalk was 110°. (factual)

The hot sidewalk sizzled as the rain began to fall. (sensory)

1. The house was deserted.

   a. _____

   _____

   _____

   b. _____

   _____

   _____

2. The students were obviously intelligent.

   a. _____

   _____

   _____

   b. _____

   _____

   _____

3. The young athlete became an outstanding quarterback.

   a. _____

   _____

   _____

b. _____

_____

_____

4. The lawyer worked very hard.

    a. _____

_____

_____

    b. _____

_____

_____

5. Traffic on the freeway has become a serious problem.

    a. _____

_____

_____

    b. _____

_____

_____

6. My grandfather planted a lovely garden.

    a. _____

_____

_____

    b. _____

_____

_____

7. The train sped down the track.

a. _____

_____

_____

b. _____

_____

_____

8. The telephone operator was busy.

a. _____

_____

_____

b. _____

_____

_____

9. It was a cold November.

a. _____

_____

_____

b. _____

_____

_____

10. Computers have changed our lives.

a. _____

_____

_____

b. _____

_____

_____

COORDINATION AND SUBORDINATION OF DETAILS

Effective paragraphs include specific facts and details that support the main idea. Since the details are more specific than the main idea, they are considered _subordinate_ to it. But the details themselves may be equally specific. If so, we say that they are _coordinate_. However, some details may be more specific than others. A detail that is more specific than another is considered _subordinate_ to it.

Thus, all the details in a paragraph are subordinate to the main idea, but some details are coordinate (equal to others), and some are subordinate to others (more specific than others).

Coordinate Details

One way to develop the main idea of a paragraph is to use all coordinate, or equally specific, details. For example, the supporting details in the paragraph below are coordinate.

(1) Mexico offers visitors a world of contrasts. (2) Its pyramids and ancient ruins give us a glimpse of the past while its modern cities provide us with the best of today's technology. (3) Its mountains offer cool weather and majestic peaks while, only a few miles away, its beaches tempt us with brilliant sun and white sand. (4) Its elegant restaurants serve the most sophisticated continental cuisine while, across the street or down the block, sidewalk vendors sell the simplest of native foods. (5) Thus the traveler to Mexico is faced with a series of delightful decisions.

Choppy sentences without transition.

In this paragraph, the main idea, which is stated in sentence (1), is supported by three equally specific, or coordinate, supporting details: sentences (2), (3), and (4). Sentence (5) concludes the paragraph and reinforces the main idea. This paragraph can be diagrammed as shown below.

FIGURE 13

Main idea (sentence 1)	
	Coordinate detail (sentence 2)
	Coordinate detail (sentence 3)
	Coordinate detail (sentence 4)
Conclusion (sentence 5)	

FIGURE 14

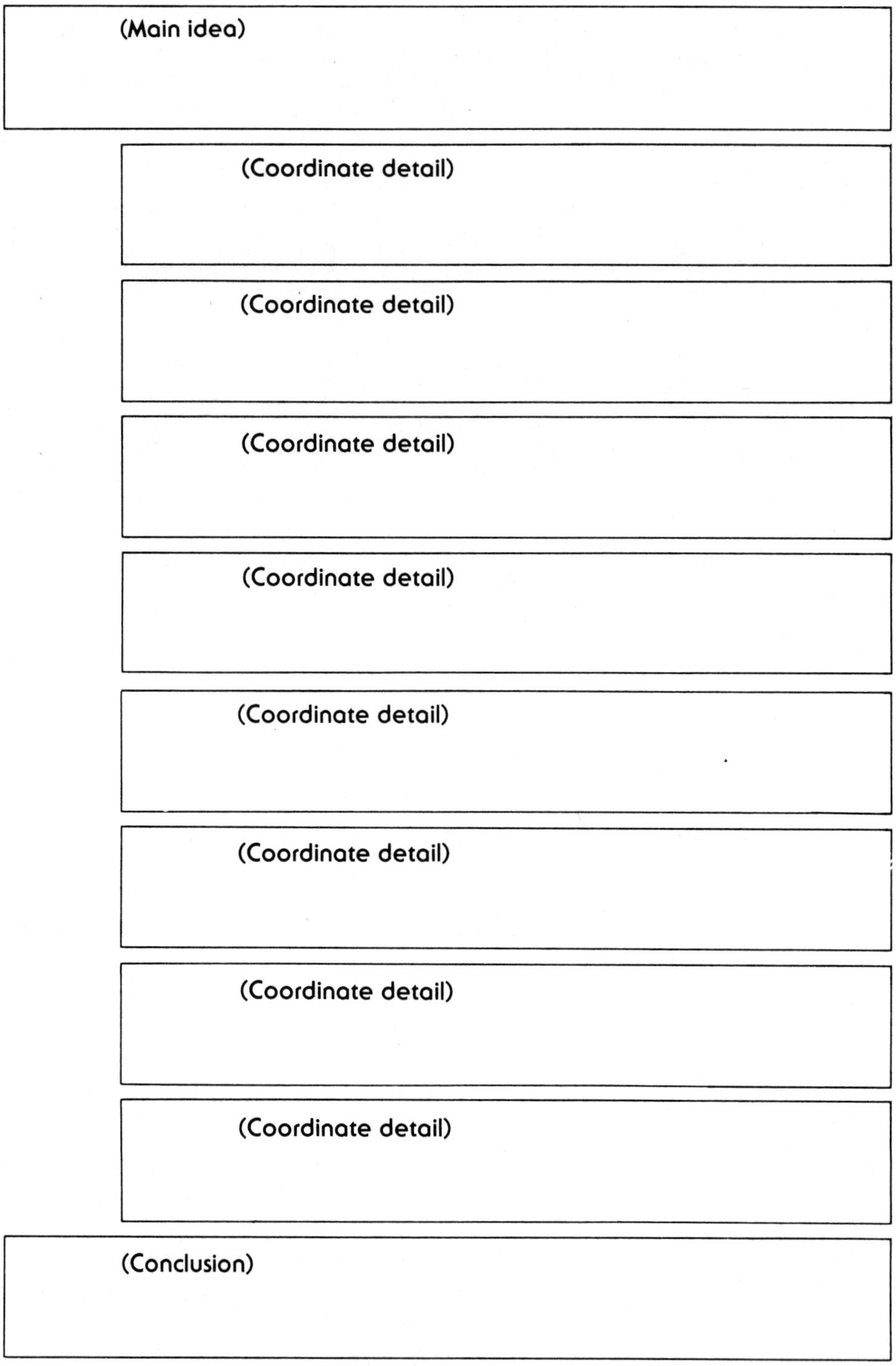

(Main idea)

(Coordinate detail)

(Coordinate detail)

(Coordinate detail)

(Coordinate detail)

(Coordinate detail)

(Coordinate detail)

(Coordinate detail)

(Coordinate detail)

(Conclusion)

EXERCISE 4.2

Write a paragraph telling what you do in the morning to get ready to go to class or to work. Develop your paragraph with factual and sensory details that are coordinate, or equally specific. Use the block form on page 78 (Figure 14) to write your rough draft. You should write a different sentence in each block, but you may not need to use all of the blocks.

Subordinate Details

Another way to develop the main idea of a paragraph is to use subordinate details. In this pattern, each detail is subordinate to (more specific than) the one before it. For example, the details in the paragraph below are increasingly subordinate, with each detail being more specific than the previous one.

Deductive paragraph

topic

(1) Clothes make the woman as well as the man. (2) Many business and professional women are realizing that clothes are an asset not just to their appearance but also to their careers. (3) A female lawyer or doctor must select clothes that inspire confidence in her clients or patients. (4) Sexy high heels, gaudy jewelry, and frilly ruffles do not reflect the competence that people expect in doctors and lawyers.

In this paragraph the main idea, which is stated in sentence (1), is a general statement about clothes and women. Sentence (2) is more specific, narrowing to the effect that clothes have on the careers of business and professional women. Sentence (3) is still more specific, focusing on women in two particular professions, medicine and law. Finally, sentence (4) cites specific types of clothing that are inappropriate for female doctors and lawyers to wear to work.

FIGURE 15

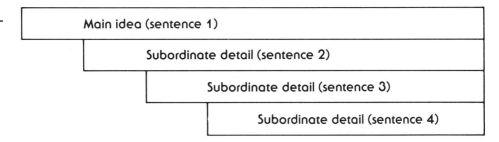

EXERCISE 4.3

Write a paragraph describing your favorite clothing—what you most enjoy wearing. Develop your paragraph with factual and sensory details that are subordinate, or increasingly specific. Use the following block form (Figure 16) to write your rough draft. Write a different sentence in each block.

FIGURE 16

(Main idea)

(Subordinate detail)

(Subordinate detail)

(Subordinate detail)

Coordinate and Subordinate Details

Another important way to support the main idea of a paragraph is to combine coordinate and subordinate details. That is, we may use two, three, or more supporting details that are coordinate, or equally specific, and then develop each of the coordinate details further by adding one or more subordinate, or more specific, details.

The coordination/subordination pattern is illustrated for you in the paragraph below. This paragraph contains three coordinate details, each of which is further supported by one subordinate detail. As you read the paragraph, try to decide which sentences contain the coordinate details and which contain the subordinate details.

(1) My father's death, which occurred when I was nine years old, had several important effects on me. (2) First of all, I felt great sadness and loneliness. (3) For the first few months, my loneliness was so great that I often dreamed that my father would miraculously return. (4) In addition, throughout the rest of my childhood, I was afraid of losing someone else whom I loved. (5) Whenever my mother was away from home, I was always nervous until she returned. (6) Finally, the loss of my father caused me to develop a greater sense of responsibility. (7) For example, I believed that with my father gone I was responsible for helping my mother with her chores. (8) My father's death, therefore, left me lonely, frightened, and responsible—a young child with adult feelings.

In this paragraph, the main idea is stated in sentence (1); the coordinate supporting details are stated in sentences (2), (4), and (6); the subordinate supporting details occur in sentences (3), (5), and (7); and sentence (8) briefly summarizes the paragraph. This paragraph pattern can be diagrammed as shown in Figure 17.

FIGURE 17

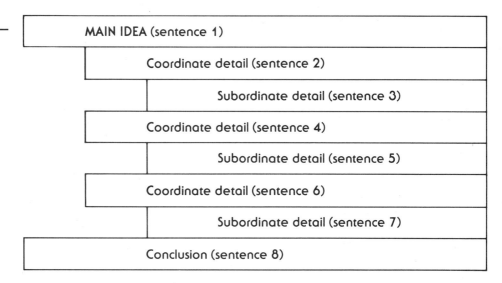

A popular variation of the coordination/subordination pattern is illustrated in the following paragraph, which also contains three coordinate supporting details. However, in this pattern, each coordinate detail is itself supported by not one but two subordinate details. As you read the paragraph, try to determine which sentences contain the coordinate supporting details and which contain the subordinate supporting details. (*Note:* The subordinate details are also coordinate, or equal, to one another. However, they are more accurately called subordinate details because they are not only subordinate to the main idea but also to the coordinate details.)

(1) The older woman who returns to school faces a number of problems. (2) For one thing, upon enrolling in college, she immediately becomes a minority. (3) She is no longer surrounded by her peers—other women who have shared experiences—but by young people, many of whom are the age of her own children. (4) Very often the only person in a class who is as old as she is the instructor (and even he or she may be much younger). (5) In addition, an older woman who re-enters the academic world assumes the double burden of managing a household while being a student. (6) She may still have children at home or a husband who makes demands on her time. (7) If she is divorced or widowed, she faces problems such as managing finances, maintaining a car, and mowing the lawn. (8) Finally, a woman middle-aged or older who decides to complete her education faces the challenge of developing a new image of herself—one that is not related to her roles as wife and mother. (9) This problem may prove to be the most difficult one of all, for it is not easy to assume a new identity, especially if the former one has been comfortable and secure. (10) In order to make the transition from housewife to student, a woman must think of herself as an individual rather than as a person whose identity depends upon her relationships to other people. (11) Although her maturity may well prove to be an asset as she continues her studies, the older co-ed initially finds herself in a challenging situation.

In this paragraph, the main idea is stated in sentence (1); the coordinate supporting details are stated in sentences (2), (5), and (8); subordinate supporting details are stated in sentences (3) and (4), (6) and (7), and (9) and (10); and the concluding statement comes in sentence (11). This paragraph can be illustrated as shown in Figure 18.

FIGURE 18

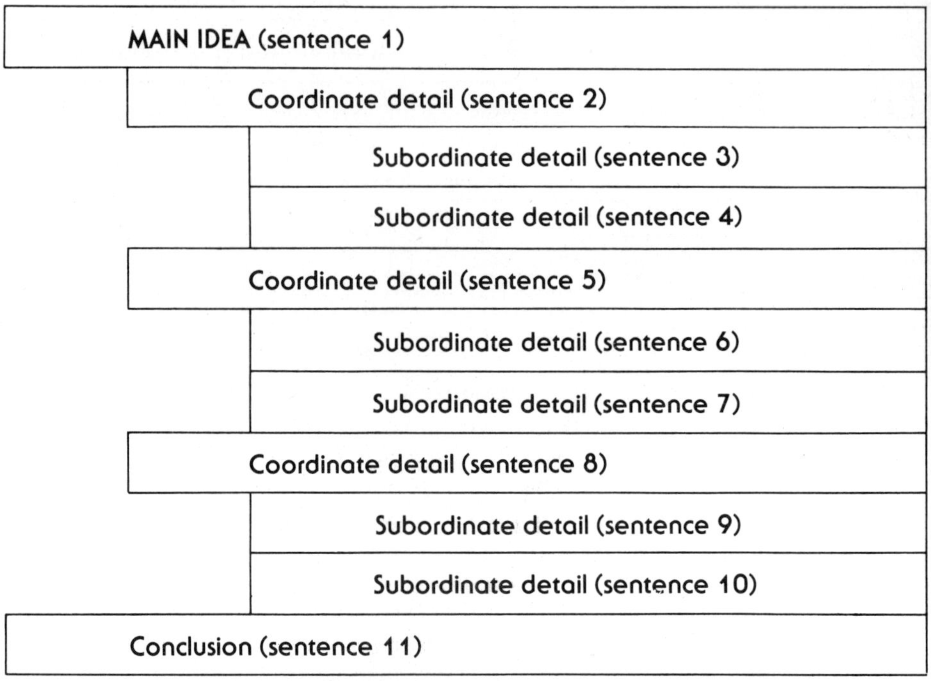

MAIN IDEA (sentence 1)
Coordinate detail (sentence 2)
Subordinate detail (sentence 3)
Subordinate detail (sentence 4)
Coordinate detail (sentence 5)
Subordinate detail (sentence 6)
Subordinate detail (sentence 7)
Coordinate detail (sentence 8)
Subordinate detail (sentence 9)
Subordinate detail (sentence 10)
Conclusion (sentence 11)

EXERCISE 4.4

Write a paragraph telling what you like about your favorite place to eat—a cafeteria, a restaurant, or your home. Use both factual and sensory details, and develop your paragraph according to the coordination/subordination model you have just studied. Use two or three coordinate details, developing each with one or, better yet, two subordinate details. Use the block form shown in Figure 19 to write your rough draft. You should write a different sentence in each block, but you may not need to use all of the blocks.

The paragraph patterns illustrated in this chapter should give you some idea of how supporting details can be arranged. You should remember, however, that these are only three of several possible patterns. In the exercises that follow, you will be able to identify these patterns in some of the paragraphs. In other paragraphs, however, supporting details may be arranged in different ways.

FIGURE 19

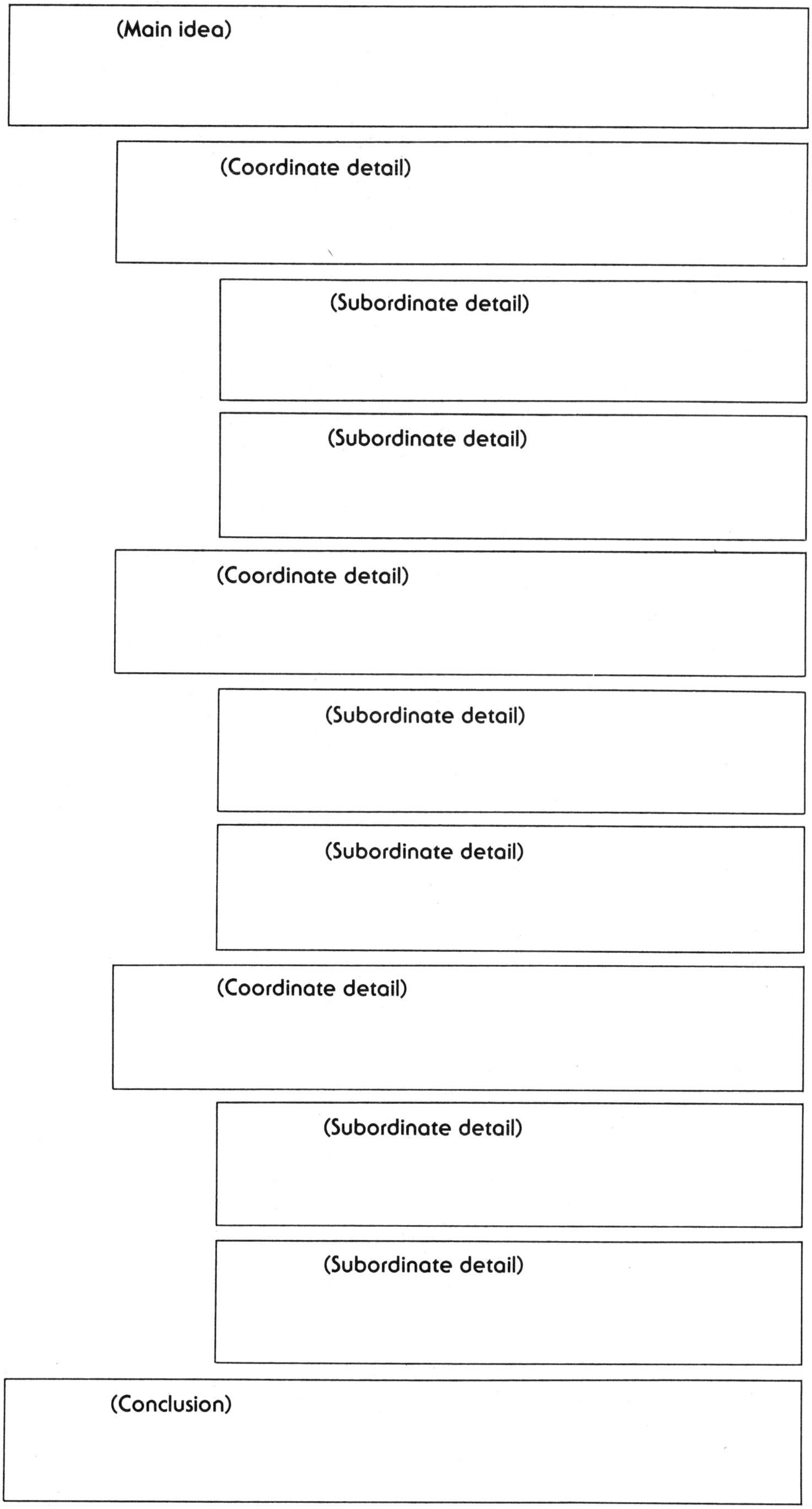

(Main idea)

(Coordinate detail)

(Subordinate detail)

(Subordinate detail)

(Coordinate detail)

(Subordinate detail)

(Subordinate detail)

(Coordinate detail)

(Subordinate detail)

(Subordinate detail)

(Conclusion)

EXERCISE 4.5

The following paragraphs were written by freshman English students. Read each paragraph and then answer the questions that follow.

PARAGRAPH A

On a sunny Sunday afternoon the sandy beach attracts several different types of visitors. Young mothers go to the beach to take their children to swim and surf in the warm water. Teen-age girls go to lie down on the sandy beach to get a sun tan and to watch the beauty of the blue water. Young men and teen-age boys go to play on the sand dunes with their four-wheel-drive trucks to see which truck doesn't get stuck. Others, like me, just go to watch the pretty girls sun bathing on the sand dunes.

Paul Noyola

1. What is the main idea of the paragraph?

   _____

   _____

2. Are the supporting details equal or unequal in importance? In other words, are the details coordinate? Or are some subordinate to others?

   _____

3. In the space below, briefly list three supporting details.

   a. _____

   _____

   b. _____

   _____

   c. _____

   _____

PARAGRAPH B

My bedroom at home was the sunniest, brightest, and neatest room in our house. My room was full of the sun. I was usually awakened in the early morning hours by it beaming through my east window. My sheer curtains let the sun shine in all day. In addition, the room was decorated in bright colors—mostly yellow and white with green accents. My bedposts were painted lemon yellow, and I had a dresser painted to match. I had a green lamp sitting on a white table with four tiers that could be arranged the way I wanted them. I had limited space in my room, so I made sure everything was kept neatly in its place. The closet in my room was well organized, with all my clothes color coordinated and all the lengths matched. My odds and ends were kept in boxes in one corner of the room, making the room seem spacious instead of cluttered. Returning home and staying in this room always makes me feel happy and safe because it has come to represent a simpler time in my life.

Debbie Rodriguez

1. What is the main idea of the paragraph?

_____

_____

2. What are the three coordinate details in the paragraph?

a. _____

_____

_____

b. _____

_____

_____

c. _____

_____

_____

3. Write below one of these coordinate details and the subordinate details used to develop the paragraph.

Coordinate supporting detail: _____

_____

_____

Subordinate supporting details: _____

_____

_____

_____

_____

PARAGRAPH C

There are many differences between college and high school football. Of course, the most obvious difference is the age of the players, a difference which makes college football a harder hitting and physically stronger game. But there are bigger and more technical differences than this obvious one. The first is the difference in practice sessions. In high school there is much teaching of techniques and conditioning of the body. In college there is only hard-hitting practice with the teaching coming at night during "skull sessions." Another difference is the purpose of the games. High school games are played for fun. They are played to give the townspeople something to do on Friday nights, and there is very little competition. On the other hand, college football games are played for money. The players are playing for scholarships, and the fans are paying to see the competition.

Glenn Regmund

1. What is the main idea of this paragraph?

_____

_____

_____

2. This paragraph contains both coordinate and subordinate support- ing details. What are the two coordinate details in the paragraph?

  a. _____

  b. _____

3. The last coordinate detail is developed by two subordinate details, each of which is further developed by even more specific details. Fill in the diagram in Figure 20 to show the relationships of the details under the coordinate statement in the first block. (*Note:* One sentence may contain two details.)

FIGURE 20

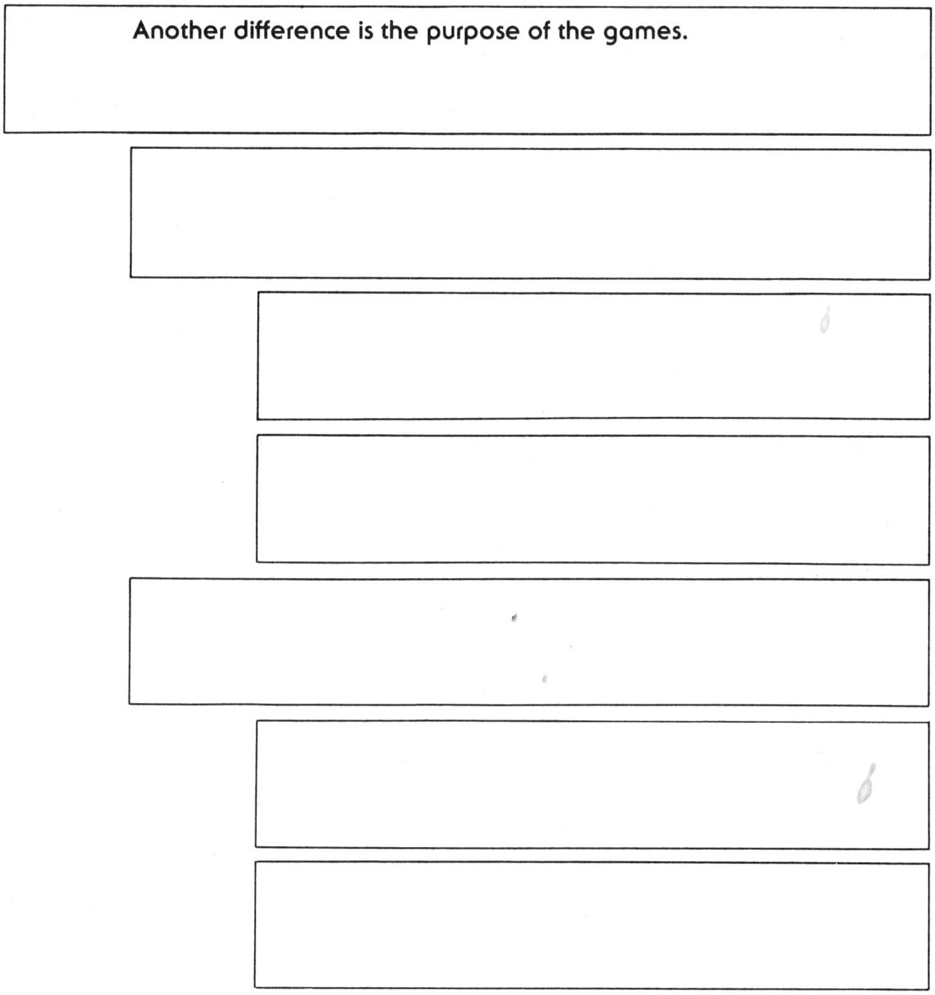

Another difference is the purpose of the games.

EXERCISE 4.6

The following paragraphs were taken from freshman textbooks. Read each paragraph and then answer the questions that follow it.

PARAGRAPH A

We will begin by dividing the whole writing process into three stages: prewriting, writing, and rewriting. In the prewriting stage you try to get clear in your mind what your specific approach to the subject should be, what kinds of materials you need, how these materials should be organized and presented for the particular kind of reader you have in mind; in short, you plan the organization and content of your projected paper. In the writing stage you work out your plan in detail through the first draft. In rewriting you examine what you have done and consider where and how the first draft can be improved.

James M. McCrimmon, *Writing with a Purpose*

1. What is the main idea of this paragraph?

   The main idea of this paragraph is writing process

2. Are the supporting sentences coordinate (equal) or subordinate (unequal)?

   The supporting sentences are subordinate

3. In the spaces below, rewrite in your own words the supporting ideas.

   a. _____

   _____

   b. _____

   _____

   c. _____

   _____

PARAGRAPH B

(1) Against Britain's armies of well-trained regulars, the Patriots seemed ill-matched. (2) For one thing, the soldiers of the Continental Army had little experience in military tactics and fighting in open battle. (3) Their training had been limited largely to frontier warfare against the Indians and the French. (4) Their officers, too, had little experience compared to British officers. (4) What is more, the Continental Army was loosely organized. (5) Patriots had joined up, not because they had been ordered to do so, but of their own free will. (6) Such volunteers felt free to return to their homes whenever their short terms of service were finished. (7) As a result, the leaders of the army could hardly tell from day to day how many troops were under their command. (7) Also, the colonies had no real navy. (8) Against the strongest navy in the world the Americans could send not one first-class fighting ship.

Howard B. Wilder et al., *This Is America's Story*

1. What is the main idea of this paragraph?

   The main idea of this paragraph is to compare Britain's armies and the Continental Army.

2. This paragraph includes both coordinate and subordinate details. How many coordinate details does it include?

_____

3. What are the coordinate details?

   a. _____

   _____

   b. _____

   _____

   c. _____

   _____

4. What subordinate details support the first coordinate detail?

   a. _____

   _____

   b. _____

   _____

5. What subordinate details support the second coordinate detail?

   a. _____

   _____

   b. _____

   _____

   c. _____

   _____

PARAGRAPH C

Four basic terms are often used by geographers in describing the surface of the land. You probably know about *hills* and *mountains*. The other two terms—*plains* and *plateaus*—both describe areas that are flatter than hills or mountains. A large, flat, low area of land is called a *plain*. Some plains are very flat, and you can see for a great distance in all directions. Other plains are rolling, but the slopes are not as steep as hills. A large area that stands higher than the land around it is called a *plateau*. Sometimes a plateau is called a tableland, because it is raised like a table above the land around it. Plateaus are fairly level, but some of them have deep valleys where streams and rivers have cut through the land.

Arthur Getis and Judith M. Getis, Geography

1. What is the main idea of the paragraph?

   _____

   _____

2. This paragraph combines coordinate and subordinate details. The first coordinate detail—"You probably know about hills and mountains"—is not developed by further details. However, a second detail of equal importance to this one is developed. What is this detail?

   _____

   _____

3. This second major coordinate detail is developed by both coordinate and subordinate details. Show the relationship between these details by writing them in the appropriate spaces in Figure 21 on page 91.

PARAGRAPH D

The North and South were also divided on the issue of federal regulation of commerce. The North, which derived much of its income from commerce, wanted the federal government to be able to make protective commercial regulations and to use a low tariff on imports as a source of revenue. On the other hand, the South, which made its money by exporting staple produce, such as tobacco and rice, feared that a government with the power to regulate commerce might legislate high export duties on such items. The South therefore demanded that all acts regulating commerce be passed by a two-thirds majority in Congress. The South also demanded assurance that Congress would not interfere with the slave trade.

Rebecca Brooks Gruver, An American History

1. What is the main idea of the paragraph?

   _____

   _____

FIGURE 21

The other two terms—*plains* and *plateaus*—both describe areas that are flatter than hills or mountains.

2. How many coordinate details does the paragraph contain?

_____

3. What are the coordinate details?

   a. _____

   _____

   _____

   b. _____

   _____

   _____

4. Which coordinate detail is supported by subordinate details?

_____

5. In your own words, what is one of these subordinate details?

_____

OUTLINING SUPPORTING DETAILS

An outline is essentially a visual representation of general and specific relationships. General statements form the main headings of an outline, and specific statements form the subheadings. But, to outline, you must determine the relationships among the various supporting statements, and to do that you need to understand coordination and subordination.

Since coordinate ideas are equal, they should be represented on your outline in the same (parallel) manner. If there are more specific details, these should be parallel to one another but subordinate to the more general statements. For example, social sciences, physical sciences, and humanities are three general categories of subjects you study in college. On an outline, therefore, you would arrange them as three equal, or coordinate, headings:

EXAMPLE

Social sciences

Physical sciences

Humanities

If you included some specific examples of each of these three general categories, you would arrange them under the appropriate headings. For example, if you wanted to list psychology, sociology, and anthropology under social sciences, you would list these equally specific examples in a coordinate pattern.

EXAMPLE

Social sciences

    Psychology

    Sociology

    Anthropology

The numbers and letters you use in your outline should reinforce the coordinate and subordinate patterns:

EXAMPLE

I. Social sciences
  A. Psychology
  B. Sociology
  C. Anthropology

If you add additional details that are even more specific, you should indicate that these details are subordinate to those that are more general but are coordinate to one another. For example, you could add two specific types of psychology courses and could indicate this further level of subordination in the formal outline below:

EXAMPLE

I. Social sciences
  A. Psychology
    1. Abnormal psychology
    2. Experimental psychology
  B. Sociology
  C. Anthropology

EXERCISE 4.7

Complete the formal outline below by adding the names of specific courses under the appropriate general headings. If necessary, use your college catalog to find this information.

I. Social science
  A. Psychology
    1. Abnormal psychology
    2. Experimental psychology
  B. Sociology
    1. _Introduction to Sociology_
    2. _Minorities in America_

C. Anthropology
    1. _____
    2. _____

II. Physical science
    A. _____Tennis_____
        1. _____Beginning_____
        2. _____Intermediate skills_____
    B. _____Golf_____
        1. _____Beginning_____
        2. _____Intermediate_____

III. Humanities
    A. _____Humor in America_____
    B. _____Art History & Apprec_____
    C. _____Hist / Radio_____

Planning Outlines

Remember, however, that not all outlines have to be formal. If you are using an outline to plan what you are going to write, you can use any form that communicates clearly to you. Planning outlines can assume a variety of forms as long as they communicate accurately the relationships that exist among the different items of information included. For example, you could use the following informal outline to represent the same information that you illustrated in the formal outline above:

FIGURE 22

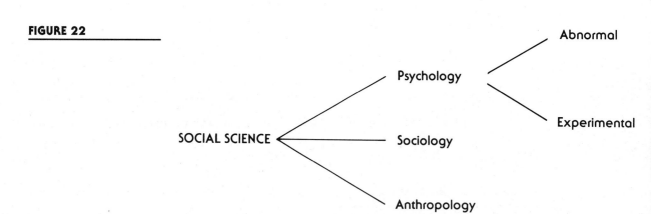

The form that a planning outline takes depends on you, since you are the one who will be using it. Some people call these planning outlines "scratch" outlines because they can be little more than scratches on a paper if the writer who makes them understands what those scratches mean.

You could communicate the same information in the following way:

FIGURE 23

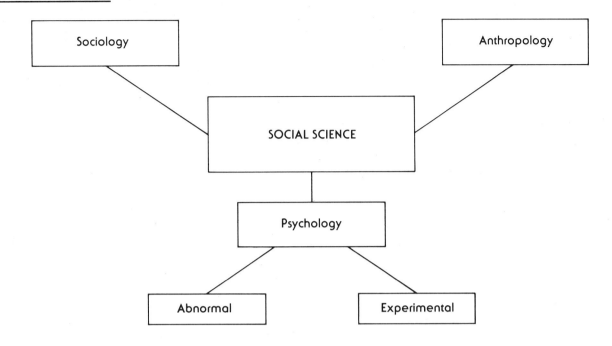

EXERCISE 4.8

On a sheet of paper, make an informal planning outline of a paragraph explaining to a new college student the different disciplines under which college courses are organized. You will need to indicate the same relationships between the general categories and specific courses that you used in the formal outline on pages 93 and 94, but choose a different format—one similar to the informal outlines illustrated above or one that you make up yourself.

READING/WRITING ASSIGNMENT 4A

A KIOWA GRANDMOTHER
N. Scott Momaday

Pre-Reading/Writing Exercise

In previous chapters you learned to use the prewriting strategies of journal writing, freewriting, and brainstorming. Another helpful prewriting technique is *mapping*. Mapping, like other prewriting techniques, helps you generate ideas through association. Mapping is a particularly helpful strategy for producing increasingly specific associations from a broad, general topic.

If your instructor asked you to write a paper on the general topic "college," for example, you might begin by mapping the topic—adding to it related examples, ideas, and associations. For instance, college suggests the more specific subtopics "classes," "goals," "careers," and "registration." A map shows in visual form the relationships among these ideas. You might circle and cluster related ideas around the word *college,* as shown below:

FIGURE 24

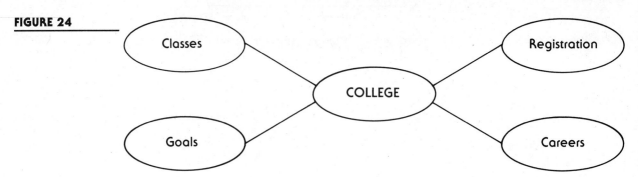

Or you might write the topic and then branch down and away from it as shown here:

FIGURE 25

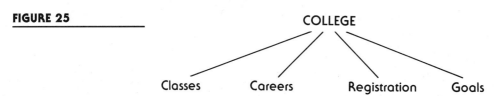

Each of these subtopics in turn suggests even more specific ideas and examples. Eventually, as illustrated below, you will have generated a number of ideas, associations, and details related to the original general topic. The most specific ideas—and therefore probably the best ideas for writing—will be on the outer edges of your mapping.

FIGURE 26

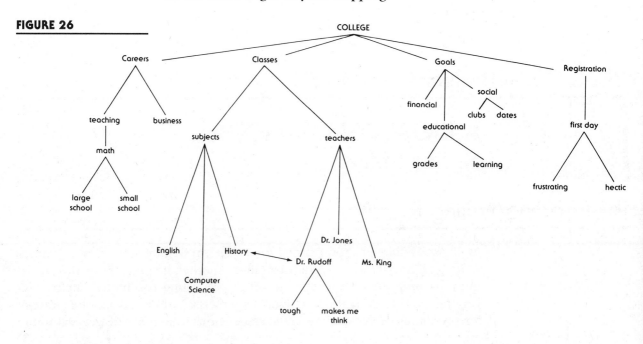

After completing this mapping, you might decide to write a paragraph about the social goals of college, about your career objective to teach math in a large high school, or about how your history teacher Dr. Rudoff makes you think for yourself.

Now, to prepare for your Reading/Writing Assignment, do a mapping exercise on the general topic "interesting people." Be sure to continue mapping until you have listed not only types of people but also specific individuals and specific details about several of these individuals.

After you complete your mapping, decide which of your ideas interests you most. Then freewrite for five or ten minutes about this specific idea.

Reading Exercise

As you read the following paragraph, determine Momaday's purpose and his main idea. In addition, notice how he uses both factual and sensory details.

Now that I can have her only in memory, I see my grandmother in the several postures that were peculiar to her: standing at the wood stove on a winter morning and turning meat in a great iron skillet; sitting at the south window, bent above her beadwork, and afterwards, when her vision failed, looking down for a long time into the fold of her hands; going out upon a cane, very slowly as she did when the weight of age came upon her; praying. I remember her most often at prayer. She made long, rambling prayers out of suffering and hope, having seen many things. I was never sure that I had the right to hear, so exclusive were they of all mere custom and company. The last time I saw her she prayed standing by the side of her bed at night, naked to the waist, the light of a kerosene lamp moving upon her dark skin. Her long, black hair, always drawn and braided in the day, lay upon her shoulders and against her breasts like a shawl. I do not speak Kiowa, and I never understood her prayers, but there was something inherently sad in the sound, some merest hesitation upon the syllables of sorrow. She began in a high and descending pitch, exhausting her breath to silence; then again and again—and always the same intensity of effort, of something that is, and is not, like urgency in the human voice. Transported so in the dancing light among the shadows of her room, she seemed beyond the reach of time. But that was illusion; I think I knew then that I should not see her again.

N. Scott Momaday, *The Way to Rainy Mountain*

1. What is Momaday's purpose in this paragraph?

_____

_____

2. What is the main idea of Momaday's paragraph?

_____

_____

3. One sentence of the paragraph includes several coordinate details listing different postures of Momaday's grandmother. What are three of these coordinate details?

a. _____

b. _____

c. _____

Which detail is fully developed in the last part of the paragraph?

_____

4. Momaday uses both *factual* and *sensory* details in the paragraph. Which kind of details does he use more frequently?

_____

What are two factual details in the paragraph?

_____

_____

What are three effective sensory details?

a. _____

_____

_____

b. _____

_____

_____

c. _____

_____

_____

To which of the five senses does Momaday appeal most effectively?

_____

5. Which details best reveal the character and personality of Momaday's grandmother?

_____

_____

_____

6. What does Momaday suggest about his grandmother in his conclusion?

_____

_____

7. Context not only gives clues to word meaning; it may also determine which of several possible word meanings is relevant to a particular usage. For example, *posture* often means "a characteristic way of bearing one's body." However, Momaday uses the word *posture* to mean not only the position of his grandmother's body but also her position or role (cooking, praying). Other words that may have more than one meaning are *pitch, descending,* and *transported. Pitch* is probably most familiar to you as a verb meaning "to toss" or a noun meaning "a thrown ball." In Momaday's paragraph, however, the word means

_____

_____

Descending is usually used in a geographical context, meaning "to go downward." As used by Momaday, however, the word means

_____

_____

Transported is also typically used in a geographical context meaning "to carry from one place to another," but Momaday uses it to mean

_____

_____

Writing Exercise

Use your mapping and freewriting as the basis for a well-developed paragraph in which you describe an interesting person—a new roommate, a special teacher, a store clerk, or your high school coach, for example. Assume that your audience is a classmate who has never seen this person. Use specific details—both factual and sensory—to recreate not only the physical details but also the personality and character of the person you are describing.

The following questions and suggestions will help you in planning and developing an effective paragraph:

1. Do you have a limited subject? What is it?

2. What is your focus? That is, what point do you want to make about the personality or character of the person you are describing? Do you want to show your subject to be intelligent, friendly, messy, kind, pathetic, unreasonable?

3. Look carefully at your Pre-Reading/Writing Exercise. What factual details can you use to describe the person you are writing about? What sensory details can you use? To which senses—seeing, hearing, touching, tasting, or smelling—will these details appeal?

4. Review the organizational patterns of coordination and subordination you have practiced in this chapter. Do the details you plan to include in your descriptive paragraph fit one of these patterns? Or can you use one of the patterns to generate even more effective details?

Rewriting Exercise

After all the members of the class have written their first drafts, work in groups of three or four students to review and make suggestions for revising these drafts. Remember as you read one another's papers that your peer reviews will be most helpful if you give honest but tactful critiques. If you make only positive comments about your classmates' papers, you will not provide them with any direction for revision. If, on the other hand, you make only negative comments, you may discourage your classmates from trying to improve their papers.

Use the following questions as an editing guide in reading each paper and writing comments about it.

1. What do you like best about the paragraph?
2. What is the topic sentence?
   a. What is its subject? Is the subject sufficiently limited? How could it be further limited?
   b. What is its focus? Is the focus adequately narrowed? How could it be further narrowed?
3. Does the paragraph contain both factual and sensory details?
   a. What are the most effective factual details?
   b. What are the most effective sensory details?
   c. What other details could be added?
   d. Should any details be omitted because they do not support the topic sentence? If so, which one(s)?
4. On what organizational pattern is the paragraph based? That is, does it use coordinate details, subordinate details, or a combination of coordinate and subordinate details? If the paragraph uses a combination of coordinate and subordinate details, what are the major coordinate details?

5. What is the purpose of the paragraph? Does the paragraph achieve its purpose and communicate to its audience? Why or why not?

After you and your classmates have evaluated one another's drafts and exchanged oral and written suggestions for revisions, rewrite your paragraphs. Remember that in a peer evaluation session, the final decisions are yours. Accept helpful suggestions but reject those you do not believe will improve your paragraph. After you have revised your paragraph, edit and proofread it.

READING/WRITING ASSIGNMENT 4B

MY NATIVE PLACE
John Steinbeck

Pre-Reading/Writing Exercise

Think about a place to which you have a strong reaction. You may react to this place because it is new or different, or you may react to it because you like or dislike it. Think about not only *how* you react to this place but *why*. What particular details affect you? In your journal, write about this place for ten minutes without stopping. At this point, do not be concerned with the form or correctness of your writing; just try to get your thoughts on paper.

Now, on a separate sheet of paper, list rapidly any details that come to mind that describe this particular place. Try to think of as many specific details as possible. Don't worry about the order in which you list the details or even whether all of them are appropriate or accurate. You are merely brainstorming, retrieving from your memory details that you associate with this place. For example, suppose you have chosen to describe Fifth Avenue in Manhattan on Christmas Eve. Your list might include the following:

lights	expensive shops
decorations	skyscrapers
concrete	Christmas trees
crowds	furs
wind	decorations
shoppers	marble
cars	voices
horns	cold
jewels	trash
music	vendors

street people	gasoline fumes
St. Patrick's	odor of chestnuts
Tiffany's	taxis

Once you have made a fairly long list, look back over it. Do some of your details seem more important or interesting than others? Are some related to one another? Draw lines connecting those that are related. Do these connecting lines indicate any relationships that you had not thought of before? Can you identify one particular cluster, or group, of related details that interests you more than the others? Look, for example, at the brainstorming list below. Notice the details that have been connected. Do you see a relationship among these details?

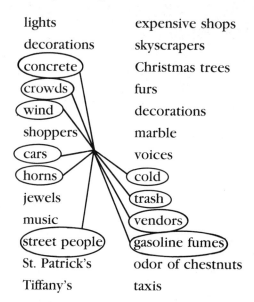

lights	expensive shops
decorations	skyscrapers
concrete	Christmas trees
crowds	furs
wind	decorations
shoppers	marble
cars	voices
horns	cold
jewels	trash
music	vendors
street people	gasoline fumes
St. Patrick's	odor of chestnuts
Tiffany's	taxis

After you have examined your list to identify connecting or related details, you should be able to make a statement that expresses the main ideas suggested by these related details. In the list above, for example, we have connected details related to the unpleasant aspects of life on a busy street in mid-Manhattan rather than to the glitter and excitement that also are found in this place, especially at Christmas time. We can express the idea suggested by this relationship in the following statement:

> In the midst of the glamour and excitement of Manhattan on Christmas Eve, Fifth Avenue also has a harsh reality.

Reading Exercise

In the descriptive paragraph below, John Steinbeck writes of his reaction to his "native place" in northern California. As you read this paragraph, think about why it was difficult for Steinbeck to write about this place where he once lived.

I find it difficult to write about my native place, northern California. It should be the easiest, because I knew that strip angled against the Pacific better than any place in the world. But I find it not one thing but many—one printed over another until the whole thing blurs. What it is is warped with memory of what it was and that with what happened there to me, the whole bundle wracked until objectiveness is nigh impossible. This four-lane concrete highway slashed with speeding cars I remember as a narrow, twisted mountain road where the wood teams moved, drawn by steady mules. They signaled their coming with the high, sweet jangle of hame bells. This was a little little town, a general store under a tree and a blacksmith shop and a bench in front on which to sit and listen to the clang of hammer on anvil. Now little houses, each one like the next, particularly since they try to be different, spread for a mile in all directions. That was a woody hill with live oaks dark green against the parched grass where the coyotes sang on moonlit nights. The top is shaved off and a television relay station lunges at the sky and feeds a nervous picture to thousands of tiny houses clustered like aphids beside the road.

John Steinbeck, *Travels with Charley*

1. Is the main idea of Steinbeck's paragraph stated or implied? What is the main idea?

_____

_____

_____

2. Compare Steinbeck's reactions to northern California today with his reactions to the northern California that he remembers.

_____

_____

_____

3. Why does Steinbeck have difficulty writing about his native place?

_____

_____

_____

4. What are some factual details used in this passage?

_____

_____

_____

5. To what senses does Steinbeck's description appeal (sight, hearing, taste, touch, or smell)? Give examples.

_____

_____

_____

_____

6. Does Steinbeck succeed in making you have a "sense of place" about northern California? How?

_____

_____

7. Notice Steinbeck's imaginative choice of verbs. In one sentence, for example, he writes of a "highway *slashed* with speeding cars," and in another he states that "a television relay station *lunges* at the sky and *feeds* a nervous picture to thousands of tiny houses." This use of specific, vivid words helps the reader to see the scene that Steinbeck is describing. What other effective verbs does Steinbeck use?

_____

8. Because Steinbeck is describing this place as it was in the past as well as the way it appears now, he uses a number of words that you may not be familiar with because they refer to objects that are uncommon today. For example, you may want to look up the following words in your dictionary:

a. hame (bells) _____

_____

_____

b. anvil _____

_____

_____

9. What is an *aphid?*

_____

What does Steinbeck's comparison of houses to aphids suggest about the houses and the people who live in them?

_____

_____

_____

Writing Exercise

Use your journal entry and your brainstorming list as the basis for a well-developed paragraph in which you describe your reaction to a specific place—a particular room, building, river, park, store, stadium, or other place that you remember in detail. Assume that your audience is a classmate who has never seen this place; use specific details, both factual and sensory, to help your reader see and feel exactly as you do about the place you are describing.

The following suggestions will help you plan and develop an effective paragraph:

1. Have you limited your topic as much as possible? Instead of writing about Yellowstone National Park, for example, you might write about a particular scene or view that you can see when standing in one specific place in the park or a small area of the park that you found especially interesting.

2. What reaction do you have to the place you are writing about? Is it frightening, awesome, peaceful, exciting? What is the focus of your paragraph?

3. Look carefully at your Pre-Reading/Writing Exercise. What sensory details have you used to describe the place that you are writing about? Does your language appeal to the senses of sight, hearing, touch, taste, or smell? What factual details can you use to describe this place?

4. Choose one of the organizational patterns of coordination and subordination that you worked with in this chapter. See whether the details you want to include in your descriptive paragraph follow one of these patterns. You might want to think of additional details to include so that your paragraph is organized according to one of the patterns.

Rewriting Exercise

Using the questions below as a guide, revise your paragraph independently or as part of a peer review group.

1. What do you like best about the paragraph?

2. Can you identify the topic sentence of the paragraph? What is the topic sentence?
   a. What is its subject? Is the subject sufficiently limited? How could it be further limited?
   b. What is its focus? Is the focus adequately narrowed? How could it be further narrowed?
3. Does the paragraph contain both factual and sensory details?
   a. What are the most effective factual details?
   b. What are the most effective sensory details?
   c. What other details could be added?
   d. Should any details be omitted because they do not support the topic sentence? If so, which one(s)?
4. On what organizational pattern is the paragraph based? That is, does it use coordinate details, subordinate details, or a combination of coordinate and subordinate details? If the paragraph uses a combination of coordinate and subordinate details, what are the major coordinate details?
5. What is the purpose of the paragraph? Does the paragraph achieve its purpose and communicate to its audience? Why or why not?

Rewrite your paragraph, making any necessary additions or deletions. After you have made the revisions necessary to communicate clearly to your audience, edit your revised draft. Your editing will be more successful if you reread your paragraph several times, concentrating on one type of error, such as spelling, in each separate reading. When you have edited your paragraph so that it is as clear and correct as possible, write your final copy and proofread it to be sure you have written exactly what you intended to write. Remember to read word by word and sentence by sentence during the proofreading stage.

Chapter 5

DEVELOPING MAIN IDEAS

METHODS OF DEVELOPMENT

The traditional methods of developing main ideas are almost as old as language itself. Even before writing was invented, people used these familiar methods to explore and develop their ideas. They are, essentially, methods of thinking—ways of approaching and exploring a topic that enable you to expand your knowledge. Learning to use these common methods of development will improve your ability to generate information and support a topic when you write and to recognize familiar patterns of thought and development when you read.

Most paragraphs, and certainly most longer pieces of writing, are combinations of different methods of development; for example, a story, which is primarily narration, often includes description. In fact, we seldom find any single method of development in isolation. However, in studying these methods, we will examine them first individually.

Narration

Most simply, narration is a story. It is probably the oldest and is certainly the best known of all methods of development. We have all had experiences with stories—listening to them, telling them, watching them on television or movie screens—even before we learned to read and write. But not all narratives are stories about people. Since a narrative is a sequence of events, it can also be a historical account or a scientific process. A narrative relates what happened. It can tell what happened to you, to someone else, or to something else. A novel tells you what happened to the characters in the story. Your history text tells you what happened at Valley Forge or during the Great Depression. And your biology text tells you what happens when trees lose their leaves or a cell divides.

The following paragraphs illustrate three different kinds of narration:

Eight children were there at play, seven sisters and their brother. Suddenly the boy was struck dumb; he trembled and began to run upon his hands and feet. His fingers became claws, and his body was covered with fur. Directly there was a bear where the boy had been. The sisters were terrified; they ran, and the bear after them. They came to the stump of a great tree, and the tree spoke to them. It bade them climb upon it, and as they did so it began to rise into the air. The bear came to kill them, but they were just beyond its reach. It reared against the tree and scored the bark all around with its claws. The seven sisters were borne into the sky, and they became the stars of the Big Dipper.

N. Scott Momaday
The Way to Rainy Mountain

When they arrived at Love Field, Congressman Henry Gonzalez said jokingly, "Well, I'm taking my risks. I haven't got my steel vest yet." The President, disembarking, walked immediately across the sunlit field to the crowd and shook hands. Then they entered the cars to drive from the airport to the center of the city. The people in the outskirts, Kenneth O'Donnell later said, were "not unfriendly nor terribly enthusiastic. They waved. But were reserved, I thought." The crowds increased as they entered the city—"still very orderly, but cheerful." In downtown Dallas enthusiasm grew. Soon even O'Donnell was satisfied. The car turned off Main Street, the President happy and waving, Jacqueline erect and proud by his side, and Mrs. Connally saying, "You certainly can't say that the people of Dallas haven't given you a nice welcome," and the automobile turning on to Elm Street and down the slope past the Texas School Book Depository, and the shots, faint and frightening, suddenly distinct over the roar of the motorcade, and the quizzical look on the President's face before he pitched over, and Jacqueline crying, "Oh, no, no. . . . Oh, my God, they have shot my husband," and the horror, the vacancy.

Arthur M. Schlesinger, Jr., A Thousand Days

After paralyzing the tarantula, the wasp cleans herself by dragging her body along the ground and rubbing her feet, sucks the drop of blood oozing from the wound in the spider's abdomen, then grabs a leg of the flabby, helpless animal in her jaws and drags it down to the bottom of the grave. She stays there for many minutes, sometimes for several hours, and what she does all that time in the dark we do not know. Eventually she lays her egg and attaches it to the side of the spider's abdomen with a sticky secretion. Then she emerges, fills the grave with soil carried bit by bit in her jaws, and finally tramples the ground all around to hide any trace of the grave from prowlers. Then she flies away, leaving her descendant safely started in life.

Alexander Petrunkevitch, "The Spider and the Wasp"

The first of these narratives is a Kiowa myth that explains how the Big Dipper came to be. This myth is the most familiar type of narrative—one that tells a simple story. The second tells of the assassination of President Kennedy, and the third is an account of how a wasp kills a spider and attaches her egg to its dead body. All three narratives tell "what happened" in a clear, interesting way. Below are some of the reasons these are good narratives.

1. **All three narratives include a lot of specific details.** They are not just a series of general statements but include "telling" details that help

you create vivid images of what happened. For example, the Kiowa myth about the Big Dipper doesn't just say that the boy became a bear. The story provides you with specific details about the boy's fingers becoming claws and his body becoming covered with fur. The historical account of President Kennedy's death includes the words of several people who were present, describes the weather and the crowds, and gives the specific route (including street names) that the president's motorcade followed. Finally, the story of the spider and the wasp provides very graphic, almost gruesome details about how the wasp kills the spider, sucks its blood, grabs a leg in her jaws, and then drags her prey into a "grave."

2. **The specific details in these narratives are arranged so you can follow them easily.** In most narratives, the details are arranged in chronological order—that is, according to the order in which they occurred. For example, in the myth you learn that the boy became a·bear before you learn that the bear chased his sisters or that they climbed a tree, which carried them up into the sky. In the account of President Kennedy's death, you are given signals that emphasize the passing of time. For example, the author uses terms such as *when, then, immediately,* and *soon* to indicate the sequence in which the events occurred. Similarly, the author of the narrative about the spider and the wasp uses words such as *eventually, then,* and *finally* to emphasize that the events being described occurred in a certain order.

3. **All of these narratives make a point or have a purpose.** Although they do not have a stated topic sentence, each has an implied topic sentence—an idea that underlies and gives significance to the sequence of events. The myth explains the Kiowa's belief about how the Big Dipper came into existence. The account of Kennedy's assassination emphasizes the suddenness and unexpectedness of loss that his death represented. And the story of the spider and the wasp illustrates the close, natural relationship between life and death. Although narratives may be told just to entertain, they frequently serve another purpose. They illustrate a point, explain a process, develop an idea, or provide information.

In the past you have probably thought of narration only as a way of entertaining or being entertained, but as a college student you need to broaden your understanding of this important method of development. Although you will continue to enjoy stories for their own sakes, you should also learn to see them as ways of developing ideas and persuading readers.

EXERCISE 5.1

Think of something that happened to you that caused you to be angry. Write below a sentence in which you explain what happened:

I was angry when _____

_____

_____

Now list below what happened—the specific events that led to your anger. Be careful to list them in the order in which they occurred:

_____

_____

_____

_____

Now think for a moment about what happened to you and why it made you angry. Was it the only time this sort of thing made you angry, or do you frequently respond with anger when something similar happens? Do you think your anger was justified, or were you later sorry that you became angry? Can you reach some conclusion, or generalization, about this incident and why it made you angry? Write your generalization on the lines below:

_____

_____

_____

Revise the generalization you have written above and use it as the topic sentence for a paragraph in which you tell what happened when you became angry. Be sure to include all of the steps or incidents you listed above, but as you write your paragraph, develop each part of your narrative by including as many specific details as possible. The details you include will help your reader understand why you felt angry.

Description

Like narration, description is a common method of development. We can describe how a character in a story looks, how a glass of wine tastes, how a headache feels, how garbage stinks, or how a symphony sounds. Description can be part of many different types of writing—fiction, poetry, history, science, biography, philosophy, and business. Description is used heavily in advertising copy and technical manuals, but it can also be found in the most sophisticated novel and the simplest story, in the most formal speech and the most casual conversation.

Effective description suggests images to the reader. It provides the reader with sense impressions—sights, sounds, smells, tastes, and feelings. To describe something effectively, you must be a good observer. You must see people, places, objects, and events with a sharp eye and be able to relate your impressions using both sensory and factual details. Thus, writing an effective description involves more than using many adjectives and adverbs. It requires noticing, selecting, and ordering details so that they effectively communicate to a reader.

Although description, even more than the other methods of development, is seldom found in isolation, the following paragraphs are primarily descriptive:

She saw green fields wrapped in the thickening gloom. It was as if they had left the earth, those fields, and were floating slowly skyward. The afterglow lingered, red, dying, somehow tenderly sad. And far away, in front of her, earth and sky met in a soft swoon of shadow. A cricket chirped, sharp and lonely; and it seemed she could hear it chirping long after it had stopped.

Richard Wright, "Long Black Song," in *Uncle Tom's Children*

Another time I saw another wonder: sharks off the Atlantic coast of Florida. There is a way a wave rises above the ocean horizon, a triangular wedge against the sky. If you stand where the ocean breaks on a shallow beach, you see the raised water in a wave is translucent, shot with lights. One late afternoon at low tide a hundred big sharks passed the beach near the mouth of a tidal river in a feeding frenzy. As each green wave rose from the churning water, it illuminated within itself the six- or eight-foot-long bodies of twisting sharks. The sharks disappeared as each wave rolled toward me; then a new wave would swell above the horizon, containing in it, like scorpions in amber, sharks that roiled and heaved. The sight held awesome wonders: power and beauty, grace tangled in a rapture with violence.

Annie Dillard, *Pilgrim at Tinker Creek*

These descriptive paragraphs focus on very different subjects and serve different purposes, but both enable you to share the writers' experiences—to see what they saw, hear what they heard, and feel what they felt. Below are some of the elements that make these descriptions effective.

1. **Like the narrative paragraphs, descriptive paragraphs are very detailed.** The writers use specific details to make their descriptions as vivid as possible. You are told precisely where the writer stood ("where the ocean breaks on a shallow beach") when she viewed the sharks. And you are told specifically how the cricket sounded ("sharp and lonely") when it chirped. Each of these writers provides you with the specific details you need to translate the image into one you "understand."

2. **The descriptions use factual as well as sensory details.** For example, in the description of the sharks, the writer tells us that she saw "a hundred . . . sharks" and that their "six- or eight-foot-long bodies" were "twisting."

3. **The writers do not rely exclusively on visual details.** Although each of the descriptions includes many visual details, the other senses are not ignored. In the first paragraph, the writer who is describing the fields includes the sound of the cricket chirping as well as the sight of the sky. In the second paragraph, the writer tells you not only what she saw but how she felt ("The sight held awesome wonders: power and beauty, grace tangled in a rapture with violence.").

4. **The writers arrange their supporting details in some familiar or logical order.** You can recognize or visualize the details because you

are familiar with the patterns of arrangement used. Descriptive details can be arranged spatially (according to their actual arrangement in space), chronologically (according to a time sequence), or in order of importance (according to their importance in the mind of the writer).

Both of these paragraphs use chronological order. In the description of the green fields, even though no action is involved, the scene changes as the woman watches it, and the writer presents the details in the order in which the woman viewed them—first the green fields, appearing to float upward, then the red afterglow on the horizon, and finally the chirping of the cricket. Similarly, the description of the sharks is chronological. The writer describes what she saw in the sequence in which it occurred.

5. **In both of these paragraphs, the description is used to support a main idea.** In the description of the green fields, the main idea (the woman's loneliness and sadness) is implied. The description of the sharks begins with a clearly stated topic sentence: "Another time I saw another wonder." The author then describes the "wonder" she saw. Like narration, description is often used to support an implied, rather than a stated, main idea, but both methods of development can be effectively used to support and develop an idea.

EXERCISE 5.2

Look around you at the classroom in which you are sitting. Study not only its appearance but also how it feels and smells and sounds. List below details— both factual and sensory—about the classroom.

_____

_____

_____

_____

_____

_____

_____

Now determine the appropriate arrangement for your details. You might arrange them spatially—floor to ceiling, front to back, right to left. Or you might arrange them chronologically, in the order in which you experience them as you walk in the door and through the room. Or you might simply list them in order of importance—putting what you consider most important first and least important last.

Next, determine the main idea you wish to communicate. You may state this idea as a topic sentence or merely use it as the controlling idea of your paragraph. Write it below.

_____

_____

_____

_____

Now write a paragraph in which you use the details you have listed above to support your main idea.

Illustration

Main ideas are frequently developed by illustration, or example. Examples give readers specific instances of the general idea expressed in the topic sentence. Sometimes a single example can adequately develop a topic sentence; other times several brief examples are needed. In either case, illustration is an effective method of development that is commonly used, especially in informative writing.

Below is a paragraph that is developed by a series of specific examples.

There is something peculiarly American in the fact that, while boxing is our most controversial sport, it is also the sport that pays its top athletes the most money. In spite of the controversy, boxing has never been healthier financially. The three highest paid athletes in the world in both 1983 and 1984 were boxers; a boxer with a long career like heavyweight champion Larry Holmes—48 fights in 13 years as a professional—can expect to earn somewhere beyond $50 million. (Holmes said that after retirement what he would miss most about boxing is his million-dollar checks.) Dempsey, who said that a man fights for one thing only—money—made somewhere beyond $3,500,000 in the ring in his long and varied career. Now $1.5 million is a fairly common figure for a single fight. Thomas Hearns made at least $7 million in his fight with Hagler while Hagler made at least $7.5 million. For the first of his highly publicized matches with Roberto Duran in 1980—which he lost on a decision—the popular black welterweight champion Sugar Ray Leonard received a staggering $10 million to Duran's $1.3 million. And none of these figures takes into account various subsidiary earnings (from television commercials, for instance) which in Leonard's case are probably as high as his income was from boxing.

Joyce Carol Oates, "On Boxing"

Notice how the writer of this paragraph arranged her examples. Why do you think she arranged them as she did?

_____

_____

_____

_____

Writers often arrange their examples in order of importance. In the paragraph about boxing, the author begins with the smaller amounts of money paid to boxers and progresses to the largest amount of money paid to a boxer for a single fight. You will see this pattern (from least to most important) repeated frequently in many different types of writing. Like spatial and chronological order, order of importance is a common pattern of organization.

Rather than a series of examples, you can also use a single extended example to illustrate a point. An extended example is often a brief narration or a description. Notice in the paragraph below that the writer uses the act of climbing stairs to illustrate subconscious knowledge.

English grammar is just one of many things you know subconsciously far better than you know consciously. When you walk up a flight of stairs, for example, you can do so without having to think about how to do it. You can climb stairs while carrying on a conversation, while composing a love sonnet, even while walking in your sleep. Although many hundreds of muscles are finely coordinated in the task of climbing stairs, you perform it errorlessly and even gracefully, and without any apparent mental effort. Yet if you or I were asked to describe how we climb stairs we would do it very inaccurately at best: "Let's see," we might say. "First you bring the right leg up and bend the knee. You point the toe up, shift your weight forward, and bring the sole down on the next step. Then. . . ." Of course you would not have begun to describe which muscles you use when you bend the knee. Your description is a long way from capturing the directions your brain gives to your body as you move. The fact is that unless you are a highly trained physiologist, you do not "know" much about how you climb stairs. And yet in another sense you "know" how to do it quite well, since you do it all the time. Your conscious knowledge of the task cannot come close to matching what you know subconsciously.

Richard Veit, *Discovering English Grammar*

EXERCISE 5.3

Working with a small group of your classmates, think of a problem (complicated registration procedures, restrictions on parking, strict attendance policy, poorly lighted parking lots, etc.) that exists on your campus. Write a general statement that clearly expresses this problem. Then, as a group, decide on a single, extended example that develops your main idea. Your example can be narrative or descriptive or both. Next, think of several specific details or facts that illustrate your main idea. Finally, still working as a group, write a paragraph using either a single, extended example or a series of specific examples to develop your main idea.

Comparison/Contrast

Another way that writers develop their ideas is by comparing or contrasting something that is unfamiliar with something that is familiar. For example, a writer may compare something new, such as a computer's storage capacity, to something well known, such as a human's memory. Often, such comparisons are quite brief, only a sentence or two or perhaps just a phrase or word. At other times, an entire paragraph or even a longer piece of writing may be developed through the use of comparison or contrast. Both of the paragraphs below use comparison/contrast as their primary method of development, but they are not organized in the same way.

Sex can be defined fairly adequately in physiological terms as consisting of the building up of bodily tensions and their release. Eros, in contrast, is the experiencing of the personal intentions and meaning of the act. Whereas sex is a rhythm of stimulus and response, eros is a state of being. The pleasure in sex is described by Freud and others as the reduction of tension; in eros, on the contrary, we wish not to be released from the excitement but rather to hang on to it, to bask in it, and even to increase it. The end toward which sex points is gratification and relaxation, whereas eros is a desiring, longing, a forever reaching out, seeking to expand.

Rollo May, *Love and Will*

This comparison/contrast paragraph is organized in an alternating pattern. That is, the writer alternately discusses one subject (sex) and the other (eros). Notice that he is careful to give approximately the same attention to each subject so that the result is a balanced view. Figure 27 on the next page illustrates this pattern:

FIGURE 27 **Alternating Pattern**

Topic sentence	General statement about A and B

1.
 	
  A.
 	
  B.
	Supporting detail (A and B)

2.
 	
  A.
 	
  B.
	Supporting detail (A and B)

3.
 	
  A.
 	
  B.
	Supporting detail (A and B)

Conclusion	General statement about A and B

Now read the next comparison/contrast paragraph, noticing especially how it is organized:

Urbanites do far better at enjoying their space than people in small towns. In fact, space in small towns is not really defined or used; it is just *there*. A French friend remarked that these towns seemed sad because one never saw any people in them, and while this is an exaggeration, Americans, in towns and villages at least, do not seem to use space as city-dwellers do. For one thing, small town Americans don't walk unless they absolutely have to; for another, there is no place for them to stop when they do walk; for a third, there isn't anything much to look at when they do stop. Small towns have parks, but people tend to go there to *do* something—play baseball or have picnics or let the children swing. . . . But in cities, which are supposed to be full of harried people, one sees people just sitting, perhaps reading or writing a letter or part of an article like this. One of the many marvelous things in Manhattan is a small park in midtown, the width of a building, with benches, some potted greenery, and a sheet of water cascading down a wall of pebbles set in concrete. This little space was financed privately in memory of someone whose name I do not recall but whose legacy is unforgettable.

Adapted from Robert M. Davis, "Just Enough for the City"

This comparison/contrast paragraph is organized in a divided pattern. That is, the writer discusses first one subject (the way people in small towns use space) and then the other (the way people in a large city use space). Notice that he uses the transition signal *but* to indicate to his readers the shift from one subject to the other. The diagram below illustrates this pattern:

FIGURE 28   **Divided Pattern**

Topic sentence	A general statement about both A and B

A.
 	
  1.
 	
  2.
 	
  3.
	Supporting details that describe or illustrate A

B.
 	
  1.
 	
  2.
 	
  3.
	Supporting details that describe or illustrate B

Conclusion	A general statement about both A and B

EXERCISE 5.4

Reread the paragraph that compares sex and eros. Notice especially the alternating pattern of the supporting sentences. Rewrite the paragraph, changing the alternating pattern to a divided pattern. Read the resulting paragraph and decide whether you prefer this arrangement to the original.

Classification

Classification is another useful method of development. In classification, you organize information by placing things into groups with other things that have similar characteristics. When you classify a subject, you divide it into categories. Thus, only plural subjects can be classified. For example, you can classify students, colleges, computers, pizzas, cars, and television shows, but you can't classify a single student, college, computer, pizza, car, or television show.

Classification is used not only by writers but also by a variety of other people for a variety of different reasons. Scientists and technical writers are fond of classification; so are sociologists and psychologists. Teachers tend to classify students (as bright, dull, irritating, impossible), and students like to classify teachers (as hard, easy, interesting, impossible). Classification can be serious or humorous, but good classification always makes a point. The point, or main idea, developed by the classification may be stated or implied, but it should be clear to the reader. Often, the main idea of a paragraph developed by classification merely states the system of classification. For example, if you are classifying types of plants, you might have a topic sentence similar to this one:

> Although plants come in all shapes and sizes, they can all be divided into two groups—those that are easy to grow and those that are difficult to grow.

This topic sentence not only identifies your categories but also implies that plants should be selected on the basis of how much care they require.

To develop a system of classification, you must first determine a basis for classifying; that is, you need a criterion on which to base your classification. For example, you can classify people according to their occupations, their physical features, their personalities, or their incomes. You can classify cities according to their size, climate, cost of living, or crime rate. However, you must be sure to classify on the basis of a single criterion. For example, you can classify cars according to how much they cost or where they are made but not according to both of these criteria at the same time.

Cost
1. Luxury cars
   a. Cadillac
   b. Mercedes Benz
   c. BMW

2. Economy cars
   a. Ford
   b. Toyota
   c. Chevrolet

Origin
1. American cars
   a. Cadillac
   b. Ford
   c. Chevrolet

2. Foreign cars
   a. Mercedes Benz
   b. BMW
   c. Toyota

Classification nearly always involves other methods of development, especially description, comparison/contrast, and illustration. But it is also frequently used as the primary method of developing a paragraph or longer piece of writing. For example, the following paragraph is developed primarily by classification, but the writer also uses several other methods of development:

There are medium friends, and pretty good friends, and very good friends indeed, and these friendships are defined by their level of intimacy. . . . We might tell a medium friend, for example, that yesterday we had a fight with our husband. And we might tell a pretty good friend that this fight with our husband made us so mad that we slept on the couch. And we might tell a very good friend that the reason we got so mad in that fight that we slept on the couch had something to do with that girl who works in his office. But it's only to our very best friends that we're willing to tell all, to tell what's going on with that girl in his office.

Judith Viorst, ''Friends, Good Friends''

Can you identify the criterion on which this writer bases her classification of friends?

_____

Notice the paragraph's topic sentence. It is very direct, identifying both the main idea and the basis for classification. The sentences that follow, which describe each of the three kinds of friends, develop this topic sentence so that, by the end of the paragraph, you can infer the author's attitude toward her subject. Write in your own words the point you think the writer wants to make about friends:

_____

_____

_____

What other methods of development does the writer use in this paragraph?

_____

_____

EXERCISE 5.5

On a separate sheet of paper, make a list of as many types of college students as you can think of.

Now, see if you can classify these different types of students into three categories. Write the names of your categories below and then list under them the appropriate types or examples of students.

Category #1 _____

    a. _____

    b. _____

Category #2 _____

    a. _____

    b. _____

Category #3 _____

    a. _____

    b. _____

Write below a topic sentence in which you state your subject and the categories you have identified:

_____

_____

_____

Next, write a paragraph in which you develop this topic sentence by briefly describing each of the categories of students you have identified.

Cause and Effect

Another method of developing a main idea is to explore its causes or effects. Like the other methods of development, cause and effect is not just a way of writing but also a way of thinking. In our culture, we commonly think in terms of what caused something or what effects something will have. For example, we say that smoking causes lung cancer. In other words,

> smoking = cause
>
> lung cancer = effect

In developing a main idea, you can consider either causes or effects or both. The important thing is that you explore the relationship between the cause and effect. Thus, you can begin with a cause and explain its effect, or you can begin with the effect and explore the cause. With cause and effect, you are always moving between the two. Sometimes this movement is clearly in one direction or the other:

> cause → effect
>
> effect → cause

The paragraphs below are developed primarily by explaining cause and effect. In one of them, the writer moves from cause to effect. In the other, the writer begins with the effect and then discusses the cause. As you read the two paragraphs, see if you can determine which is which.

Once I shot an Iguana. I thought that I should be able to make some pretty things from his skin. A strange thing happened then, that I have never afterwards forgotten. As I went up to him, where he was laying dead upon his stone, and actually while I was walking the few steps, he faded and grew pale, all color died out of him as in one long sigh, and by the time that I touched him he was grey and dull like a lump of concrete. It was the live impetuous blood pulsating within the animal, which had radiated out all that glow and splendor. Now that the flame was put out, and the soul had flown, the Iguana was as dead as a sandbag.

Isak Dinesen, "The Iguana," in Out of Africa

I passed all the other courses that I took at my university, but I could never pass botany. This was because all botany students had to spend several hours a week in a laboratory looking through a microscope at plant cells, and I could never see through a microscope. I never once saw a cell through a microscope. This used to enrage my instructor. He would wander around the laboratory pleased with the progress all the students were making in drawing the involved and, so I am told, interesting structure of flower cells, until he came to me. I would just be standing there. "I can't see anything," I would say.

James Thurber, "University Days," in My Life & Hard Times

Did you decide that the paragraph about the iguana begins with cause ("Once I shot an Iguana.") and that the paragraph about failing botany begins with effect ("I could never pass botany.")? The writer of the first paragraph tells us the *effects* of killing the iguana; the writer of the second paragraph tells us *why* he failed botany (because he could not see through a microscope).

Notice that both of these paragraphs, although they are developed primarily by cause and effect, also include narration and description. The iguana paragraph also uses comparison ("he was grey and dull like a lump of concrete").

EXERCISE 5.6

Write a paragraph in which you discuss some of the causes of high school drop-out. Then write another paragraph in which you discuss the effects dropping out of school can have on a young person's life. Finally, combine these two paragraphs into one in which you explore both the causes and the effects of this problem.

Definition

The last method of development we will discuss, definition, is not really a different method so much as it is a combination of all the other methods. Your main concern in defining a subject is to explore the subject's "whatness." In other words, when you define something, you are telling what it is. You can define a subject by describing, illustrating, comparing, or classifying it. You can even define a subject by telling a story about it or analyzing its causes or effects. In definition, you use any and all of the other methods to explain your subject.

Formal definitions, the kind found in dictionaries, are usually brief. A formal definition places the subject (or term) into a class (as in classification) and then tells how it differs from the other members of that class (as in contrast). For instance, we can define a lullaby by placing it in the general category of songs and then specify the characteristics that make it different from other songs. We might arrive at the definition that "a lullaby is a song that is used to encourage sleep."

However, not all definitions are formal definitions. Longer definitions, sometimes called *extended definitions,* are not limited to the specifications of the formal definition. When you define a subject, you are free to use any methods of development that will help your reader arrive at a clear understanding of your subject. You can describe it (using both factual and sensory details), give an example of it, compare or contrast it with something else, or classify it. For example, an extended definition of *lullaby* might include a description of how a lullaby sounds (soothing), an example of it ("Rock-a-bye-baby in the tree top"), or a comparison with another type of music (rock-and-roll). As you read the following definitions, notice the different methods of development used in each:

Robotics is the science that deals with the construction, capabilities, and applications of robots. Most robots are used to perform tedious, dangerous, or otherwise undesirable work in factories. . . . These industrial robots can work where humans cannot, and do not need protective devices. They never need time off; a typical industrial robot is up and running 97 percent of the time! And the quality of work never suffers. Further, management never has to contend with sick, tired, or bored robots. The machines never complain, go on strike, or ask for higher wages.

Steven L. Mandell, *Introduction to Computers*

Falling in love is an experience that almost everyone has at least once and usually several times. To fall into love is to fall into a profound set of emotional experiences. There may be a range of physical symptoms such as dry mouth, pounding heart, flushed face, and knotted stomach. The mind may race, and fantasy, especially about the loved one, is rampant. Motivation to work, play, indeed for anything except the lover, may fall to zero. As the love feelings develop, strong feelings of passion may occur. In fact, passionate love is essentially the same as romantic love, except that the focus is more specifically on the emotional intensity and sexual passion.

Clyde Hendrick and Susan Hendrick, *Liking, Loving, & Relating*

In the appropriate spaces below, list the different methods of development you identified in each of the definitions:

1. Robotics

_____

_____

_____

2. Falling in love

_____

_____

_____

EXERCISE 5.7

Choose a subject to define. Your subject does not have to be an object; it can be an action, an emotion, an event, a type of person, or anything else that interests you and that you know enough about to define for a reader. Once you have selected your subject, think about the different methods you might use to define it. Can you describe it, compare or contrast it with something or someone else, illustrate it, discuss its causes or effects, and so on? Decide which of the methods would explain your subject most clearly to a reader and write a paragraph using at least two different methods of development.

RECOGNIZING DIFFERENT METHODS OF DEVELOPMENT

As a reader, you will use your knowledge of the different methods of development to understand what you read. Recognizing a familiar pattern of development helps you anticipate how writers are going to present their ideas or information and therefore helps you understand them better. The following exercise will give you practice in recognizing different methods of development.

EXERCISE 5.8

Read the following paragraphs carefully. Then (1) write the main idea of the paragraph in your own words and (2) state its primary pattern of organization (narration, description, illustration, comparison/contrast, classification, cause and effect, or definition). If you discover that other patterns of organization have been used to support the primary pattern, list them in parentheses.

PARAGRAPH A

So Grant and Lee were in complete contrast, representing two diametrically opposed elements in American life. Grant was the modern man emerging; beyond him, ready to come on the stage, was the great age of steel and machinery, of crowded cities and a restless burgeoning vitality. Lee might have ridden down from the old age of chivalry, lance in hand, silken banner fluttering over his head. Each man was the perfect champion of his cause, drawing both his strengths and his weaknesses from the people he led.

Bruce Catton, *Grant and Lee: A Study in Contrasts*

Main idea: _____

_____

Method(s) of paragraph development: _____

_____

PARAGRAPH B

Melody is that element of music which makes the widest and most direct appeal. It has been called the soul of music. It is generally what we remember and whistle and hum. We know a good melody when we hear it and we recognize its unique power to move us, although we might be hard put to explain wherein its power lies. The world has always lavished a special affection upon the creators of melody; nothing is more intimately associated with inspiration, not only in the popular mind but also among musicians.

Adapted from Joseph Machlis, *The Enjoyment of Music*

Main idea: _____

_____

Method(s) of paragraph development: _____

_____

PARAGRAPH C

If the system involves the use of a computer, one or more computer programmers may be asked to write a computer program for a particular procedure. For example, a computer programmer may be asked to write a program for computing the gross and net pay for each pay period. Another programmer may be asked to program the procedure for the preparation of paychecks and employee earnings statements. Another may be asked to program the procedure for preparing the quarterly tax reports required by the federal government. Each of these programs will be part of the payroll data processing system.

Beryl Robichaud et al., *Introduction to Data Processing*

Main idea: _____

_____

Method(s) of paragraph development: _____

_____

PARAGRAPH D

Landforms, arbitrarily but conveniently, may be divided into four categories: plains, hills, plateaus, and mountains. Hills are not only lower than mountains but are usually more rounded and more gently sloping. Plateaus are simply elevated plains. Elevation, however, is less important than *local relief.* Local relief includes the degree of slope of the ground, how much difference there is between the highest and the lowest parts of an area, and how much of the area as a whole is level or sloping. A high plateau may be more usable than a rough, low-lying area. Many areas labeled mountains may actually contain extensive sections of low relief, and many plains may be interrupted by high relief.

Rhoades Murphy, *Patterns of the Earth*

Main idea: _____

_____

Method(s) of paragraph development: _____

_____

PARAGRAPH E

One night a moth flew into the candle, was caught, burnt dry, and held. I must have been staring at the candle, or maybe I looked up when a shadow crossed my page; at any rate, I saw it all. A golden female moth, a biggish one with a two-inch wingspread, flapped into the fire, dropped abdomen into the wet wax, struck, flamed, and frazzled in a second. Her moving wings ignited like tissue paper, like angels' wings, enlarging the circle of light in the clearing and creating out of the darkness the sudden blue sleeves of my sweater, the green leaves of jewelweed by my side, the ragged red trunk of a pine; at once the light contracted again and the moth's wings vanished in a fine, foul smoke. At the same time, her six legs clawed, curled, blackened, and ceased, disappearing utterly. And her head jerked in spasms, making a spattering noise; her antennae crisped and burnt away and her heaving mouthparts cracked like pistol fire. When it was all over, her head was, so far as I could determine, gone, gone the long way of her wings and legs. Her head was a hole lost to time. All that was left was the glowing horn shell of her abdomen and thorax—a fraying, partially collapsed gold tube jammed upright in the candle's round pool.

Annie Dillard, "Death of a Moth," in *Pilgrim at Tinker Creek*

Main idea: _____

_____

Method(s) of paragraph development: _____

_____

PARAGRAPH F

Hiroshima was a fan-shaped city, lying mostly on the six islands formed by the seven estuarial rivers that branch out from the Ota River; its main commercial and residential districts, covering about four square miles in the center of the city, contained three-quarters of its population, which had been reduced by several evacuation programs from a wartime peak of 380,000 to about 245,000. Factories and other residential districts, or suburbs, lay compactly around the edges of the city. To the south were the docks, an airport, and the island-studded Inland Sea. A rim of mountains runs around the other three sides of the delta. . . .

Adapted from John Hersey, *Hiroshima*

Main idea: _____

_____

Method(s) of paragraph development: _____

_____

PARAGRAPH G

Despite these common assumptions, television highlighted not the candidates' words but their manner of presentation. Radio listeners, who were not distracted by visual appearances, reacted favorably to Nixon's speeches. But the television cameras accentuated the vice president's heavy "five o'clock shadow" and dark eye sockets. His makeup dripped, and his body movements seemed stiff. Suffering from a severe cold, he looked unhealthy, if not unsavory. In contrast, Kennedy brought a dramatic flair to the television screen. He seemed comfortable and confident. The television format, by projecting the candidates as equals, added to Kennedy's national reputation. Subsequent polls indicated that the debates may have influenced as many as four million voters; of these, Kennedy gathered three-quarters.

David W. Noble et al., *Twentieth Century Limited*

Main idea: _____

_____

Method(s) of paragraph development: _____

_____

PARAGRAPH H

On week days Polk Street was very lively. It woke to its work about seven o'clock, at the time when the newsboys made their appearance together with the day laborers. The laborers went trudging past in a straggling file— plumbers' apprentices, their pockets stuffed with sections of lead pipe, tweezers, and pliers; carpenters, carrying nothing but their little paste-board lunch baskets painted to imitate leather; gangs of street workers, their overalls soiled with yellow clay, their picks and long-handled shovels over their shoulders; plasterers, spotted with lime from head to foot. This little army of workers, tramping steadily in one direction, met and mingled with other toilers of a different description—conductors and "swing men" of the cable company going on duty; heavy-eyed night clerks from the drug stores on their way home to sleep; roundsmen returning to the precinct police station to make their night report, the Chinese market gardeners teetering past under their heavy baskets. The cable cars began to fill up; all along the street could be seen the shop keepers taking down their shutters.

Frank Norris, *McTeague*

Main idea: _____

_____

Method(s) of paragraph development: _____

_____

READING/WRITING ASSIGNMENT 5A

WHAT IS AN AMERICAN?
James Baldwin

Pre-Reading/Writing Exercise

You can use different methods of development not only to *organize* ideas in your reading and writing but also to *generate* ideas for writing. One such method for generating or creating ideas is a variation of freewriting called *cubing.* Cubing encourages you to consider a topic—an object, person, place, or idea—from six different points of view. That is, you examine the topic from each of the six sides of an imaginary "cube." These six viewpoints are listed below:

1. *Describe it.* Look at the subject closely and describe what you see. Colors, shapes, sizes, and so forth.

2. *Compare it.* What is it similar to? What is it different from?

3. *Associate it.* What does it make you think of? What comes into your mind? It can be similar things, or you can think of different things, different times, places, people. Just let your mind go and see what associations you have for this subject.

4. *Analyze it.* Tell how it's made. (You don't have to *know;* you can make it up.)

5. *Apply it.* Tell what you can do with it, how it can be used.

6. *Argue for or against it.* Go ahead and take a stand. Use any kind of reasons you want to—rational, silly, or anywhere in between.

Gregory Cowan and Elizabeth Cowan, *Writing*

With the help of this prewriting technique, you will be able to focus on ideas before reading about them and to see possibilities for writing in the most unlikely subjects. For example, the following cubing of a clock suggests two or three interesting possibilities for writing:

1. **Describe it:** The clock is about three inches square and light ivory in color with a white face. The white face has black numbers with a black minute hand and a black hour hand. The turquoise second hand constantly turns clockwise, and a little gold alarm hand is nearly hidden under the other larger hands. The brand name *General Electric* is written in small black letters on the lower portion of the inner circle of numbers. The time is . . .

2. **Compare it:** This small alarm clock can be compared with a much larger clock, to the battery clock over our mantel, for instance, or to a large grandfather clock in a beautiful wooden cabinet. Of course, this little clock costs only a fraction of the price of a grandfather clock. The little alarm clock can also be compared with a smaller timepiece such as a pocket watch or a wristwatch. Size doesn't necessarily make a smaller timepiece less expensive, however; a small wristwatch may cost as much as a grandfather clock. And yet the inexpensive alarm clock can tell time just as accurately as . . .

3. **Associate it:** The clock reminds me of deadlines, of unfinished tasks, of getting up in the morning before I am ready to get up. It also reminds me of sleepless nights looking at the clock ticking away beside my bed, of jerking awake and looking at it in the middle of the night when the phone rings with emergency calls from the hospital about sick parents. The clock can be beneficial, but I have mostly negative associations about . . .

4. **Analyze it:** The clock itself can be broken down into its various parts: its outer covering, the clock face and its parts, the inner gears, and the cord that connects it to its life force of electricity. Perhaps, though, the clock suggests a more interesting analysis—that of time itself, of what time means to me and other people I know, of how important time is in our country as compared with countries in South America or Europe, for example.

5. **Apply it:** To apply the clock, I must think about how I use it. I check the clock when I wake up in the morning to see how long I can snooze before I get up. I check it when I go to bed at night to see how long I have to sleep. When it is in sight, I look at it before I check my watch.

6. **Argue for or against it:** A clock is necessary to my life, but sometimes I would like to throw it out the window! I get tired of deadlines, of rushing from one class to another, from one meeting to another. Sometimes I wish I could get rid of all these deadlines and go back to a life of more natural rhythms—one where I could determine my life instead of the clock's determining it. Yet as I think about it, a baby's life is one of natural rhythms but of no real purpose other than existence, and I wouldn't want to go back to that kind of life. So I guess I need the clock even though I don't really like it.

From this cubing, you could write a narrative of the events surrounding a particular emergency call, a comparison of different kinds of timepieces, or a cause-and-effect paragraph about how you react to deadlines. Now, practice the cubing technique by applying it to the topic *American*. Spend approximately three minutes on each angle. As in your regular freewriting, just try to get your ideas down on paper without worrying about form or correctness. When your instructor gives you the signal to switch points of view, stop—even in midsentence—and switch to the new point of view. When you finish your cubing exercise, you will be surprised not only at how much you have written but also at what interesting ideas you have discovered. Your instructor may ask you to read and discuss your cubings in pairs or small groups.

Reading Exercise

James Baldwin wrote the following paragraph after living and writing in Paris, France. Disillusioned with America, Baldwin had gone to Paris to escape American prejudice against black writers, but while he was in France, he came to understand more about what it means to be an American. As you read Baldwin's paragraph, determine his purpose, main idea, and primary method of development.

"It is a complex fate to be an American," Henry James observed, and the principal discovery an American writer makes in Europe is just how complex this fate is. America's history, her aspirations, her peculiar triumphs, her even more peculiar defeats, and her position in the world—yesterday and today—are all so profoundly and stubbornly unique that the very word "America" remains a new, almost completely undefined and extremely controversial proper noun. No one in the world seems to know exactly what it describes, not even we motley millions who call ourselves Americans.

James Baldwin, *Nobody Knows My Name: More Notes of a Native Son*

1. Is Baldwin's main idea stated or implied?

_____

What is his main idea?

_____

_____

2. What is the paragraph's primary method of development?

_____

3. What are some of the unique causes of America's complexity?

_____

4. Baldwin avoids the traps of triteness (overused language) and senti-mentality (overly emotional language) that writers often fall into when writ-ing about highly personal or emotional topics such as country, parents, children, or religion. For example, he could have used a trite phrase such as "the American way of life" to try to capture audience sympathy without earning it. Or he might have used such words as *un-American, reactionary,* or *bigot* to trigger an automatically negative response. Instead of relying on trite or sentimental expressions such as *brave, loyal,* and *true,* Baldwin describes Americans in a fresh and original way. For example, he describes the American character—or "fate"—as *complex* and then proceeds to sug-gest several aspects of that complexity. Other words that Baldwin uses to describe Americans are *unique* and *motley.* What does *unique* suggest about the American character?

What does *motley* suggest about Americans?

5. What is Baldwin's *stated* purpose in the paragraph?

What is Baldwin's *implied* purpose (note the title of the book from which the paragraph was taken)?

Discussion Questions

1. How has America's history determined her fate?
2. What aspirations do you associate with being an American?
3. What are some of America's triumphs?
4. What are some of America's defeats?
5. Has America had moral as well as physical triumphs and defeats? Give some examples.

6. What is America's position in the world? For example, how is America viewed by people in other countries (militarily, economically, etc.)?

7. How are American tourists viewed in other countries?

Writing Exercise

Look back at your cubing exercise on the topic *American*. Put check marks by the part or parts of the cubing that produced the most interesting descriptions, memories, or ideas about America or the American character.

If you were born in the United States, think about how you could explain some feature or incident that typifies American character to someone from another country. For example, you could describe a person or event that illustrates a particularly American quality such as independence or pride, you could discuss the causes or effects of such an American quality, you could provide examples of a particular freedom such as freedom of speech or religion, you could provide a narrative illustration of an American tourist abroad, or you could consider whether a particular heritage—German, Scandinavian, African, Spanish, or Chinese—makes an individual more or less of an American.

If you were not born in the United States, write to an American audience about some particularly American custom or characteristic that interests you or even confuses you. You might compare a custom in America with one in your native country. After you decide on your particular purpose, draft your topic sentence, being sure your subject is limited and your focus clear. Then determine the best method(s) of development and most effective supporting details. Use the space below to plan your paragraph:

Purpose: _____

Topic sentence: _____

_____

Method(s) of development: _____

_____

Major supporting details: _____

_____

_____

_____

_____

Audience: _____

Now write the first draft of your paragraph.

Rewriting Exercise

Reread your draft to see whether you have achieved your purpose and communicated your ideas to your audience. If your class is composed of both Americans and students from other countries, divide into groups or pairs with different backgrounds to see whether each paragraph communicates to its intended audience. As you read one another's paragraphs, answer these questions.

1. What is the purpose of the paragraph? Who is the audience? Is the purpose clear to the audience?
2. Does the paragraph have a clearly stated (or implied) topic sentence? What is the topic sentence?
   a. What is the subject? Is the subject sufficiently limited? How can it be further limited?
   b. What is the focus? Is the focus adequately narrowed? How can it be further narrowed?
3. What is the primary method of development?
4. Does the paragraph contain enough supporting details? Which details are the most effective? What other details could be added? Does the paragraph contain any details that should be omitted because they do not support the topic sentence? If so, which one(s)?
5. Is the word choice clear and original? If the paragraph contains any trite or sentimental words or phrases, what are they?
6. Does the paragraph achieve its purpose and communicate to its audience? Why or why not?

After you have evaluated your draft, rewrite your paragraph, making any additions, deletions, or other changes necessary to achieve your purpose and communicate to your audience. Then edit your paper for errors in sentence structure, usage, spelling, and punctuation, and proofread your final copy carefully.

Optional Rewriting Exercise

1. Rewrite your paragraph for the same audience using another method of organization. Does this revision change your purpose?

2. Rewrite your paragraph using the same method of development but changing your audience. How does this revision affect your word choice?

SHOULD MEN CRY?
Ashley Montagu

Pre-Reading/Writing Exercise

Emotions and feelings are an essential part of being human. However, people express their emotions and feelings in different ways for different situations. Some people laugh at weddings; others cry. Some people cry at funerals; others do not. In preparation for Reading/Writing Assignment 5B, think about the last time you cried or saw another adult cry. Then write a journal entry about this experience. At this time, concentrate on recording your thoughts and feelings rather than on form or correctness.

Reading Exercise

Now read the following paragraphs about crying. As you read, compare the author's attitude about crying, especially about men crying, with your own attitudes and experiences. Do you think that it is unmanly for a male to cry? Or should men be encouraged to cry as freely as women do?

1   American men don't cry because it is considered unmasculine to do so. Only sissies cry. Crying is a "weakness" characteristic of the female, and no American male wants to be identified with anything in the least weak or feminine. Crying, in our culture, is identified with childishness, with weakness and dependence. No one likes a crybaby, and we disapprove of crying even in children, discouraging it in them as early as possible. In a land so devoted to the pursuit of happiness as ours, crying really is rather un-American. Adults must learn not to cry in situations in which it is permissible for a child to cry. Women being the "weaker" and "dependent" sex, it is only natural that they should cry in certain emotional situations. In women, crying is excusable. But in men, crying is a mark of weakness. So goes the American credo with regard to crying.

2   "A little man," we impress on our male children, "never cries. Only sissies and crybabies do." And so we condition males in America not to cry whenever they feel like doing so. It is not that American males are unable to cry because of some biological time clock within them which causes them to run down in that capacity as they grow older, but that they are trained not to cry. No "little man" wants to be like that "inferior creature," the female. And the worst thing you can call him is a sissy or crybaby. And so the "little man" represses his desire to cry and goes on doing so until he is unable to cry even when he wants to. Thus do we produce a trained incapacity in the American male to cry. And this is bad. Why is it bad? Because crying is a

natural function of the human organism which is designed to restore the emotionally disequilibrated person to a state of equilibrium. The return of the disequilibrated organ systems of the body to steady states or dynamic stability is known as homeostasis. Crying serves a homeostatic function for the organism as a whole. Any interference with homeostatic mechanisms is likely to be damaging to the organism. And there is good reason to believe that the American male's trained incapacity to cry is seriously damaging to him.

Ashley Montagu, *The American Way of Life*

1. Is the main idea of Montagu's first paragraph stated or implied?

_____

What is the main idea?

_____

_____

2. In order to understand Montagu's purpose in writing this paragraph and therefore his main idea, you must understand his attitude and tone. A writer's attitude or feelings toward himself, his subject, and his readers determines his tone. *Tone* is the mood, atmosphere, or attitude expressed in a piece of writing. As the diagram below shows, then, tone is closely related to subject, purpose, and audience.

FIGURE 29 _____

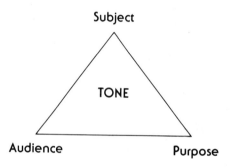

Tone may be sad or humorous, serious or light, friendly or unfriendly, straightforward or ironic. The tone of previous reading selections has been fairly straightforward: Adler's tone was informative, Angelou's was excited, and Steinbeck's was nostalgic. In this selection, however, Montagu's tone is ironic. That is, although the first paragraph states that "in men, crying is a mark of weakness," Montagu's real purpose is to disagree with this statement. Thus, the actual main idea is the opposite of what is stated. Reread your main idea statement in Question 1 and, if necessary, revise it below:

_____

_____

3. The primary method of development in the second paragraph is cause and effect. Does the paragraph begin with cause and then move to effect, or does it begin with effect and then move to cause?

_____

What are the effects?

_____

_____

_____

4. In this reading selection, Montagu uses certain words toward which most readers have stereotyped feelings. For example, how do you react toward the word *crybaby?* If you look up the word in a dictionary, you will find that its denotation, or dictionary meaning, is "a person who cries or complains frequently, with little cause" (*American Heritage Dictionary*). Though this meaning is negative enough, most of us have connotations of this word that are even more negative. That is, most of us have similar mental pictures of a crying, sniveling kid, and some of us may have specific memories of a particular "crybaby" or of being called a "crybaby." A word's connotations are those associations or suggestions that are connected with it. A word's denotation determines our understanding of its basic meaning; a word's connotations determine our attitudes toward it. Now, for each of the following words, write the denotation, your connotations, and what you believe to be Montagu's connotations of the word.
   a. feminine

   (1) denotation _____

   _____

   _____

   (2) your connotations _____

   _____

   (3) Montagu's connotations _____

   _____

   _____

   b. masculine

   (1) denotation _____

   _____

(2) your connotations _____

_____

(3) Montagu's connotations _____

_____

_____

_____

5. Montagu has put the terms *weakness, weaker, dependent, little man,* and *inferior creature* in quotation marks. What does this technique show about his attitude toward men and women?

_____

_____

_____

_____

_____

_____

_____

6. The words *equilibrium, disequilibrated,* and *homeostasis* look complex, but you can figure them out easily from their parts: *dis-* means "not, lack of, or removal"; *equi-* means "equal"; *libra* means "balance"; *homeo-* means "similar or same"; and *stasis* means "motionless." Define these words below.

a. equilibrium _____

b. disequilibrated _____

_____

c. homeostasis _____

Discussion Questions

1. Is it acceptable in our society for men to cry in certain situations but not in others? Why or why not? How can different situations justify different reactions?

2. What specific reasons or situations could cause a man or a woman to cry?

3. Have you seen a male whom you admire crying? Did you find this person weak or unmanly because you saw him cry? Why or why not?

4. If you are a female, have you ever known your father, husband, or boyfriend to cry? What is your reaction to a man or boy who cries? Do you find him less attractive, less strong, or more appealing?

5. Do you know of a boy who is afraid to cry? How does this refusal to cry affect him and those about him?

6. Do you think adults should consciously try to teach children that little boys should not cry? Why or why not?

7. Do you think females are emotionally healthier because our culture allows, even encourages, them to cry?

8. What attitudes do people in other cultures have toward a man's crying? Compare and contrast those attitudes with American attitudes.

Writing Exercise

Write a paragraph about how American men and/or women express their emotions. Review your journal entry and the discussion questions above to help you decide on your specific subject, purpose, method of development, and audience. You might write a comparison/contrast paragraph about attitudes toward crying in the United States and in another country, such as France or Mexico, about attitudes of younger and older men in America, or about attitudes of men and women. You might illustrate or classify the physical or emotional effects of a man's stifling his need to cry. Or you might describe a particularly emotional scene you have observed and explain how you felt about the incident. Your audience might be students in another country, men who are developing high blood pressure because of repressed feelings, or your own classmates or family. Use the space below to plan your paragraph:

Purpose: _____

Topic sentence: _____

_____

Method(s) of development: _____

Major supporting details: _____

_____

_____

_____

_____

Audience: _____

Now write the first draft of your paragraph.

Rewriting Exercise

Reread your paragraph to see if you have achieved your purpose and communicated to your audience. Use the questions below to help you revise it.

1. What is the purpose of the paragraph? Who is the audience? Is the purpose clear to the audience?

2. Does the paragraph have a clearly stated (or implied) topic sentence? What is the topic sentence?
    a. What is the subject? Is the subject sufficiently limited? How can it be further limited?
    b. What is the focus? Is the focus adequately narrowed? How can it be further narrowed?

3. What is the primary method of development?

4. Does the paragraph contain enough supporting details? Which details are the most effective? What other details could be added? Does the paragraph contain any details that should be omitted because they do not support the topic sentence? If so, which one(s)?

5. Does the paragraph achieve its purpose and communicate to its audience? Why or why not?

After you have revised your paper, edit it for errors in sentence structure, usage, spelling, and punctuation that will detract from your overall purpose. You may even want to type your paper so you can see your errors more clearly as you edit and proofread.

Optional Rewriting Exercises

1. Rewrite your paragraph for the same audience using another method of development.

2. Rewrite your paragraph using the same method of development but for a different audience. How does the change affect your tone?

ARRANGING and CONNECTING IDEAS

For a paragraph to be comprehensible to a reader, it must be unified and coherent. That is, the ideas in the paragraph must be logically arranged and connected so that a reader understands why they occur as they do. A paragraph is coherent if the different ideas in the paragraph function as a unit, or whole, and not as a series of individual, unconnected sentences. In the following sections of this chapter, you will learn more about coherence—how sentences in a paragraph relate to one another—and the signals that writers and readers use to communicate about these relationships.

ARRANGEMENT

Writers achieve coherence primarily by using a pattern of arrangement that is familiar to readers. The most common pattern of arrangement is the simple general-to-specific pattern, in which a writer begins with a general idea and supports it with specific details. But additional patterns are often needed for arranging the specific details within a paragraph. Three of the most frequently used patterns of arranging specific details are time order, space order, and order of importance. You are already familiar with these patterns, but the following reviews and exercises will help you see how writers and readers use them to communicate effectively.

Time Order

Most narrative paragraphs—those that tell a story, relate a series of events, or describe a process—are arranged in chronological order; that is, they are arranged in the order in which the events of the narrative occurred. Paragraphs arranged in chronological order often include references to the time of day, day of the week, or specific dates. Or they include signal words such as *first, then, next,* and *last* to indicate the passage of time. The following paragraph is arranged in chronological order:

Crime has invaded even the most respectable neighborhoods of our towns and cities. On the evening of August 18, 1985, Dr. Alice James was returning home from a late emergency-room call. As she pulled into the garage of her expensive brick home in one of the most prestigous areas of Salt Lake City, she noticed that it was nearly midnight. She simultaneously pushed the remote-control button to lower the garage door and opened the car door. At that precise moment, a man, who had apparently been waiting in the bushes just outside the garage, dashed under the closing garage door and hit her on the head with a heavy object. The next morning, the maid arrived to find the house burglarized and Dr. James lying unconscious on the floor of the garage. Three months later, on November 22, Dr. James finally regained consciousness. Today, two years later, she is still afraid to live alone, and the burglar is still at large, never caught by the police even though a number of Dr. James's possessions have appeared at local pawn shops.

Space Order

Many paragraphs, especially those that describe places or people, are arranged in space order; that is, the objects or details are arranged in the order in which they are observed in space. In a description of a room, for example, the writer may describe objects from left to right, from floor to ceiling, or from the outside walls to the center of the room. Paragraphs arranged by space order often include references to directions, such as *right, left, up, down, east, west, under, over, beyond, in front of, behind,* and so on. The following paragraph illustrates space order.

The view from the front door was breathtaking. Immediately in front of the house, to the west, was a small dirt road, and beyond this road the land dropped sharply so that the entire valley was visible. This broad valley was cut down the center by the Snake River, a curving blue-white scar across the pale green sage brush that covered most of the valley. On the far side of the valley, sandstone cliffs rose abruptly from the gently rolling valley floor. Rising above the cliffs were the distant mountains, majestic peaks crowned with snow and ice.

Order of Importance

The details in a paragraph may also be arranged according to order of importance. That is, writers may begin with the most important supporting point and end with the least important; however, more frequently, writers begin with the least important point and end with the most important. The latter pattern allows a writer to build to a high point, or climax. In either arrangement, writers may help their readers by emphasizing the points with signal words such as *first* and *second* or with descriptive phrases such as *more important* and *most important.* As you read the following paragraph, notice how the details progress from the least important to the most important:

Several considerations should influence your choice of a career. First, you should choose a career that will provide the lifestyle you want. If living in an expensive house and driving a big car are your goals, you should not decide to be a schoolteacher or a paramedic. Although it is possible to make a good living in these professions, most teachers and paramedics make rather modest salaries, especially at the beginning of their careers. Second, and more important, you should choose a career for which you have an aptitude. Even though you may love art, if you have no talent as an artist, you will not be successful. Finally, and most important, you should choose a career you will enjoy. Deciding to be a mechanic because you are good at repairing cars is not wise if you do not find car maintenance interesting or enjoyable. Becoming a lawyer if you do not enjoy writing briefs or researching legal issues is a mistake. You will spend countless hours working at whatever career you choose. Those hours will be more rewarding and less tiring if they are spent in work that you enjoy.

EXERCISE 6.1

Each of the following groups of sentences may be rearranged in a logical paragraph based on time order. Study each group of sentences, looking for the logical time sequence and for other transitional clues, such as signal words and repetition. More than one arrangement may be possible for the sentences in each group, but decide what you believe is the best order and number the sentences accordingly.

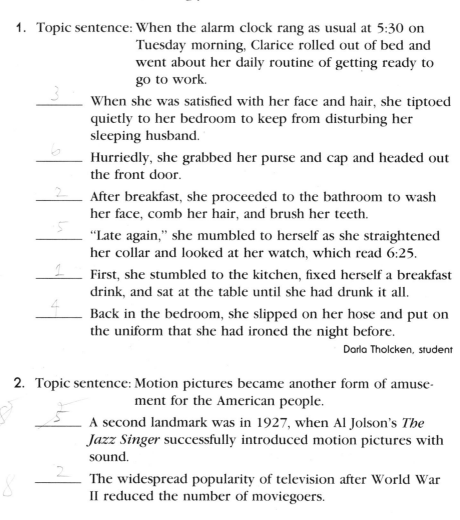

1. Topic sentence: When the alarm clock rang as usual at 5:30 on Tuesday morning, Clarice rolled out of bed and went about her daily routine of getting ready to go to work.

   __3__ When she was satisfied with her face and hair, she tiptoed quietly to her bedroom to keep from disturbing her sleeping husband.

   __6__ Hurriedly, she grabbed her purse and cap and headed out the front door.

   __2__ After breakfast, she proceeded to the bathroom to wash her face, comb her hair, and brush her teeth.

   __5__ "Late again," she mumbled to herself as she straightened her collar and looked at her watch, which read 6:25.

   __1__ First, she stumbled to the kitchen, fixed herself a breakfast drink, and sat at the table until she had drunk it all.

   __4__ Back in the bedroom, she slipped on her hose and put on the uniform that she had ironed the night before.

   Darla Tholcken, student

2. Topic sentence: Motion pictures became another form of amusement for the American people.

   __5__ A second landmark was in 1927, when Al Jolson's *The Jazz Singer* successfully introduced motion pictures with sound.

   __2__ The widespread popularity of television after World War II reduced the number of moviegoers.

_____1_____ Pioneered in America by Thomas Edison, the earliest motion pictures were different from those we see today.

_____3_____ However, through the years to the present, "going to the movies" has continued to be the favorite recreation of millions of Americans.

_____2_____ In these early movies, the film flickered and was dim; the motions of the actors were quick and jerky; and the actors' facial expressions as they showed fear, joy, or sadness would seem rather silly to us.

_____3_____ But the movies improved rapidly.

_____6_____ Then, during the 1930s, pictures in color added to the enjoyment of moviegoers.

_____4_____ In the thirties and forties, as many as 100 million people went to the movies each week.

_____4_____ In 1915, the success of *Birth of a Nation* encouraged the building of silent-movie theaters in cities and towns throughout the country.

Adapted from Howard B. Wilder et al., This Is America's Story

EXERCISE 6.2

Each of the following groups of sentences may be arranged in a logical paragraph based on space order. Study each group of sentences, looking for the logical spatial sequence, for signal words, and for other clues in the repetition of structures and ideas. More than one arrangement may be possible for the sentences in each group, but in Paragraph 1 the best arrangement is from the house outward, and in Paragraph 2 the best order is from back to front and from inside to outside. Number the sentences in the order in which they should be arranged in a paragraph.

1. Topic sentence: Skillful landscaping distinguishes the professor's white stucco house.

   _____ A low trellis separates these flowers from the evenly manicured lawn, which is broken only by a circular planter filled with more geraniums and centered with a fountain.

   _____ In front of the brick wall of the courtyard is a carefully shaped box hedge.

   _____ At the edge of the street, this lawn drops sharply three feet to a street-level sidewalk.

   _____ Directly in front of the house is a small brick courtyard in which cacti and yucca plants have been attractively arranged.

   _____ Next to this hedge grow rows of brightly colored flowers—red geraniums and white periwinkles.

2. Topic sentence: The scene is a spacious, handsome, and tastefully furnished home.

_6_ Through the windowpanes in the front room can be seen part of a verandah outside and trees covered with autumn foliage.

_1_ In the back of the house is a drawing room, which has a wide doorway, with curtains drawn back.

_3_ This front room is the same style as the drawing room.

_4_ In the righthand wall of the front room is a folding door leading out to the hall.

_2_ This wide doorway leads into a smaller front room.

_5_ In the opposite wall, on the left, is a glass door which also has the curtains drawn back.

Adapted from Henrik Ibsen, *Hedda Gabler*, Act I

EXERCISE 6.3

Each of the following groups of sentences may be arranged in a logical classification paragraph based on order of importance. Study each group of sentences, looking for a logical order, for signal words, and for clues of repetition. More than one arrangement may be possible for the sentences in each group, but you should determine the best order and number the sentences accordingly.

1. Topic sentence: During the Middle Ages, England had a very strict class structure based on the manor, a self-supporting landed estate.

_3_ Above the serf and below the lords was a large group of freemen, including tenants, shop owners, craftsmen, clergymen, soldiers, and lesser nobles.

_4_ Finally, at the very top of the class structure was the king, to whom the nobleman owed his allegiance.

_2_ The least important member of the class system was the serf, a servant who was bound to the soil of the manor and to the nobleman who owned it.

_1_ Near the top of the hierarchy was the lord who owned the estate.

2. Topic sentence: All organisms can be classified on the basis of their specializations into more or less well-defined types of categories.

_1_ Within a phylum, the next highest rank is the class.

_3_ Within the living world as a whole, the highest taxonomic rank usually recognized is the kingdom.

<u> 4 </u> Using criteria of likenesses and differences among and within groups, one may recognize orders within a class, families within an order, genera within a family, and species within a genus.

<u> 5 </u> The species normally is the lowest unit.

<u> 2 </u> The next highest rank within the kingdom is the division, or the phylum.

Adapted from Paul Weisz, *The Science of Biology*

TRANSITION   *make paragraphs becomes coherent.*

Ideas within a paragraph are held together primarily by logical arrangement. One idea usually follows another because readers and writers have agreed that certain arrangements, or patterns, are logical. For example, it is "logical" to discuss how to dress for an interview before discussing what to say (time order), to describe the front of a house before describing the rear of the house (space order), and to consider the most important reason for choosing to attend a certain college after you have considered the less important reasons (order of importance). But readers often need help to see your logic. Even though you arrange your ideas in a familiar, logical pattern, a reader may not perceive the pattern or the logic without assistance. The assistance a writer gives a reader is called *transition*.

Transition can be defined as the clues, or signals, a writer provides to help a reader see the connections between ideas. If the connections between the ideas are obvious, transitions are usually not needed; if they are less obvious, clear transitions become essential. In general, good writers are sensitive to the needs of their readers and give them as much assistance as possible.

The three basic methods of indicating transition are (1) repetition of words and ideas, (2) repetition of structure, and (3) use of transition words and phrases to signal the appropriate relationships.

Repetition of Key Words and Ideas

One of the most common means of providing transition in a paragraph is to repeat key words or ideas. This repetition reinforces the main idea stated in the topic sentence and connects supporting details to the main idea and to one another. In writing, you may reinforce, clarify, or elaborate a key word or idea by (1) repeating the same word, (2) using a more specific word or phrase for the same idea, (3) using a word or phrase with a similar meaning (a synonym), or (4) substituting a pronoun. Below you will find examples of each of these types of repetition:

1. **Repetition of exact word:** The *woman* was beautiful, but the *woman* was also dangerous.

2. **Repetition through more specific words:** In literature, *birds* often appear as symbols. For example, the *robin* may symbolize hope and the *raven* death.

3. **Repetition through synonyms:** Joe made an *attempt* to catch the bus, but his *try* was unsuccessful.
4. **Repetition through pronouns:** The *professor* started his lecture on the Constitution, but *he* was unable to finish it before the bell rang.

Much of the coherence of the following paragraph comes from the effective use of various types of repetition to reinforce the main topic, "dangerous chemicals." Key words or phrases that repeat or reinforce this topic have been boxed for you. In addition, marginal notes indicate how the author has used repetition to make the paragraph cohere, or "stick together."

Topic sentence	(1) For the first time in the history of the world, every human being is now
Key phrase	subjected to contact with dangerous chemicals from the moment of con-
Repetition through pronoun	ception until death. (2) In the less than two decades of their use, the
Repetition through synonym	synthetic pesticides have been so thoroughly distributed throughout the ani-
	mate and inanimate world that they occur virtually everywhere.
Repetition through pronouns	(3) They have been recovered from most of the major river systems and
	even from streams of groundwater flowing unseen through the earth.
Repetition through more specific phrase	(4) Residues of these chemicals linger in soil to which they may have
Repetition through pronouns	been applied a dozen years before. (5) They have entered and lodged in
	the bodies of fish, birds, reptiles, and domestic and wild animals so univer-
	sally that scientists carrying on animal experiments find it almost impossible to
Repetition through related word (synonym)	locate subjects free from such contamination. (6) They have been found in
Repetition through pronoun	fish in remote mountain lakes, in earthworms burrowing in soil, in the eggs of
Repetition through exact word	birds—and in man himself. (7) For these chemicals are now stored in the
Repetition through pronoun	bodies of the vast majority of human beings, regardless of age. (8) They
	occur in the mother's milk, and probably in the tissues of the unborn child.

Rachel Carson, Silent Spring

As you read the paragraph above, did you notice that the writer has reinforced the key words "dangerous chemicals" with all four types of repetition of key words or ideas? If she had used only one type of repetition—repetition through exact words or through pronouns, for example—the paragraph would be repetitious and dull. To see how different the effect would have been, reread the paragraph and substitute the exact word *chemicals* for each boxed word. As you have just discovered, it is not just repetition but repetition with variation that provides the most effective transition within a paragraph.

EXERCISE 6.4

The coherence of the following paragraph comes primarily from the effective use of repetition. Study the paragraph and underline once all the words and phrases that refer to the subject "arithmetic."

In reality <u>arithmetic</u> is always a means to an end, never an end in itself—except in school. Indeed, very few activities call for actual skill in arithmetic nowadays. With computers, elaborate cash registers, and now the small electronic calculators, the mechanics of arithmetic take second place, in practice, to choosing the necessary calculations and the right numbers to work with. Thus, we ask children to spend several years learning difficult, tedious skills that are rapidly coming to be of limited value. In doing so, we inadvertently teach that mathematics is not only hard but also not very useful. Rote arithmetic is a difficult and tedious branch of mathematics—a poor starting point for most students.

Mitchell Lazarus, "Rx for Mathophobia"

Repetition of Structure

Repetition of structure can also improve paragraph transition and coherence. When as writers we present information in obviously similar, or parallel, structures, we help our readers focus on our ideas and on the relationships among those ideas. In contrast, when we present related details and ideas in forms that have different, or nonparallel, structures, our awkward or unclear presentation of those ideas may keep our readers from understanding them. For example, which sentence below is easier to read and understand?

1. A successful lawyer must have education, experienced, and courageous.
2. A successful lawyer must have education, experience, and courage.

Do you agree that the second sentence is clearer? The first sentence is awkward because the writer has not used parallel forms in a situation in which the reader expects similar forms or structures to be repeated. In contrast to the first sentence, which uses a noun (*education*), a verb form (*experienced*), and an adjective (*courageous*), the second sentence clearly emphasizes three necessary attributes of a lawyer by repeating them in parallel noun forms.

As a writer, you can add coherence to your paragraphs by repeating parallel (1) word forms, (2) phrases, (3) clauses, and (4) sentences. As a reader, you can use such repetition of structure to help you identify important supporting details and their relationships to one another. Examples of the four major types of repetition of structure are given below:

1. **Repetition of word form:** The coach *fired* the punter, *traded* a running back, and *hired* a new wide receiver. (repetition of verbs of similar structure)

2. **Repetition of phrases:** He looked everywhere—*in the closet, behind the door,* and *under the bed.* (repetition of phrases of similar structure)

3. **Repetition of clauses:** It was obvious *that I had failed* and *that she had passed.* (repetition of clauses of similar structure)

4. **Repetition of sentences:** *I was tired. I was hungry. I was lost.* And, suddenly, *I was afraid.* (repetition of sentences of similar structure)

Now read aloud the following paragraph. As you read, notice how the writer repeats similar structures to make his paragraph more coherent, more readable, and more rhythmic. As you read the paragraph, notice especially the repetition of the word *it* and the repeated structure of *it* plus a verb, which occurs throughout the paragraph. The repeated, or parallel, structures have been underlined and noted for you in the margins.

[margin notes:]
Repetition of phrases
  from dawn
  to dusk
  to dawn
Repetition of sentences
  It trembles
  It moves
  It is
Repetition of word forms
  swell when hot
  contract when cold
  its great veins
  its span
Repetition of phrases
  in summer
  in winter
Repetition of nouns and "who" clauses
  romantics <u>who</u> gaze
  escapists <u>who</u> jump
  girl <u>who</u> lumbers
  motorists <u>who</u>
    cross

[handwritten margin notes:]
phrase : No S, no V
clause : S + V

(1) In New York <u>from dawn/to dusk/to dawn</u>, day after day, you can hear the steady rumble of tires against the concrete span of the George Washington Bridge. (2) The Bridge is never completely still. (3) <u>It trembles</u> with traffic. (4) <u>It moves</u> in the wind. (5) <u>Its great veins</u> of steel <u>swell when hot</u> and <u>contract when cold;</u> <u>its span</u> often is ten feet closer to the Hudson River <u>in summer</u> than <u>in winter</u>. (6) <u>It is</u> an almost restless structure of graceful beauty which, like an irresistible seductress, withholds secrets from <u>the romantics who gaze</u> upon it, <u>the escapists who jump</u> off it, <u>the chubby girl who lumbers</u> across its 3,500-foot span trying to reduce, and <u>the</u>

smash
shortchange
get jammed

100,000 motorists who each day <u>cross it</u>, <u>smash into it</u>, <u>shortchange it</u>, <u>get</u> <u>jammed up on it</u>.

Gay Talese, "New York"

By repeating the same structures, the writer is able to emphasize the various activities of the different people who use the bridge. Indeed, his repetition of structure creates a rhythm that reminds us of traffic rushing back and forth across the bridge. By repeating similar structures but varying the content of those structures, you can make your writing clearer and more interesting for your reader. Moreover, you can improve the sound and rhythm of your writing and learn to be more aware of the rhythms in your reading.

EXERCISE 6.5

The following paragraph also makes effective use of repetition of structure. Read the paragraph aloud and listen to its rhythm. Then reread the paragraph and look for structures that are repeated. Finally, fill in the blanks in the diagram that follows the paragraph.

On Wednesday morning at quarter past five came the earthquake. A minute later the flames were leaping upward. In a dozen different quarters south of Market Street, in the working class ghetto and in the factories, fires started. There was no opposing the flames. There was no organization, no communication. All the cunning adjustments of a twentieth century city had been smashed by the earthquake. The streets were humped into ridges and depressions, and piled with the debris of fallen walls. The steel rails were twisted into perpendicular and horizontal angles. The telephone and telegraph systems were disrupted. And the great water mains had burst. All the shrewd contrivances and safeguards of man had been thrown out of gear by thirty seconds' twitching of the earthcrust.

Jack London, "San Francisco Earthquake"

1. Repetition of phrases

     a. In _____

     b. in _____

     c. in _____

2. Repetition of sentence structures and phrases

     a. There _____

     b. There _____

          no _____

3. Repetition of sentence structures

   a. All the cunning _____

   _____

   _____

   b. All _____

   _____

   _____

4. Repetition of sentence structures, phrases, and word forms

   a. The streets were humped _____

   and _____

   b. The steel rails _____

   _____

   c. The _____ and _____

   d. And _____

Transition Signals

Probably the most common type of transitional device is the use of specific transition words and phrases to indicate relationships within and between sentences. These words and phrases signal changes and thus alert readers to "shift gears" or to take a new direction. For example, the word *however* signals contrast, and the words *next* and *then* signal progression.

Transition within the following paragraph is clear because signal words indicate specific relationships among ideas. As you read the paragraph, be sure you understand the appropriateness of each signal word. The signal words have been underlined for you, and the relationships that they indicate have been noted for you in the margin.

Addition   (1) Self-employed people can <u>and</u> do reduce their Social Security taxes

Manner   simply by failing to report all of their income. (2) <u>As</u> we shall see, this

Contrast   practice is clearly illegal. (3) <u>Nevertheless</u>, the high Social Security tax rate

Addition   <u>and</u> maximum-earnings limit make it very profitable to work for cash <u>and</u>

Addition/contrast	not report the income. (4) <u>Even though</u> the probability of getting caught
Time	may be small for "careful" cheaters, their tax savings <u>now</u> could spell seri-
Condition	ous consequences <u>if</u> they or their families need to use the coverages that
Condition	Social Security can provide. (5) <u>If</u> you avoid the mandatory tax premiums,

you won't be eligible for the coverage either.

Adapted from Daniel McGowan, *Contemporary Personal Finance*

This passage is particularly easy to read because the writer has made effective use of signal words.

As readers, we know to expect a contrasting idea when we see the word *nevertheless,* a similar idea when we see *and,* and a condition when we see *if.* Therefore, these words help us to "guess" or predict the general idea or type of idea that follows them. Such words help us understand the content of the passage well enough that we are not surprised and confused as we read through it. If we read the signal incorrectly, or if the writer gives us a faulty signal—if, for example, he had written *although* instead of *if* in the last sentence—we must go back and reread to comprehend the passage.

Just as readers take advantage of signal words as they read to predict the content of a passage, writers use signal words in their writing to help readers find their way from one idea to another. However, you do not want to add too many signal words or inappropriate ones. You should arrange your sentences so that one idea follows another in some type of logical progression. The signal words you use should serve primarily to reflect and reinforce the order of arrangement you have chosen. The following lists suggest some of the most common signal words and phrases. Notice that they are divided into categories on the basis of the type of development or order of arrangement with which they can be used.

TIME ORDER

first	then
second	soon
third, etc.	sometime(s)
now	next
before	last
after(ward)	finally
later	immediately
until	suddenly
while	gradually
when(ever)	meanwhile

SPACE ORDER

where(ever)	in front
behind	in back

before	to the left
under	to the right
in	at the top
out	at the bottom
over	to the north
above	to the south
within	to the east
outside	to the west
around	up/down
upon	through

ORDER OF IMPORTANCE

first	furthermore
second	finally
third, etc.	last
then	moreover
next	also
more important	foremost
most important	especially
primarily	less important
in addition	least important

ILLUSTRATION

for example	such as
for instance	like
that is	as
to illustrate	

COMPARISON/CONTRAST

however	instead
but	still
yet	rather
nevertheless	although
like	though
likewise	even though
similarly	whereas
on the contrary	in contrast
on the one hand/ on the other hand	

CAUSE AND EFFECT

therefore	since
consequently	because
accordingly	for
as a result	so that
hence	due to
thus	

EXERCISE 6.6

For practice in using signal words, read the following paragraph carefully and then write appropriate signal words in the blanks. Be sure to read the paragraph through completely before you start to fill in the blanks, and reread as much as necessary to determine the relationships among words and ideas.

The Indians of North and South America differed in their civilizations and in their governments. The South American Indians—such as the Aztecs and the Incas—had extremely sophisticated civilizations. Both tribes used highly developed agricultural techniques _____ (1) irrigation, terracing, and fertilizing. _____ (2), the Aztecs developed a hieroglyphic writing system and were skilled in the sciences _____ (3) in the arts. The Incas were skilled in textile weaving _____ (4) dyeing. _____ (5), the civilizations of the North American Indians were not as highly developed as those of the South American Indians, although the Pueblos built communal adobe cities _____ (6) the Natchez built burial mounds, which they later used as platforms for temples. The government of the South American Indians was organized around the concept of the empire, with the Inca government being harsh and dictatorial _____ (7) the Aztec government being more loosely administered. In North America the Natchez were ruled by an absolute monarch, _____ (8) most tribes either had leaders who were

only advisers, as in the Plains tribe, _____ had democratic governments,
                                    (9)

_____ in the Iroquois confederation.
  (10)

EXERCISE 6.7

The paragraph below lacks effective transitions. Rewrite the paragraph, adding transition signals and using repetition of words and structure where appropriate. You may want to combine sentences or rearrange words to make the paragraph more readable.

In the 1970s, Archie Bunker became a member of many American families. We knew that he was imperfect. He was temperamental and stingy. He fussed at Edith. He was ignorant and uneducated. He often used words incorrectly, confusing one with another. He would say, "I'll spend the hold rest of my life with a guilty complexion." He would say, "Ever since I'm unemployed, I'm totally impudent in bed." Archie was an unabashed WASP bigot, prejudiced against all ethnic minorities. He got a job as a custodian. He told his boss, "I'm gonna be the best janitor a white man can be." Archie had many human faults. We accepted him—even forgave him. We saw our own weaknesses reflected in his humorous, sometimes pathetic, actions.

READING/WRITING ASSIGNMENT 6A

I WANT A WIFE
Judy Syfers

Pre-Reading/Writing Exercise

Think for a few minutes about the responsibilities of a wife and those of a husband. What should a husband and wife expect of each other? What should they not expect? What should children expect of a mother or a father? What should they not expect? Now brainstorm about this topic, making two lists, one of a wife's responsibilities and one of a husband's. Then study your lists and draw lines to connect items that are related.

Reading Exercise

The paragraph below is part of a longer essay by Judy Syfers entitled "I Want a Wife." Syfers wrote this essay after observing a recently divorced male friend who was "obviously looking for another wife." Syfers writes, "As I thought about him while I was ironing one evening, it suddenly occurred to me that I, too, would like a wife." Read the paragraph to find out why she would like a "wife."

I want a wife who will take care of my physical needs. I want a wife who will keep my house clean, a wife who will pick up after me. I want a wife who will keep my clothes clean, ironed, mended, replaced when need be, and who will see to it that my personal things are kept in their proper place so that I can find what I need the minute I need it. I want a wife who cooks the meals, a wife who is a *good* cook. I want a wife who will plan the menus, do the necessary grocery shopping, prepare the meals, serve them pleasantly, and then do the cleaning up while I do my studying. I want a wife who will care for me when I am sick and sympathize with my pain and loss of time from school. I want a wife to go along when our family takes a vacation so that someone can continue to care for me and my children when I need a rest and change of scene.

Adapted from Judy Syfers, "I Want a Wife"

1. What is the topic sentence of Syfer's paragraph?

_____

2. Give examples of repetition that tie the paragraph together and emphasize both its main idea and its major supporting details.

_____

_____

_____

_____

_____

_____

3. What is the tone of Syfers's paragraph?

_____

4. "I Want a Wife" was first published in *Ms. Magazine* in 1972. What does this suggest about the audience for whom Syfers was writing?

_____

_____

5. This paragraph does not have any obviously difficult words, but it does have several simple words that are used, or could be used, in more than

one way. For example, in the first sentence *care* is a noun meaning "charge" or "responsibility," as in "to take charge of." Later, however, *care* is used as a verb meaning "to be concerned about." Thus, the context, the surrounding words, determines the meaning. Two other words that are used in different ways are *cook(s)* and *need(s)*. For each use of these words write below (1) the context and (2) the definition.

    a. cook(s)

        (1) Context: _____

              Definition: _____

        (2) Context: _____

              Definition: _____

    b. need(s)

        (1) Context: _____

              Definition: _____

        (2) Context: _____

              Definition: _____

        (3) Context: _____

              Definition: _____

        (4) Context: _____

              Definition: _____

Discussion Questions

1. Does Syfers think wives are treated fairly or unfairly? Do you agree or disagree with her? Are husbands also treated unfairly at times? How?

2. In the rest of her essay, Syfers writes that she would like a wife not only to take care of her physical needs but also to send her to school, to care for her children, to listen to her problems, to take care of her social life, and to be sensitive to her sexual needs. Do these responsibilities belong to the wife alone?

3. At the end of her essay, Syfers somewhat sarcastically says that when she finishes school and goes to work, she wants "her" wife to quit her job and stay at home to "take care of a wife's duties." What do you consider to be a wife's "duties"? Should a wife stay at home or have a career? Can she do both? How?

Writing Exercise

Write a paragraph about a wife's and/or husband's responsibilities. You might write to an audience that consists primarily of women (as Syfers did) or primarily of men, to a group of young engaged couples, or to middle-aged couples who have been married for several years.

To find your specific subject and focus, look back at your two lists and at the discussion questions about Syfers's paragraph on page 155. Your purpose might be to compare or contrast the responsibilities for a specific duty, such as preparing meals; to show the effects of neglected responsibilities, such as money management; or to show through example or narration the importance of a particular responsibility, such as child care. After you decide on your audience, purpose, main idea, and method of development, write a rough draft of your paragraph.

Rewriting Exercise

Reread your paragraph to see whether you have achieved your purpose and communicated to your audience. Use the questions below to help you revise it.

1. What is the purpose of the paragraph? Who is the audience?
2. Does the paragraph have a clearly stated (or implied) topic sentence? What is the topic sentence?
   a. What is the subject? Is the subject sufficiently limited? If not, limit it further.
   b. What is the focus? Is the focus adequately narrowed? If not, narrow it further.
3. What is the primary method of development?
4. What are your major supporting details? What other details could be added? Does the paragraph contain any details that should be omitted because they do not support the topic sentence? If so, which one(s)?
5. How are the supporting details arranged (time order, order of importance, etc.)? Can they be arranged more effectively? If so, how?
6. What forms of transition does the paragraph contain? What additional transition, if any, is needed?
7. Does the paragraph achieve its purpose and communicate to its audience? Why or why not?

After you have revised your paragraph, edit it for problems in sentence structure, punctuation, spelling, and word choice. Then proofread for minor errors and omissions.

MAKING CAMP
Stewart Edward White

Pre-Reading/Writing Exercise

Think about an activity or hobby that you particularly enjoy and that you do well. For example, you might be an expert at swimming, snow skiing, water skiing, hunting, fishing, dancing, typing, or playing basketball, football, baseball, or tennis. Brainstorm about this activity for a few minutes, listing on one side of your page what you most enjoy about the activity and on the other side important steps to follow in performing this activity or a part of it.

Reading Exercise

The following passage is taken from *The Forest* by Stewart Edward White. As you read, notice how clearly White describes the process of making camp.

1   When five or six o'clock draws near, begin to look about you for a good level dry place, elevated some few feet above the surroundings. Drop your pack or beach your canoe. Examine the location carefully. You will want two trees about ten feet apart, from which to suspend your tent, and a bit of flat ground underneath them. Of course the flat ground need not be particularly unencumbered by brush or saplings, so the combination ought not to be hard to discover. Now return to your canoe. Do not unpack the tent.

2   With the little axe clear the ground thoroughly. By bending a sapling over strongly with the left hand, clipping sharply at the strained fibers, and then bending it as strongly the other way to repeat the axe stroke on the other side, you will find that treelets of even two or three inches diameter can be felled by two blows. In a very few moments you will have accomplished a hole in the forest, and your two supporting trees will stand sentinel at either end of a most respectable-looking clearing. Do not unpack the tent.

3   Now, although the ground seems free of all but unimportant growths, go over it thoroughly for little shrubs and leaves. They look soft and yielding, but are often possessed of unexpectedly abrasive roots. Besides, they mask the face of the ground. When you have finished pulling them up by the roots, you will find that your supposedly level plot is knobby with hummocks. Stand directly over each little mound; swing the back of your axe vigorously against it, adze-wise, between your legs. Nine times our of ten it will crumble, and the tenth time means merely a root to cut or a stone to pry out. At length you are possessed of a plot of clean, fresh earth, level and soft, free from projections. But do not unpack your tent.

4   Lay a young birch or maple an inch or so in diameter across a log. Two clips will produce you a tent-peg. If you are inexperienced, and cherish memories of striped lawn markees, you will cut them about six inches long. If you are wise and old and gray in woods experience, you will multiply that length by four. Then your loops will not slip off, and you will have a real grip on mother earth, than which nothing can be more desirable in the event of a heavy rain and wind squall about midnight. If your axe is as sharp as it ought to be, you can point them more neatly by holding them suspended in front of you while you snip at their ends with the axe, rather than by resting them against a solid base. Pile them together at the edge of the clearing. Cut a crotched sapling eight or ten feet long. Now unpack your tent.

5   In a wooded country you will not take the time to fool with tent-poles. A stout line run through the eyelets and along the apex will string it successfully between your two trees. Draw the line as tight as possible, but do not be too unhappy if, after your best efforts, it still sags a little. That is what your long crotched stick is for. Stake out your four corners. If you get them in a good rectangle and in such relation to the apex as to form two isosceles triangles of the ends, your tent will stand smoothly. Therefore, be an artist and do it right. Once the four corners are well placed, the rest follows naturally. Occasionally in the North Country it will be found that the soil is too thin, over the rocks, to grip the tent-pegs. In that case drive them at a sharp angle as deep as they will go, and then lay a large flat stone across the slant of them. Thus anchored, you will ride out a gale. Finally, wedge your long sapling crotch under the line—outside the tent, of course—to tighten it. Your shelter is up. If you are a woodsman, ten or fifteen minutes has sufficed to accomplish this.

Stewart Edward White, *The Forest*

1. What is the purpose of this passage?

_____

_____

2. White's description of making camp is not only enjoyable but also technically accurate. What are some factual details that describe exactly how to make camp?

_____

_____

_____

3. White also uses sensory details to create a sense of atmosphere and background. List some of the most effective sensory details.

_____

_____

_____

4. Writers may use several methods of development in explaining a process. Most writers use narration, explaining the essential steps in the process in the order in which they occur. In addition, writers may define the process itself or important terms necessary to the process; they may show the effects of one or more steps in the process; or they may describe in detail one or more steps. What primary method of development does White use?

_____

5. White uses many transition words and phrases to clarify the process of making camp. Write below some of the transition words and phrases used in the last paragraph.

_____

_____

6. White provides unity and coherence between paragraphs by the repetition of a sentence. What is this sentence?

_____

_____

7. Process explanations such as White's often use technical words and phrases to provide accurate step-by-step descriptions. Writers may even use illustrations or diagrams to explain a process as accurately and completely as possible. Define and draw an illustration of each of the following technical words. You may use your previous knowledge of the word, the context, or a dictionary to help you.

  a. adze-wise _____

   _____

   _____

  Illustration:

  b. crotched _____

   _____

Illustration:

c. apex _____

_____

Illustration:

d. isosceles _____

_____

Illustration:

Writing Exercise

Look back at your brainstorming about a favorite hobby. Then, following one of the specific assignments below, write a paragraph about this activity.

1. Explain to a beginner the process involved in this activity. Since you are writing only a paragraph instead of an essay, limit your explanation to one part of the process and describe that part fully. For example, if your favorite hobby is swimming, focus on the process of floating or doing the breast stroke. Include in your explanation of the process all the steps your reader—a beginner—would need to know. Arrange the steps of the process

in a clear and logical order and provide clear transitions, such as *first, then, before,* and *after.* Also, include any illustrations or diagrams necessary to make the process clear to your reader. Finally, define in context any terms that might be unfamiliar to your reader.

2. Write to a friend or classmate explaining why you enjoy your favorite hobby. Support your topic sentence with reasons, examples, or a narrative illustration. Arrange your support logically (time order, order of importance, etc.), and provide clear transitions.

Rewriting Exercise

Reread your paragraph to see whether you have achieved your purpose and communicated to your audience. Use the questions below to help you revise it.

1. What is the purpose of the paragraph? Who is the audience?
2. Does the paragraph have a clearly stated (or implied) topic sentence? What is the topic sentence?
   a. What is the subject? Is the subject sufficiently limited? If not, limit it further.
   b. What is the focus? Is the focus adequately narrowed? If not, narrow it further.
3. What is the primary method of development?
4. What steps or details have been included? What steps or details should be added? Does the paragraph contain any details that should be omitted because they do not support the topic sentence or because they detract from the explanation of the process? If so, which one(s)?
5. Do illustrations or diagrams need to be added, revised, or omitted? Explain.
6. How are the supporting details arranged (time order, order of importance, etc.)? Can they be arranged more effectively? If so, how?
7. What forms of transition does the paragraph contain? What additional transition, if any, is needed?
8. If your paragraph is an explanation of a process, could a beginner use it to complete the process? Why or why not?

After you have revised your paragraph, edit it for problems in sentence structure, punctuation, spelling, and word choice. Then proofread for minor errors and omissions.

Chapter 7

Read 162–171
Do exercise 7.1

READING and WRITING ESSAYS

Thus far in this book our primary concern has been the paragraph. But, as a college student, you are frequently required to read and write longer compositions, especially essays. Your knowledge of paragraph structure will be very helpful to you as you begin to work with essays because the basic structure of an essay is the same as that of a paragraph. An essay, like a paragraph, consists of an introduction, a body, and a conclusion. However, an essay is composed of a series of related paragraphs, whereas a paragraph consists of a series of related sentences.

A good essay is composed of *well-developed paragraphs,* which in turn develop the main idea of the essay. Many readers and writers make the mistake of ignoring the structure of the paragraph once it is part of an essay. Although the paragraphs that make up the body of an essay may not be able to stand alone as compositions, they often have essentially the same structure as a paragraph that is meant to stand on its own. Therefore, as you read and write essays, you will continue to use your knowledge of paragraphs.

The essay diagrammed in Figure 30 consists of five paragraphs: an introductory paragraph, three body paragraphs, and a concluding paragraph. The number of paragraphs varies widely from one essay to another. Some essays are very brief; others are quite long. But the five-paragraph essay serves as a convenient model.

INTRODUCTION: STATEMENT OF THESIS

Essays, like paragraphs, develop one main idea. The main idea of an essay is called a *thesis statement,* and it is expressed in the introduction, usually at the end of the introduction. Like the main idea of a paragraph, a thesis is a general statement. The general statement that serves as a thesis for an essay is often more general than the topic sentence of a paragraph but not as general as a thesis of a book.

Disciplinary ('disaplaneri') adj

school/military discipline

EXAMPLE

Topic sentence of a paragraph: My sixth-grade teacher was a strict disciplinarian.

'disaplin

Thesis of an essay: Discipline problems created a poor environment for learning in my high school.

162

FIGURE 30

PARAGRAPH   **ESSAY**

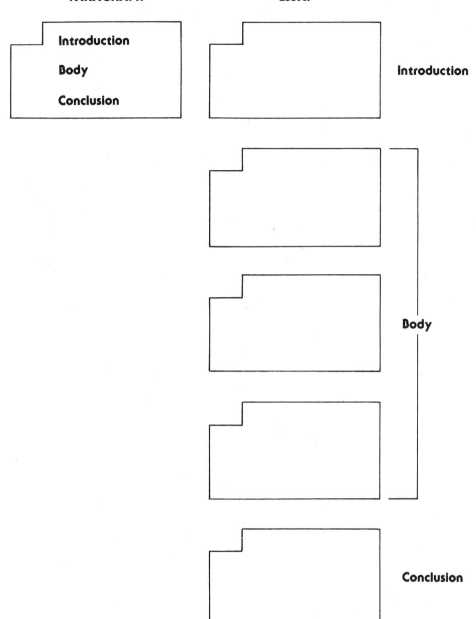

Thesis of a book: One of the major problems with the United States' system of education is its failure to deal effectively with discipline problems.

Notice that the topic sentence of the paragraph is limited to a partic-ular person (sixth-grade teacher) and to a specific aspect of that person (role as disciplinarian). The paragraph that develops this topic sentence will not merely describe the sixth-grade teacher but will focus on how he disciplined the class. The thesis of the essay, in contrast, is broad enough to include a discussion of several problems that contributed to discipline in the high school, but it is limited to a particular high school at a particular time and to the experience of one person. The essay that develops this thesis will not discuss every aspect of the writer's high school experience—just the problems in the school associated with discipline. The thesis of a book, however, is much broader, allowing for a complex, complete discussion of how the problem of discipline affects the United States' entire school system.

Thus, the general statement that serves as the controlling idea of an essay should not be *too* general. In fact, many times the same idea that served as the topic sentence of a paragraph can be used effectively as the thesis of an essay. A very broad, vague, overly general statement is inappropriate as the thesis of an essay. If you narrow your main idea so that your focus is fairly limited, you will have less difficulty writing your essay and will write a better essay.

As a reader, you should look carefully at the introduction of an essay to determine the thesis. Although not all writers place the thesis statement in the introduction, most writers—especially writers of textbooks, newspapers, magazines, and reports—include in their introduction a thesis statement that explains clearly the point they wish to make. It is a good idea, therefore, to read the introduction very carefully, looking especially for the thesis statement. Since everything else in the essay will be related to the thesis, you must understand it before you can understand the essay as a whole.

Occasionally, a writer will not include a thesis statement. At least, he or she will not express the main idea in a single sentence that can be identified as a thesis. But every essay has a main idea; if there is no stated thesis, you should formulate in your own words what you think the writer's thesis is. Read the introduction several times if necessary to determine what the subject is and what the writer is going to say about that subject. You will not understand clearly the remainder of the essay unless you begin your reading with a clear idea of the writer's thesis. You may also want to return to the introduction after you have read the entire essay (or chapter or article) in order to review the thesis statement. Sometimes after you have read an essay, its thesis statement will have more meaning. Reviewing the thesis after you have read an essay will also help you remember the main points of the essay.

Writing Introductions

An introduction serves as a contract between a writer and his or her readers. In the introduction, a writer makes specific commitments that must then be fulfilled. The most important of these is the thesis statement, which commits the writer to a specific focus. In effect, it provides the reader with an accurate expectation of what the writer plans to do—the main idea that the writer plans to develop.

In general, a good introduction accomplishes three purposes:

1. It attracts the reader's interest.
2. It provides the reader with background information.
3. It focuses the reader's attention on the main idea of the essay.

For example, the following paragraph could serve as an introduction to an essay on the discipline problems that affected one person's high school education.

<table>
<tr><td>Background information</td><td>From 1972 to 1976, I attended an inner-city high school in Chicago. The school was located in an area that was rapidly changing from residential to commercial. It was an old, respected school that had formerly educated the children of the families in the neighborhood. Many of the teachers were dedicated, competent professionals, who had taught in this school for years. Others were inexperienced, young teachers who were encountering their</td></tr>
<tr><td>Transition</td><td>first students. However, neither the experienced nor the inexperienced teachers were able to handle the undisciplined, unmotivated students who attended their classes. As a result,</td></tr>
<tr><td>Thesis statement</td><td>discipline problems created a poor environment for learning in the high school.</td></tr>
</table>

Notice that the writer devotes several sentences to background information, supplying the reader with a context for what is to follow. The sentence about the problems the teachers had in controlling the students serves as a transition, focusing the reader's attention on the thesis statement that follows. The writer and the reader are now ready to explore this thesis statement in the body of the essay.

As a writer, you want your introduction to be not only clear but interesting. A dull or trite introduction can discourage a reader from continuing to the main part of the essay. But attempts at cuteness and cleverness often fail, resulting in an introduction that is not only unclear but also embarrassingly inappropriate. One strategy for composing effective introductions is to use one of the methods of development discussed in Chapter 5. For example, we could vary the introduction about the inner-city Chicago school by using different methods of development.

NARRATION

In 1972 I enrolled in an old high school located in the midst of an area that was rapidly changing from residential to commercial. During my freshman year, I was too nervous to think about anything except finding my classes and deciding which clubs to join. But by the time I was a sophomore, I began to notice the discipline problems that all too often disrupted classes. Many of the students were obviously not interested in learning. As I entered my junior year, I began to resent the troublemakers and to sympathize with the teachers who struggled each day to teach those students who wanted to learn. By the time I was a senior I was really angry because I realized that the discipline problems had created a poor environment for learning in my high school.

DESCRIPTION

The boys' restroom at my high school was disgusting. The concrete walls of the restroom carried crude messages scratched into their fading green paint. All of the doors had been torn off the hinges, so there was no privacy. And the drains were nearly always clogged with the paper towels that had been left in the sinks rather than thrown in the trash. Paper towels, cigarette butts, and candy wrappers littered the dirty, wet floor. But the thing I found most disgusting was the tobacco juice that stained everything—toilets, wash basins, even the floors. This filthy bathroom reflected the attitudes of the students in this inner-city school who had as little respect for authority and learning as they did for property.

ILLUSTRATION

The high school I attended was run, not by the teachers and administrators, but by a group of students who had no interest in learning. On one occasion, they actually took control of the school building and refused to let the teachers inside. Another time, they organized a boycott of classes by threatening all of us if we went to any of our classes. Even worse, these undisciplined students disrupted every class that was held in the school. As a result, the environment in the school was never one that encouraged learning.

COMPARISON/CONTRAST

During my first two years of high school, I attended a school in a quiet suburb of Chicago. When I was a junior, I transferred to a large inner-city high school. The students at the suburban high school were, for the most part, well behaved and highly motivated. However, most of the students at the inner-city school were totally undisciplined and unmotivated. The modest brick building in the suburbs was not fancy but was clean and well maintained. The inner-city school was dirty and run down. At the suburban high school a discipline problem usually consisted of a student's talking back to a teacher or skipping class. At the inner-city school, discipline problems ranged from verbal and physical abuse of teachers to violent, occasionally fatal, fights among the students themselves. As a result of the poor learning environment, my last two years of high school were a complete waste of time.

CLASSIFICATION

Like the beds in the house of the three bears that Goldilocks tried, some schools are too hard, some are too soft, and some are just right. A school in which the rules restrict the imagination and creativity of the students is too hard. One in which there are too few rules often lacks an environment that encourages learning. The best school is one that has enough rules to ensure that students' and teachers' rights are not violated but that also allows everyone the freedom that is essential to real learning.

CAUSE AND EFFECT

The high school I attended was ruled by a gang of disruptive students. All of us, especially the teachers, were frightened of these bullies. They freely broke the rules, intimidated the teachers, and generally did as they pleased. As a result, discipline problems created a poor environment for learning in the high school.

DEFINITION

We all have different environments in which we exist; we live in one environment, work in another, and often play in still another. These different environments are the contexts that give our lives meaning. If they are supportive, we can operate within them in positive, productive ways. If they are hostile and nonsupportive, we cannot. A school provides a learning environment for its students. To a great extent, that environment, more than the teachers and books, determines what students learn. My high school failed to provide an environment that encouraged learning.

Although each of these introductions is based primarily on one specific method of development, most of them actually employ several methods. For example, the one that is developed by illustration also includes narration and description. But you can see how useful it is when writing introductions to think in terms of these various methods of development. Below are some additional suggestions for writing effective introductions.

SUGGESTIONS FOR WRITING EFFECTIVE INTRODUCTIONS

1. Be clear and direct (clarity is more important than cleverness).
2. Provide the background information your reader needs to understand your subject.
3. Avoid trite expressions, such as "In the world today" or "For as long as man has existed."
4. End your introduction with a clear statement of your thesis.

EXERCISE 7.1

Write an introduction for an essay about friendship. Use one of the methods of development (narration, description, illustration, comparison/contrast, classification, cause and effect, or definition) as the basis for your introduction. Then, using the same or a similar thesis statement, write a second introduction using a different method of development.

BODY: DEVELOPMENT OF THESIS

The body of a unified, coherent essay consists of a number of related paragraphs that develop the thesis. The individual sentences within each paragraph support the main idea (topic sentence) of the paragraph, and the paragraphs support the main idea (thesis) of the essay (see Figure 31).

FIGURE 31

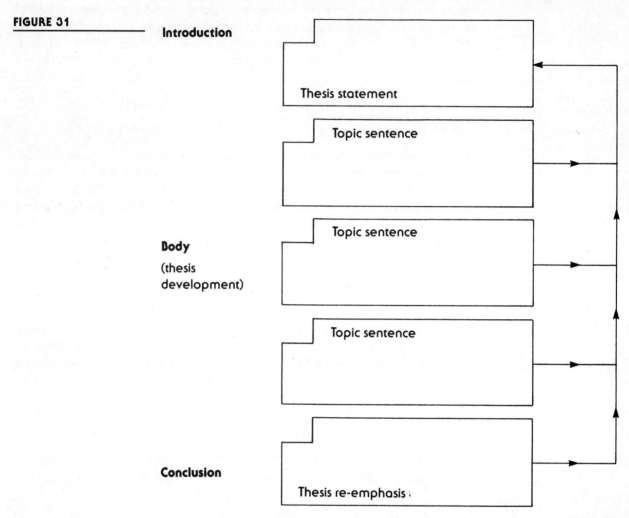

Introduction

Thesis statement

Topic sentence

Body

(thesis development)

Topic sentence

Topic sentence

Conclusion

Thesis re-emphasis

A writer develops the topic sentence of a paragraph by discussing, explaining, and expanding the idea that it expresses. A writer develops the thesis of an essay in the same way. Both topic sentences and thesis statements are general statements that must be supported by specific facts, details, and examples. In an essay, a writer usually devotes a paragraph to each *major* supporting point. Each of these supporting points is directly related to the thesis and helps develop it. But each major supporting point is also developed individually as a paragraph.

Writers often develop the paragraphs that make up the body of an essay by using the familiar methods of development—narration, description, illustration, comparison/contrast, classification, cause and effect, and definition. Although sometimes you may use a single method of development for an entire essay, it is much more likely that you will use a combination of methods. For example, if you were completing the essay on the high school that had discipline problems, you might use the following topic sentences and methods of development:

Introduction
Thesis: As a result, discipline problems created a poor environment for learning in the high school.

Paragraph 1
Topic sentence: One problem was the turmoil that always existed within the classrooms.
Methods of development: cause and effect, illustration, description, or narration

Paragraph 2
Topic sentence: An even more serious problem was the lack of authority the teachers had.
Methods of development: comparison/contrast, cause and effect, illustration, or description

Paragraph 3
Topic sentence: The most serious problem, however, was that most of the students simply refused to learn.
Methods of development: classification, cause and effect, description, or comparison/contrast

As a writer, you have many choices to make in developing the body of your essay. As a reader, you need to be aware of the choices the writer has made. Familiar patterns of organization and development can help you in both roles. In the outline above, for example, the essay is organized so that the major supporting points are listed in order of importance—a familiar pattern that readers easily recognize. The individual paragraphs are written with different methods of development that are also familiar to a reader. As a result, both writer and reader can focus on the meaning because the new ideas occur in a familiar context.

EXERCISE 7.2

Using as a starting point one of the introductions you wrote in Exercise 7.1, plan the body of an essay on friendship. Write three or more topic sentences that would appropriately develop your thesis, and decide on at least one method of development that could be used in each paragraph.

CONCLUSION: RE-EMPHASIS OF THESIS

The conclusion of an essay, like the conclusion of a paragraph, gives the reader a sense of completion. Conclusions usually refer back to the introduction or, at least re-emphasize in some way the thesis stated in the introduction. Often the conclusion briefly summarizes the thesis and the major supporting points. A good conclusion always confirms the audience's understanding of what they have read by reminding them of the writer's purpose. Like introductions, conclusions provide readers with an overview.

For example, the paragraph below would effectively conclude the essay on discipline problems in the Chicago high school.

Recently I visited my parents in Chicago and drove past my old high school. Now a warehouse for textbooks, the building looks abandoned and dilapidated. Crude, obscene messages remain scrawled on the walls, and many of the windows are broken or missing. Evidently, the discipline problems finally defeated the valiant but discouraged teachers. I am glad the school is now closed, for learning had become impossible in that environment.

Conclusions should not be cute or trite or obvious. The best conclusions are appropriate, clearly written, and straightforward. They do not strain for an effect they cannot achieve (such as humor, cleverness, or brilliance). If you have not written a good essay, your conclusion cannot save it; however, a good essay can be damaged by an ineffective or inappropriate conclusion.

Writing Conclusions

Just as an introduction can be viewed as a contract between you and your reader, a conclusion reassures your reader that you have fulfilled your contract. Your closing paragraph should leave your reader with a sense of completion—with the feeling that you have done what you intended to do and have finished what you had to say.

Several different types of conclusions accomplish this purpose:

1. **Restatement of main idea.** The main idea may be re-emphasized or reinforced. If you choose this type of conclusion, however, be sure not to merely repeat your thesis. You not only should vary the wording so that your conclusion is not too similar to your introduction but should also try to get beyond your thesis statement—to express an appropriate conclusion and to give your reader a sense of closure.

2. **General impression.** If your essay is basically a description of an experience or of some person, place, or thing, an effective conclusion might consist of a statement of the dominant impression you have attempted to convey. For example, if your essay about your high school is largely a description of what occurred to you when you were there, you might conclude with what you remember most clearly about the whole experience.

3. **Evaluation.** An essay may also conclude with a judgment based on the information presented. For example, you might end an essay on your high school by evaluating whether the experience was essentially negative or positive.

4. **Recommendation.** An essay can be concluded with a suggestion for some action the writer feels should be taken. This type of conclusion is especially appropriate if the main idea is a controversial statement or one that is persuasive in nature. For example, you might conclude your essay

about your high school's discipline problems by recommending that a new administration be hired or a new school board be elected.

5. Prediction. Even though a conclusion is the final part of an essay, it can be used to make a prediction on the basis of the major points made in the essay. This prediction should be closely related to the content of the essay, giving a reasonable explanation of what may happen. For example, you might predict in the conclusion to your essay about your high school's problems that the school will be closed down in the near future.

Regardless of the type of conclusion you choose for your essay, the conclusion should re-emphasize your thesis. It should also be a clear signal to your reader that you have completed what you had to say. Following are some suggestions that will be helpful to you in writing conclusions.

SUGGESTIONS FOR WRITING EFFECTIVE CONCLUSIONS

1. Do not contradict the point you have made.
2. Do not introduce a new topic or new information.
3. Do not conclude with a cliché ("You can't teach an old dog new tricks").
4. Do not apologize for lack of knowledge, ability, or resources.
5. Do not use obvious transition words or phrases such as *in conclusion, in summary,* and *as I have attempted to show.* You may, however, use less obvious transition words, such as *therefore, finally,* and *consequently.*
6. Do make your conclusion brief and to the point.
7. Do make the tone (serious, humorous, clever, straightforward, etc.) consistent with the overall tone of your essay.

EXERCISE 7.3

Using one of the five types of conclusion described above, write an appropriate conclusion for the essay you planned in Exercise 7.2.

FROM PARAGRAPH TO ESSAY

Read the following paragraph, which compares and contrasts two different cities. Note especially the topic sentence and the major supporting points.

Moving from Detroit, Michigan, to Hobbs, New Mexico, was not easy. First, I had to get used to the change in climate. Even though the weather in Michigan is not ideal, it was what I had known all my life, and I was used to the dampness and the cold in winter and the dampness and the heat in the summer. In Hobbs, any moisture evaporates immediately. And it is sometimes difficult to tell winter from summer since the two seasons are so much alike. My next problem was adjusting to life in a small town. Detroit is a busy, industrial city that never sleeps. Hobbs never wakes up. It is so quiet and small that I felt at first as though I were living on the fringe of civilization. But the biggest problem I had was the difference in time. I don't mean just the fact that Detroit is on Eastern Standard Time and Hobbs is on Mountain Standard Time. I mean fast versus slow. Everyone in Detroit is on the move—in a hurry, rushed, afraid of being late. In Hobbs, on the other hand, no one really cares what time it is. No one seems concerned about getting places on time, much less early. But now that I have lived in Hobbs for a year, I find that I too am slowing down. Moreover, I have found that I haven't left civilization. I've just moved to a different type—a drier, warmer, quieter, slower one.

EXERCISE 7.4

Answer the following questions about the paragraph you have just read.

1. What is the main idea of the paragraph?

   _____

   _____

2. Is the main idea expressed in a topic sentence? _____

3. Underline the topic sentence.

4. What are the major supporting points developed in the paragraph?

   a. _____

   b. _____

   c. _____

5. What is the primary method of development?

   _____

6. Reread the last sentence of the paragraph. Does this sentence serve as an effective conclusion to the paragraph?

   _____ Notice especially how the conclusion reminds you of the writer's main idea and summarizes the major supporting points.

   Now read the following essay, which has the same main idea as the paragraph you have just read. Notice, as you read, that the main difference between the paragraph and the essay is that the writer uses different paragraphs for each of the three major supporting points in the essay and that she uses many more details and examples to support each major point. Notice also that the author contrasts Hobbs with Detroit in each of the three paragraphs that make up the body of the essay. This pattern of organization is typical of many comparison/contrast essays.

1   I was born in Detroit, Michigan, and had lived there all of my life until I married and moved with my husband to Hobbs, New Mexico. The morning that my parents took us to the airport, they cried as if I were leaving the country and moving to a foreign land. Although I felt some apprehension, I thought that surely there could not be much difference between one state or city and another. After all, both Detroit and Hobbs are in the United States. People in both places speak English, eat hamburgers, and wear blue jeans. I felt confident that my life would be much the same. It did not take me long to discover, however, that moving from Detroit to Hobbs was not easy.

2   First, I had to get used to the change in climate. Even though the weather in Michigan is not ideal, it was what I had known all my life. I was used to the dampness and the cold in winter and the dampness and heat in summer. I accepted mildew and frizzy hair as facts of life. In Hobbs any moisture that may accidentally occur immediately evaporates. Even in the early morning there is no dew on the grass, and a rainfall is a major event, celebrated and talked about for days. Fog and mist are absolutely unheard of. Day after day the sun shines brightly, even relentlessly, drying out everything. In fact, it is sometimes difficult to tell winter from summer because the two seasons are so much alike.

3   My next problem was adjusting to a small town. Detroit is a busy, industrial city that never sleeps. Hobbs never wakes up. It is so quiet and small that I felt at first as though I were living on the fringe of civilization. Instead of several major newspapers, a variety of local radio and television channels, and a choice of big name entertainers and shows, Hobbs has one daily newspaper, a small radio station, and a few movies. By ten o'clock at night almost everyone is at home. And everyone knows everyone else. In Detroit, I could go all over the city and never see anyone I knew—not even a familiar face. In Hobbs, I rarely see anything but familiar faces. A stranger in town is the source of real excitement—a cause for speculation and curiosity. In Hobbs I don't dare go to the supermarket (there are only a few) with my hair in curlers, for I am sure to see people I know. In Detroit I could be anonymous when I chose; in Hobbs I am part of a small, even intimate community.

4   But the biggest problem I have had is the difference in time. I don't mean just the fact that Detroit is on Eastern Standard Time and Hobbs is on Mountain Standard Time. I mean fast versus slow. Everyone in Detroit is on the move—in a hurry, rushed, afraid of being late. In Hobbs, on the other hand, no one really cares what time it is. No one seems concerned about getting places on time, much less early. For example, soon after we arrived in Hobbs we were invited to a party. Conditioned by years of living in Detroit, where everyone strives to be punctual, my husband and I arrived at the party on time. The door was opened by a surprised hostess, who, dressed in a robe, was straightening the living room and preparing some last minute snacks for the party. She very graciously invited us in and explained that the other guests would be arriving soon ("soon" turned out to be almost an hour later). We sat uncomfortably in the deserted living room as the hostess fin-

ished dressing and preparing the food. When the other guests finally arrived, an hour after the appointed time, the party began, although guests continued to arrive late into the evening. I now realize that when people in Hobbs say a party begins at a certain time, they don't really mean at that exact time. The attitude toward time is so relaxed that it is almost impossible to be *late*. People just aren't terribly concerned with being punctual.

5   I have now lived in Hobbs for a year, and I find that I am slowing down too. I don't drive as fast as I did; I don't worry if I am a few minutes late; and I certainly don't arrive at parties on time. I am getting used to the climate too. On a recent trip back to Detroit I was terribly conscious of the humidity and nearly froze because the weather was so cold and damp. Moreover, I have discovered that moving to Hobbs has not meant that I left civilization. I've just moved to a different type of civilization—one that is drier, warmer, quieter, and slower.

EXERCISE 7.5

Answer the following questions about the essay you have just read.

1. What is the main idea of the essay? _____

_____

2. Is the main idea expressed in a thesis statement? _____

3. Underline the thesis statement.

4. What are the major supporting points developed in the essay?

a. _____

b. _____

c. _____

_____

5. Does each of these major supporting points serve as a topic sentence of a paragraph?

_____

6. Underline each of the topic sentences that expresses a major supporting point.

7. Compare these topic sentences with the three major supporting points of the original paragraph. Are they the same supporting points?

_____

8. List below several details the writer uses to support her major supporting points in the essay but not in the paragraph.

   a. _____

   _____

   b. _____

   _____

   c. _____

   _____

   d. _____

9. Compare the concluding paragraph of the essay with the concluding sentence of the paragraph. Do both refer the reader to the introduction and re-emphasize the main idea?

_____

READING/WRITING ASSIGNMENT 7A

TEEN PRIVACY
Haim G. Ginott

Pre-Reading/Writing Exercise

For a few minutes, think about being alone. Do you sometimes like to be alone? Do you have feelings, relationships, letters, or diaries that you do not like to discuss with other people? Brainstorm for a few minutes about ways in which your privacy is sometimes violated by people or things.

Reading Exercise

Read the essay "Teenager's Privacy." As you read, think about ways in which parents violate their children's privacy or ways in which children violate their parents' privacy.

1 Teenagers need privacy; it allows them to have a life of their own. By providing privacy, we demonstrate respect. We help them disengage themselves from us and grow up. Some parents pry too much. They read their teenagers' mail and listen in on their telephone calls. Such violations may cause perma-

nent resentment. Teenagers feel cheated and enraged. In their eyes, invasion of privacy is a dishonorable offense. As one girl said: "I am going to sue my mother for malpractice of parenthood. She unlocked my desk and read my diary."

2   One sixteen-year-old boy complained: "My mother has no respect for me. She invades my privacy and violates my civil rights. She comes into my room and rearranges my drawers. She can't stand disorder, she says. I wish she'd tidy up her own room and leave mine alone. I deliberately mess up my desk as soon as she cleans it up. But mother never learns."

3   Some teenagers complain that their parents participate too eagerly in their social life.

4   Bernice, age seventeen, speaks with bitterness: "My mother dresses up before my date arrives. She gossips with him while I'm getting ready. She even walks down with us to the car. When I return, I find her waiting for me, bursting with curiosity. She wants to know everything. What did he say? What did I answer? How did I feel? How much money did he spend? What are my future plans? My life is an open book; every page is a public announcement. My mother tries to be a pal. I don't want to hurt her feelings but I don't need a forty-year-old pal. I'd rather have some privacy."

5   Respect for privacy requires distance which parents find hard to maintain. They want closeness and fraternization. For all their good will, they intrude and invade. Such familiarity does not breed mutual esteem. For respect to flourish, parents and teenagers must keep some distance. They can "Stand together yet not too near together." Respect encompasses an awareness of our teenager as a distinct and unique individual, a person apart from us. In the last analysis, neither parent nor teenager "belongs" to the other. Each belongs to himself.

Haim G. Ginott, *Between Parent and Teenager*

1. What is the author's thesis?

_____

_____

2. Do you agree or disagree with the thesis? Why or why not?

_____

_____

_____

_____

3. What are the major supporting points in the essay?

a. _____

_____

b. _____

_____

c. _____

_____

4. Several of the words in this reading begin with common prefixes. Knowing the meanings of these prefixes will help you define not only these words but other words that begin with the same prefixes.

    a. The prefix *dis-* is a negative prefix that reverses the meaning of the word to which it is attached. Thus, the word *disengage,* which occurs in the third sentence—"We help them disengage themselves from us and grow up"—means "not to engage" or "to detach oneself from." The word *dishonorable* also appears in this reading. Using your knowledge of the prefix *dis-,* define the word *dishonorable:*

_____

_____

_____

    b. Another common prefix is *mal-,* which means "bad." This prefix appears in the word *malpractice,* which occurs in the sentence "I am going to sue my mother for malpractice of parenthood." Using the context in which the word appears and your knowledge of the prefix *mal-,* define the word *malpractice:*

_____

_____

_____

    The word *malpractice* does not usually refer to parents but to medical doctors. The author is deliberately using the word in a different context to suggest that children, like patients, should perhaps be protected from irresponsible or unethical treatment.

    c. A third common prefix that occurs in this reading is *re-,* which means "again." The word *rearranges* appears in the sentence "She comes into my room and rearranges my drawers." Define the word *rearrange:*

_____

_____

Discussion Questions

1. What kind of privacy does a child have a right to expect?

2. Is privacy always an advantage, or is there such a thing as too much privacy, especially for a child?

3. What are a parent's rights to privacy? Can children violate their parents' rights to privacy?

4. What is your attitude about privacy among friends your own age? If you can tell that a friend is troubled, should you respect his or her privacy or try to find out what is wrong?

Writing Exercise

Write a paragraph about the idea of privacy. Before you begin, look back at your brainstorming, think about the questions that followed your reading of Ginott's passage, and consider the questions below:

1. Do you remember times when you were growing up that a parent, teacher, or adult friend violated your privacy or trust? How did you react?

2. If you are a parent, coach, or teacher who works with young people, how do you treat their privacy?

3. Do you respect the privacy of friends your own age? Do you expect them to respect your privacy?

4. When is privacy most important to you? How do you get privacy when you need it?

5. Is "respect of privacy" ever used as an excuse for lack of concern?

Use your prewriting and these questions to help you decide on your specific subject, purpose, main idea (topic sentence), and audience (teenagers, parents, teachers, etc.). Then write a paragraph that includes two or three major supporting points that are coordinate and one or two details to support each of the major points.

After you have finished your paragraph, think about how you might expand it into an essay. In an informal outline, list your major supporting points. Then list under each major supporting point additional details and examples you can use to develop that point into a paragraph in your essay.

Now, using the topic sentence of your paragraph (or a revised version of it) as your thesis statement, write a short essay. Be sure that you have an introductory paragraph that includes your thesis. The body of your essay should consist of two or three paragraphs, one for each of your major supporting points. Remember that your essay must include *more* supporting material—more specific details, facts, examples, descriptions, and illustrations—than your paragraph. Be as specific and detailed as you can as you support each topic sentence. Your last paragraph should be a conclusion.

Rewriting Exercise

If possible, let your rough draft rest at least a day before you begin your revision. Then look carefully at the structure of your essay and answer the following questions about it.

1. What kind of introduction did you use? Does it capture reader interest, provide necessary background, and lead into your thesis? Would another type of introduction be more effective? How can you improve your introduction?

2. What is your thesis? Is it clearly stated and effectively limited and focused? Does each paragraph support your thesis by developing one of your major subpoints?

3. Reread each paragraph to be sure you have included enough specific support. What other details and examples can you add? Does each sentence in the paragraph support the topic sentence?

4. Does your essay have an effective conclusion? What type of conclusion did you use? Would another type be more effective? How can you improve your conclusion?

5. Does your essay achieve your purpose and communicate to your audience? If not, what revisions do you need to make?

Once you are satisfied with the content and structure of your essay, edit it by examining carefully your sentence structure, usage, punctuation, and word choices. Then make a final copy and proofread for errors. If possible, wait a few hours between your editing and final proofreading so that you will be more objective.

READING/WRITING ASSIGNMENT 7B

GETTING 'EM READY FOR DARRELL
Larry King

Pre-Reading/Writing Exercise

Most of you have participated in some type of sport at some time in your life or know someone who has. Try to remember what it was like as a teenager or child to be involved in an athletic contest. How did you feel when you won? When you lost? When you played well? When you played badly? Do you now see these as good experiences? Or were they harmful or hurtful to you in some way? Write in your journal about one of these experiences, including as many details as you can. Try to remember not only what happened but how you felt about the experience.

Now answer the following questions about the experience you wrote about in your journal:

1. *What* was the event or experience?

    _____

    _____

    _____

    _____

2. *When* did it occur?

    _____

    _____

3. *Where* did it occur?

    _____

    _____

4. *How* did you feel about the experience?

    _____

    _____

    _____

    _____

5. *Who* else was involved?

    _____

    _____

6. *Why* did you feel this way?

    _____

You can create ideas for writing assignments by asking yourself *what, who, when, where, how,* or *why* about a particular subject or event. These questions, often called "reporter's questions," are an effective prewriting strategy.

Reading Exercise

Now read the narrative essay "Getting 'em Ready for Darrell" about a young boy's experience with junior high football. This story is by Larry King, a Texas writer, and takes place in Midland, a town in West Texas. The Texas context is important to a reader's understanding of the story, since there are many references to people and places associated with Texas. For example, the young boy attends San Jacinto Junior High. San Jacinto is the name of a famous battle in the war Texas fought with Mexico. And, when the fathers are talking, they mention the bitter football rivalry between the University of Oklahoma and the University of Texas. The annual game between these two schools is traditionally hard fought and serious. It involves a weekend of activities and attracts enormous crowds of fans from both states. The man Darrell, who is referred to in the title and again in the conversation among the fathers, is Darrell Royal, head football coach at the University of Texas for many years. Knowing these facts will help you understand and appreciate the story. Notice that the story is told from the father's point of view. Does the essay enable you to understand both the boy's and the father's feelings?

1   The day was miserably cold and wet for mid-October, the wind cutting down from the north with a keen blade. A ghostly mist blew in about midnight. By daylight the Texas desert air knew a coastal chill, clammy and bone-numbing. Soon Midland's flat paved streets flowed like shallow rivers.

2   Seventh and eighth graders of the city's three junior high schools on awakening may have groaned into the weather's wet face, but they pulled on their football jerseys in compliance with a tradition requiring them to set themselves apart as gladiators each Thursday, which is Game Day. They would wear the jerseys in their classrooms.

3   Three hundred strong, ranging in age from 12 to 14 years, they comprised the dozen junior high football teams—four to a school, two to a grade—that play blood-and-thunder eight-game schedules with provisions for the more successful to play through to a city championship. Each team practices from two to two and one-half hours per day, except on game days; no homework is assigned to football players the night before a game.

4   A blond 12-year-old named Bradley, who weighed all of 107 pounds and limped on a swollen left knee, was having a more modest thought than of the city championship. "Maybe we can score on a wet field," he said. "We haven't done so good on a dry one." His team, the San Jacinto

Seventh Grade Blues, had not known the dignity or solace of a touchdown in four previous outings. Their frustrated coach, a chunky, red-faced young man only recently out of college, had promised to run two laps around the football field for each touchdown his Blues scored against the unbeaten Trinity Orange. This prospect made Bradley grin. "You gonna play on that bad knee?" Bradley's visiting father asked. "I played on it last week," he shrugged.

5   There were perhaps a dozen shivering spectators behind each bench—mostly parents—when the Blues kicked off to Trinity at 3:30 P.M. Bradley, who had started all four previous games, was chagrined to find himself benched. "Maybe the coach is protecting your knee," his father suggested.

6   But Bradley believed he had been benched because he had missed two practice sessions that week, due to the death of his grandfather.

7   Trinity marched through the Blues for four consecutive first downs, most of the damage done by a ponderous fullback who, though slow, had enough strength and size to run over the smaller defensive kids. Even so, his performance did not satisfy his coach. "Come on, Don," he shouted from the Orange sideline. "Duck that shoulder and go! You're just falling forward out there!"

8   Meanwhile, the Blues' coach exhorted his collapsing defense: "Get mean out there! Come on, pop 'em! Bobby Joe, dammit, I'm gonna come out there and kick you if you let that ole fat boy run over you again!" Bobby Joe, who may have weighed all of 100 pounds, sneaked a timid glance at the sideline. "You look like a girl, Bobby Joe," a man in boots and a western hat shouted through his cupped hands. "I'm his father," he said to a glaring visitor, as if that mitigated the circumstance.

9   Trinity fumbled five yards away from a certain touchdown, losing the ball. The Blues jumped and yelled in celebration, while over on the Trinity side the Orange coach tore his rain-wet hair and shouted toward the sullen heavens. "We're gonna score." "Way to *talk*, Donny!" an assistant coach said, slapping the youngster's rump as he ran on the field.

10   But scoreless San Jacinto could not move the ball. Backs, attempting double and multiple handoffs, ran into each other and fell. Orange linemen poured through to overwhelm the quarterback before he could pass. "We gonna have us some blocking practice at half time if you guys don't knock somebody down," the Blue coach screamed. As if in defiance, the Blue line next permitted several Orange linemen to roar through and block a punt near their own goal line. "Blocking practice at the half!" the Blue coach screamed, his face contorted. "I mean it, now. You dadgummed guys didn't touch a man!" The Orange in four plays plunged for a touchdown, then ran in the two-point conversion for an 8 to 0 lead.

11   "I told you guys to get in a goal-line defense, Mike!" the Blue coach raved. "Dammit, *always* get in a goal-line defense inside the ten."

12   "I thought we was *in* a goal-line defense," Mike alibied, his teeth chattering in the cold. He turned to a teammate: "Gene, wasn't we in a goal-line defense?" Gene was bent over, his head between his legs, arms hugging his ribs. "Somebody kicked me in the belly," he answered. The Blue coach missed this drama. He was up at the 50-yard line, shooing off a concerned mother attempting to wrap the substitutes in blankets she had

brought from a station wagon. "They won't be cold if they'll hit somebody," the coach shouted.

13   "Same ole thing," Bradley muttered from the bench as his team prepared to receive the kickoff. He had been inserted into the game long enough to know the indignity of having the touchdown scored over his left tackle position. "I had 'em," he said, "but then I slipped in the mud." Nobody said anything, for Bradley had clearly been driven out of the play like a dump truck.

14   Midway in the second quarter Bradley redeemed himself, fighting off two blockers to dump a ball carrier who had gotten outside the defensive end. He ended up at the bottom of a considerable pile and rose dragging his right foot, hopping back into position while grimacing at the sidelines as if in hope of relief. The coach did not see him, however, for he was busy chastising the offending end: "Paul, dammit, don't give him the outside! Protect your territory!" "Bobby Joe," his father yelled, "*crack* somebody out there. You just standin' around." Bradley played the remainder of the half, limping more on the injured ankle than on the swollen knee. Rain was coming down in windblown and near-freezing torrents when the young teams ran to their respective buses for half-time inspirations.

15   Four or five fathers shivered near the 50-yard line, asses turned to the wind, smoking and talking of the 41 to 9 crusher applied to Oklahoma by the University of Texas. "They sure looked good," one of them said. "I think ole Darrell Royal's got his best team."

16   A mother in red slacks, her coat collar turned up and her nose red, approached the men. "I think it's just terrible to play those little fellers in weather like this," she said. The men chuckled indulgently. "Well," one of them said, "we got to git 'em ready for Darrell." The men laughed.

17   A balding, portly man in a mackinaw puffed up. "How's Jerry doing?" he inquired. "Well," one of the men hedged, "none of our boys lookin' *too* good. Especially on offense." "I went to see my other boy play the first half," the newcomer said. "His bunch was ahead 19 to 0. They looked great. 'Course, they're eighth graders."

18   When the teams returned to the field the newcomer grabbed his son, a thick-legged little back. "Jerry," he said, "son, you got to get tough. Leland's lookin' tough. His team's ahead 19 to 0."

19   "We got to *hurt* some people," a stubby little towhead with the complexion of a small girl said. "We got to *kill* us some people." The men laughed.

20   Bradley, soaking wet like all his teammates, was dispirited. What had the coach said to the Blues at half time? "He said we're better than they are and that we can beat 'em." The disapproving mother had returned with her blankets. Having wrapped up the bench warmers, she approached Bradley, who shrugged warmth off with a grunt: "I'm starting." An assistant coach, moving in to confiscate the coddling blankets, thought better of it when the mother stood her ground. "Damnfool *men*," she muttered, glaring.

21   The Blues drove 60 yards in the third period, their best-sustained drive of the season, inspiring their coach to whoop and holler like a delegate to the Democratic National Convention. "Way to *go*, Jerry!" the portly father shouted on play after play as he ran up and down. "Get outta them blankets!" the assistant coach yelled at the bench warmers as soon as the corrupt-

ing mother had fled to her station wagon. "If you don't think about being cold you won't *be* cold." Ten yards short of a touchdown three Blue backs collided behind the line in attempting a tricky double reverse, fumbling the ball and losing it in the process. The coach threw his red baseball cap in the mud and stomped it some.

22   "Coach," the visiting father said, "don't you think your offense is pretty complicated for a bunch of kids? I mean, why not have simple plays they can execute?"

23   The harassed coach cast a suspicious glance at the visitor. "We teach 'em the same basic system they'll need in high school," he snapped, turning away.

24   Trinity's Orange picked up a couple of first downs and then fumbled the ball back. The Blues, trembling in a new opportunity, came to the line of scrimmage a man short of the required eleven. The coach grabbed Bradley and thrust him into the game at right guard. Four plays later, failing to pick up a first down, the Blue offense trooped off the field. Water ran down their young faces. Two little girls in short cheerleaders' skirts gave them soggy rah-rahs from beneath a tent of blankets, their voices thin and self-conscious.

25   "Coach," Bradley said, "I don't know the plays for guard."

26   "You *don't?* Well, why not? Didn't you study the playbook?"

27   "Yeah, but you never *played* me at guard before. I'm a tackle."

28   "Oh," the coach said. "Well . . . Bobby *Joe,* dern you, *hit* somebody!"

29   "Way to *go,* Jerry!" the portly father shouted, breathing heavily as he kept pace with the action, jogging up and down the sideline. He turned to a bystander, puffing and beaming: "Jerry's not the ballplayer Leland is. 'Course, Leland's an eighth grader."

30   The visiting father touched the wet arm of his downcast son. "Bradley," he said, "you're standing up on defense before you charge. That gives the blocking linemen a better angle on you. Go in low. If your first charge is forward instead of up, you'll have so much power the laws of physics will guarantee your penetration."

31   "*Wow!*" one of the teenybopper cheerleaders said. "The laws of physics! Outta sight!" Her legs were blue in the cold.

32   "Way to *go,* Jerry!"

33   On his next defensive opportunity, Bradley charged in low and powerfully, his penetration carrying him so deep into the Orange backfield that he overran the ball carrier—who immediately shot through the vacated territory for a 20-yard gain. Bradley stood back at the 50-yard-line, hands on hips, shaking his head in disgust and staring coldly at the visiting father, who suddenly studied his shoes.

34   San Jacinto's scoreless Blues got off a final fourth-quarter drive, aided by two unnecessary roughness penalties against the Orange. "Coach," one of the bench warmers sang out, "they're playing dirty."

35   "Let 'em play dirty," Jerry's father responded. "We'll take that 15 yards every *time,* baby."

36   But balls were dropped and young feet slid in the mud, and in the end the Blue drive ended ignominiously. San Jacinto's Blues were fighting off another Orange advance when the game ended. They lost again, 0 to 8; their coach was safe from running laps.

37   "We gonna work in the blocking pits next week," he promised his young charges as they ran through the rain to their bus.

38   Bradley, showered and dressed in street clothes, limped slowly to his visiting father's car. His right shoe was unlaced because of the swollen ankle; by nightfall it would show dark blue around the shinbone with bright red welts running along the heel base.

39   "I'm sorry I didn't do better," Bradley said. "I got confused. You yelled one thing at me and the coach yelled another. *You* said charge hard and *he* said just stay there and plug up the hole."

40   "Well," the visiting father said lamely, "I'm sorry I yelled anything at you." There had been too much yelling. "Can't you get heat treatment for that ankle? Or at least supporting tape?"

41   "Naw," Bradley said. "They don't give us those things until high school."

42   They drove along in the rain, the windows steaming over. They passed Robert E. Lee High School, where a squad of perhaps 60 young men drilled in the rain, padless, tuning up for their Friday-night game against Abilene. Thousands would drive the 200 miles east, some of them drunk or drinking. Probably at least one would hit another car or a telephone pole.

43   "I may not play in high school," Bradley blurted. "I may not even play next year. The eighth-grade coach came scouting around last week, and he asked me some questions and I told him I might not even *play* next year." His blond hair was wet; his creamy young face was red. He looked angry and haggard and somehow old.

44   "Way to *go*, Bradley," his visiting father said.

Larry King, *Getting 'em Ready for Darrell*

1. Is King's thesis stated or implied? _____

What is his thesis? _____

_____

_____

Do you agree or disagree with the thesis? Why or why not?

_____

_____

_____

2. How does the author portray the mothers, coaches, and other fathers in the story?

_____

_____

_____

_____

_____

_____

Do you find these character portrayals accurate and fair? Why or why not?

_____

_____

3. Why is the father consistently referred to as the "visiting father"?

_____

_____

What implications does this have for the story?

_____

_____

_____

_____

4. When Bradley's father asks him about heat treatment and supporting tape for his ankle, Bradley answers, "They don't give us those things until high school." How is Bradley's statement ironical—different from what you would expect or from what would seem appropriate?

_____

_____

_____

_____

5. What decision does Bradley make after the game?

_____

_____

Has Bradley's experience changed him? _____

How and why? _____

_____

6. When the "portly father" tells his son "Way to *go*, Jerry," he is showing his obsessive concern with his son's success in football. Obviously referring to this line, the "visiting father" reacts to his son Bradley's decision not to play football the following year by saying, "Way to *go*, Bradley." What does this statement show about the effect of the game on the father?

_____

_____

_____

7. In previous lessons, you have seen how *context*, or surrounding words, can give you clues to a word's meaning. As illustrated below, context clues can be of several different types: contrast, explanation through synonyms, explanation through restatement, example, or inference.

a. **Contrast.** Bradley has "a more *modest* thought than of the city championship." The words *more* and *than* indicate a contrast between the relatively important and ambitious thought of the championship and Bradley's "modest" thought. Therefore, *modest* means

_____

_____

b. **Explanation through synonyms.** The synonyms *strength* and *size* provide clues that *ponderous* means

_____

_____

c. **Explanation through restatement.** The definition of *penetration* is restated in the phrase "carrying him so deep into the Orange backfield." *Penetration* means

_____

_____

d. **Example.** The coach's scolding instructions to his team— "Paul, dammit, don't give him the outside! Protect your territory!"—are examples of *chastising*, which means

_____

_____

e. **Inference (suggestion).** The "portly father's" actions—"breathing heavily" and "puffing" as he jogs—implies that he is fat and heavy. Therefore, *portly* means

_____

(**Note:** The context clues "imply" the word's meaning; you "infer" the meaning.)

8. This reading passage contains other words that may be unfamiliar to you. Using context clues, write a brief definition for each of the following words. Then discuss and compare your definitions with those of your classmates.

a. solace _____

_____

b. chagrined _____

_____

c. mitigated _____

_____

d. alibied _____

_____

e. grimacing _____

_____

f. indulgently _____

_____

g. confiscate _____

_____

h. harassed _____

_____

i. ignominiously _____

_____

j. haggard _____

_____

Look back at the reading passage for other unfamiliar words. Underline these words and try to determine their meaning from the context in which they appear.

Discussion Questions

1. What is more important to most children who play competitive sports—winning or playing the game? What is more important to most parents and coaches?

2. What competitive sports do children and young people play in your home town? Are some sports too dangerous for children to play? What sports should they be allowed to play?

Writing Exercise

Write an essay about sports or athletics. You might write about an experience you have had playing, coaching, or watching a team sport such as football or baseball or an individual sport such as swimming or tennis. You might write about a sports event that you have read about or watched on television. Or you might write about gymnastics, aerobics, or exercising.

Before you begin to write, think about your audience and purpose. For whom are you writing? Athletes, young children, coaches, parents? What is your purpose? Do you want to convince your audience that sports are beneficial, harmful, fun, exciting, boring, or commercialized?

After you have made these decisions, write a paragraph in which you include your main points or make an informal outline in which you list your major supporting points. Then write your essay. Be sure that your introduction includes a statement of your thesis and that each paragraph has a topic sentence that expresses one of your major points.

Rewriting Exercise

If possible, let your rough draft rest at least a day before you begin your revision. Then look carefully at the structure and development of your essay and answer the following questions.

1. What type of introduction did you use? Does it capture reader interest, provide necessary background, and lead into your thesis? Would another type of introduction be more effective? How can you improve your introduction?

2. What is your thesis? Is it clearly stated and effectively limited and focused? How can you improve it? Does each paragraph support your thesis by developing one of your major subpoints?

3. Reread each paragraph carefully to see that each sentence within the paragraph supports the topic sentence. Notice also your use of specific details and examples. Do you include enough details to support your thesis and each topic sentence? One of the reasons Larry King's essay is effective is that he includes a great many factual and sensory details. Have you included both factual and sensory details in your essay?

4. Does your essay have an effective conclusion? What type of conclusion did you use? Would another type be more effective? How can you improve your conclusion?

5. Does your essay achieve your purpose and communicate to your audience? If not, what revisions do you need to make?

Once you are satisfied with the content and structure of your essay, edit it by examining carefully your sentence structure, usage, punctuation, and word choices. Then make a final copy and proofread for errors, examining each word and punctuation mark carefully.

Chapter 8

SUMMARIZING and REACTING TO IDEAS

The reading process varies significantly, depending on the purpose of the reader and what is being read. Browsing through the funny pages of the Sunday newspaper is not the same as reading a novel, and scanning the classified ads for a used car is not the same as reading a chapter of a textbook. Sometimes you read strictly for pleasure; other times you read for information. Reading includes browsing, skimming, studying, scanning, and memorizing. Efficient readers are aware of these different types of reading and adjust their rate and manner of reading to accommodate their purposes. In this chapter, you will learn more about how to read when your primary purpose is studying.

OUTLINING TO STUDY

Outlining can be an important aid to reading when your purpose is to learn the material being read. If you outline what you read, you force yourself to focus on your reading task and to analyze the content and structure of what you are reading. Because it involves writing, outlining also reinforces learning and retention. Furthermore, an outline provides you with a written record of the most important ideas from your reading—a record that can be invaluable when the time comes for a written assignment or a test.

Study outlines are informal outlines that help you understand and remember what you read. Study outlines, like planning outlines, do not have to conform to any certain format or any specific restrictions. They can be as informal and individual as you want to make them. But a useful study outline is one that is still comprehensible to you weeks or even months after you have written it, so your outline needs to be clear and complete. A useful study outline is also comprehensive and accurate; it includes all of the important ideas and does not distort their meaning. If you have not previously used study outlines, you may find the following general guidelines helpful.

1. Read the *entire* passage carefully.
2. Determine the author's main idea and state it in your own words.
3. Decide on the major subdivisions (be sure that all of the major supporting points are of equal importance).
4. Under each major division, list the more specific supporting points (do *not* include examples or minor details).

Guided Practice

Use the guidelines above to outline the following paragraph:

1. Read the *entire* passage carefully.

Comedy is usually defined as the opposite of tragedy. One reason definitions of comedy are rarely given is that there are two distinct types of comedy, and these two types are very different. The first type, low comedy, is loud, uninhibited, occasionally physical, and often vulgar. For example, slapstick comedy is considered low comedy. The second type, high comedy, is sophisticated, subtle, and usually romantic. The situation comedies so popular with television viewers are an example of high comedy. Because these two types of comedy are so different, it is difficult to define comedy.

2. Determine the author's main idea and state it *in your own words.*

_____

3. Decide on the major subdivisions (be sure that these major points are of equal importance).

First major point: _____

_____

Second major point: _____

_____

4. Under each major division, list the more specific supporting points (do *not* include minor details or, as a rule, examples).
Specific supporting points under first major point:

_____

_____

Specific supporting points under second major point:

_____

_____

Your outline probably does not include information from either the first or the last sentence of the paragraph. Since the first sentence is not the topic sentence but merely an introduction to the main idea (which is stated in the second sentence), it has no information that needs to be included. The last sentence serves as a conclusion and restates the main idea, so it too contains no new information. You may have also omitted the examples of the two types of comedy. However, if these examples helped you under-stand the difference between the two types, you may have included them as minor supporting points.

Now you are ready to put your outline together. Use any format with which you are comfortable, but be sure that you (1) indicate the order in which the points on your outline occur and (2) show the appropriate rela-tionships among major and minor supporting points.

When you have completed your outline, you may want to compare it with those of your classmates. Notice that the same basic outline can assume many different forms.

EXERCISE 8.1

Using the guidelines given above, outline the following paragraph. Begin by underlining the thesis statement and major supporting ideas.

Comedy, which was one of the earliest forms of drama in the United States, has also been one of the most enduring. The minstrel show is generally accepted as the first form of comedy in this country. On plantations black slaves sang and danced first for their own entertainment and later for the amusement of their masters. In the eighteenth century the minstrel shows became staged productions in which both white and black entertainers per-formed. During the last half of the nineteenth century the minstrel show was the most popular form of American entertainment. The popularity of the minstrel shows led to the evolution of the musical revue, which dominated the American stage during the first part of the twentieth century. Adding pretty girls, elaborate costumes, and contemporary music and dancing to the old minstrel routines, musical revues became a popular form of comic enter-tainment. In time, the musical revue evolved into the musical comedy, which added a story line to the songs and dances. Today, musical comedies con-tinue to be popular with American audiences.

SUMMARIZING

Many of the skills you use in outlining are also used in writing a summary—a concise restatement of a reading selection. In order to summarize, you must have a good understanding of what you have read and be able to identify clearly the main idea and the major supporting points. Then you must restate these ideas in your own words. Thus, summarizing requires both reading and writing skills.

Guidelines to Follow in Summarizing

READING THE SELECTION

Summarizing requires two important reading skills: (1) finding the main idea and (2) determining major supporting points. Neither of these skills is new to you. You simply need to see how they apply to summarizing. Below are some suggestions for reading a selection you plan to summarize.

1. *Read through the entire selection before you start to summarize.* If you try to summarize as you read, you will very likely fail to recognize the major ideas, and your summary will be too long and wordy.

2. *Identify the author's main idea.* If the main idea is expressed in a topic sentence, you might want to underline this sentence.

3. *Determine the major supporting details and their relationship to the main idea.* Again, underlining may be helpful.

WRITING THE SUMMARY

After you have read through the selection carefully and have gone back over it to determine the main idea and major supporting details, you are ready to begin writing your summary. The length of a summary depends on the length of the original selection. For example, a summary of a thirty-page textbook chapter might be several pages long. In summarizing a paragraph, however, you would probably write only one sentence, two or three at the most. A good rule of thumb is that your summary should be approximately one-third the length of the original.

Writing a summary requires all of the writing skills you have studied so far. In addition, here are several specific suggestions that may prove helpful.

1. *If you know the title and author of the selection you are summariz-ing, include them in your summary.* You may combine this information and the main idea statement in one sentence.

2. *Include only the author's main ideas and the important supporting details.* Do not insert your own ideas or irrelevant details.

3. *Write in your own words.* Use the author's ideas but not the author's words. If you include a direct quote, enclose it in quotation marks.

4. *Be brief and to the point.* The whole idea of summarizing is to condense the main ideas of the original into as few words as possible.

Guided Practice

To summarize a paragraph, you first need to read through the entire paragraph and then go back and identify the main idea and major supporting points. In the following paragraph, we have underlined the topic sentence (main idea) and the key words and phrases (major supporting points):

[main idea]

As emerging masculinities gain strength, men will no longer feel compelled to keep masculine and feminine roles separate. We can allow them to be shared. The lines of responsibility, such as his for making money and hers for taking care of the children, can soften. Most jobs are more rewarding if they are freely chosen and do not consume one's whole life. Men will be more balanced breadwinners if that responsibility is shared. Women will be more balanced caretakers if that responsibility, too, is shared. And as they are shared, they will be transformed. Some couples may wish to reverse roles completely; others may retain clearly divided roles. But if the freedom to choose is increased, the outcome, whatever its form, will be liberating for both men and women.

Mark Gerzon, *A Choice of Heroes*

One possible summary of this paragraph follows:

In *A Choice of Heroes,* Mark Gerzon predicts that when men have a new view of masculinity, there will be less separation and more sharing of male and female roles. As responsibilities for earning a living and caring for the family are re-examined, both men and women will have more freedom.

EXERCISE 8.2

Read the following paragraphs and write a summary of each:

PARAGRAPH A

As soon as the War of 1812 ended, most Americans turned their attention to domestic concerns. One important result was that Tecumseh's Indian confederacy had been crushed, opening the area east of the Mississippi to settlement. Even more importantly, American manufacturing had been forced to develop, so the country was now more self-sufficient. The most widely felt effect of the war, however, was probably the rebirth of pride in the United States.

Rebecca Brooks Gruver, *An American History*

Summary: _____

_____

_____

_____

_____

PARAGRAPH B

There are roughly three New Yorks. There is, first, the New York of the man or woman who was born here, who takes the city for granted and accepts its size and its turbulence as natural and inevitable. Second, there is the New York of the commuter—the city that is devoured by locusts each day and spat out each night. Third, there is the New York of the person who was born somewhere else and came to New York in quest of something. Of these three trembling cities the greatest is the last—the city of final destination, the city that is a goal. It is the third city that accounts for New York's high-strung disposition, its poetical deportment, its dedication to the arts, and its incomparable achievements. Commuters give the city its tidal restlessness, natives give it solidity and continuity, but the settlers give it passion. And whether it is a farmer arriving from Italy to set up a small grocery store in a slum, or a young girl arriving from a small town in Mississippi to escape the indignity of being observed by her neighbors, or a boy arriving from the Corn Belt with a manuscript in his suitcase and a pain in his heart, it makes no difference: each embraces New York with the fresh eyes of an adventurer, each generates heat and light to dwarf the Consolidated Edison Company.

E. B. White, *Essays of E. B. White*

Summary: _____

_____

_____

_____

_____

PARAGRAPH C

I believe that it is an increasingly common pattern in our culture for each one of us to believe, "Every other person must feel and think and believe the same as I do." We find it very hard to permit our children or our parents or our spouses to feel differently than we do about particular issues or problems. We cannot permit our clients or our students to differ from us or to utilize their experience in their own individual ways. On a national scale, we cannot permit another nation to think or feel differently than we do. Yet it has come to seem to me that this separateness of individuals, the right of each individual to utilize his experience in his own way and to discover his own meaning in it—this is one of the most priceless potentialities of life. Each person is an island unto himself, in a very real sense; and he can only build bridges to other islands if he is first of all willing to be himself and permitted to be himself.

Adapted from Carl Rogers, *On Becoming a Person*

Summary: _____

_____

_____

_____

_____

PARAGRAPH D

In the mid-nineteenth century, middle-class culture had developed a "cult of true womanhood" that defined respectable women as incapable of expressing sexual pleasure. Women, therefore, were supposed to be more spiritual than men. But contradicting this idea of female spirituality was the belief that women were controlled by their bodies and not by their minds. This concept justified the exclusion of women from politics because, it was claimed, they could not think as rationally as men could. Men, therefore, were put in the impossible situation of viewing their mothers and their wives as sexless but, at the same time, as being completely defined by sex. In the eyes of a man, a woman could quickly change, then, from an individual of angelic spirituality into a creature of frightening bodily appetites.

David W. Noble, *Twentieth Century Limited*

Summary: _____

_____

_____

_____

Summarizing Essays and Chapters

Writing a summary of a longer composition, such as an essay or a textbook chapter, is similar to writing a summary of a paragraph. Whether you are summarizing a paragraph or a longer passage, you must read through the entire selection and identify both the author's main idea and major supporting details. In summarizing a paragraph, you look for a stated or implied *topic sentence;* in summarizing an essay or chapter, you look for a stated or implied *thesis statement.* In writing a summary of a paragraph, you determine the major supporting details; in writing a summary of an essay, you determine the main ideas of each paragraph.

Guided Practice

Below is a passage from a college chemistry book. The thesis, or main idea, of the passage is not stated but is implied. We have identified the thesis and underlined the main supporting points in the passage. Notice also the marginal notes (Learning goals) provided by the textbook authors.

> **Thesis:** The origins of modern chemistry can be traced back to ancient civilizations.

THE ORIGINS OF CHEMISTRY

Learning goal 1
Beginnings of scientific thought

The earliest attempts to explain natural phenomena led to fanciful inventions—to myths and fantasies—but not to understanding. Around 600 B.C., a group of Greek philosophers became dissatisfied with these myths, which explained little. Stimulated by social and cultural change as well as curiosity, they began to ask questions about the world around them. They answered these questions by constructing lists of logical possibilities. Thus Greek philosophy was an attempt to discover the basic truths of nature by thinking things through, rather than by running laboratory experiments. The Greek philosophers did this so thoroughly and so brilliantly that the years between 600 and 400 B.C. are called the "golden age of philosophy."

Some of the Greek philosophers (scientists, really) believed they could find a single substance that everything else was made of. A philosopher named Thales believed that this substance was water, but another named Anaximenes thought it was air. A third, Empedocles, said that the world was composed of four elements: earth, air, fire, and water.

During this period, the Greek philosophers laid the foundation for one of our main ideas about the universe. Leucippus (about 440 B.C.) and Democritus (about 420 B.C.) were trying to determine whether there was such a thing as a smallest particle of matter. In doing so, they established the idea of the atom, a particle so tiny that it could not be seen. At that time there was no way to test whether atoms really existed, and more than 2,000 years passed before scientists proved that they do exist.

Learning goal 2
Influence of Greek philosophy on chemistry

While the Greeks were studying philosophy and mathematics, the Egyptians were practicing the art of chemistry. They were mining and purifying the metals gold, silver, and copper. They were making embalming fluids and dyes. They called this art *khemia,* and it flourished until the seventh century A.D., when it was taken over by the Arabs. The Egyptian word *khemia* became the Arabic word *alkhemia* and then the English word *alchemy.* Today our version of the word is used to mean everything that happened in chemistry between A.D. 300 and A.D. 1600.

Learning goal 3
Egyptians' role in the development of chemistry

A major goal of the alchemists was to transmute (convert) "base metals" into gold. That is, they wanted to transform less desirable elements such as lead and iron into the element gold. The ancient Arabic emperors employed many alchemists for this purpose, which, of course, was never accomplished.

Learning goal 4
Alchemists' major goals

The alchemists also tried to find the "philosopher's stone" (a supposed cure for all diseases) and the "elixir of life" (which would prolong life indefinitely). Unfortunately they failed in both attempts, but they did have some lucky accidents. In the course of their work, they discovered acetic acid, nitric acid, and ethyl alcohol, as well as many other substances used by chemists today.

Learning goal 5
Boyle's influence on the development of modern chemistry

The modern age of chemistry dawned in 1661 with the publication of the book *The Sceptical Chymist,* written by Robert Boyle, an English chemist, physicist, and theologian. Boyle was "skeptical" because he was not willing to take the word of the ancient Greeks and alchemists as truth, especially about the elements that make up the world. Instead Boyle believed that scientists must start from basic principles, and he realized that every theory had to be proved by experiment. His new and innovative scientific approach was to change the whole course of chemistry.

Alan Sherman, Sharon Sherman, and Leonard Russikoff, Basic Concepts of Chemistry, 3rd ed.

EXERCISE 8.3

In the space below, write a one-paragraph summary of the passage you have just read. The first sentence of your summary (the topic sentence) should include the author's name, the title of the reading selection, and the main idea. Write your summary in your own words. If you include specific phrases from the passage, be sure to enclose them in quotation marks. Your summary has been started for you:

"The Origins of Chemistry" by Alan Sherman, Sharon Sherman, and Leonard Russikoff states that

_____

_____

_____

_____

_____

_____

_____

_____

_____

_____

_____

_____

_____

_____

_____

DRAWING CONCLUSIONS

When writers do not state their main idea in a thesis or topic sentence, you must use the information that is provided in the paragraph to form your own conclusion. Using the information that is available to you plus your own logic, you must *infer* the main idea—that is, you must draw a conclusion.

Guided Practice

In the following paragraph, the main idea is not stated in a topic sentence. However, the writer has given you the information you need to draw a conclusion about the paragraph's main idea.

Several model communities were organized in America in the 1800s. In the 1820s Robert Owen founded New Harmony, a community in which all property was cooperatively owned and which did not allow religious worship or marriage; however, internal problems caused the community to be abandoned after only a few years. Brook Farm was organized in 1841 by several New England thinkers and writers, but the community did not succeed economically. In the 1840s, forty model communities were set up by Charles Fourier, but all of them failed, partly because they were made up of intellectuals from the city who soon became dissatisfied with rural farm life. The Oneida community, established by John Humphrey Noyes, was more successful; nevertheless, popular resentment of its practice of communal marriages caused its breakup. The only model utopian or religious community to experience any lengthy success was the Shaker community founded by Mother Ann Lee.

Using the facts and details that are given in this paragraph, what conclusion can you logically draw?

_____

_____

_____

One conclusion you might have drawn from the paragraph is that "most nineteenth-century model communities were unsuccessful." Such a conclusion is adequately supported by the information given in the paragraph. You should be careful not to make sweeping generalizations or projections that go beyond the evidence presented. For example, you could not have concluded from the information presented in the paragraph above that _all_ nineteenth-century model communities were unsuccessful. Such a conclusion ignores the clearly stated facts that the Shaker community was successful and that the Oneida community experienced limited success. Neither could you have concluded that _any_ model community established today will be unsuccessful. This conclusion makes a sweeping projection extending beyond the evidence presented, for the facts given in the paragraph refer only to model communities in nineteenth-century America. Whether you are reading or writing, you should always try to form conclusions that are adequately supported by the facts and details included in the paragraph.

EXERCISE 8.4

Following are several sets of facts. Write a logical conclusion for each set.

1. **a.** Jerry had known for two months that he had to write a research paper, but he waited until the night before it was due to write it.
   b. Although he had plenty of money, Jerry did not pay his phone bill until after the phone company threatened to take his phone out.
   c. He waited until he had nine cavities and a terrible toothache before he finally visited the dentist.

   Conclusion: _____

   _____

2. **a.** Bill works twelve hours every day.
   b. He works six days a week.
   c. He has not had a vacation in three years.
   d. He does more work than any other employee in his company.

Conclusion: _____

_____

3. a. The price of building materials has increased sharply in the last few years.
    b. Labor costs have almost doubled during the same period.
    c. Mortgage interest rates have also skyrocketed.

Conclusion: _____

_____

EXERCISE 8.5

Below are two paragraphs. Read each one, studying the information that is given to draw an appropriate conclusion.

Hands stained and brow dripping perspiration, the young man struggled to complete the task before him. He had been working for hours, and his body ached with exhaustion. His back hurt from hours of bending over his task; his head hurt from the intense concentration and mental effort he had expended; and his hand hurt from gripping the tool with which he was working. Furthermore, his mind had never felt so fatigued—so utterly depleted. Moaning to himself, he picked up his leaking pen and bent once more over his smudged paper. He must go on. The essay was due in the morning.

Conclusion: _____

_____

_____

Henry VIII became king of England in 1509. His first wife was Catherine of Aragon, who was unable to give him a male child. Dissatisfied with Catherine, Henry became interested in Anne Boleyn, for whom he challenged the Church and divorced Catherine. Anne, too, failed to bear him a male child, so she was charged with adultery and beheaded. Next, Henry married Jane Seymour, who gave him a male heir, Prince Edward, and then conveniently died. Later, Henry married Anne of Cleves on the strength of her portrait. Being disappointed in the real Anne, however, he bought her off and sent her away to a remote castle. He then married Catherine Howard, a pretty young thing who was unfaithful to him and who, not surprisingly, was beheaded for her infidelity. Finally, Henry married Catherine Parr, a young widow to whom he remained happily married until his death.

Conclusion: _____

_____

CRITICAL READING AND WRITING

Of the different types of reading, critical reading is the most demanding. Browsing through a magazine or reading a mystery novel makes very few demands on your intellect because you are reading primarily for pleasure. Reading for information requires more mental effort, for you must be sure in these instances that you understand what you are reading. Often too, when you read for information, you must try to remember what you read, so you are striving not only to comprehend but also to retain what you read. Critical reading takes you a step beyond literal comprehension. When you read critically, you are attempting not only to comprehend but also to *evaluate* the significance of the writer's assertions. The step from comprehension to evaluation is not an easy one. It requires first that you understand what you read on a literal level and then that you judge the validity of the ideas and information you have read. Ultimately, however, all educated people need to be able to read critically—to react intellectually as well as emotionally to what they read.

Every educated person also needs to be able to express his or her critical reaction in writing. Critical writing requires that you *understand* what you read, *evaluate* the information and ideas in what you read, and then *express* your evaluation clearly and coherently so that a reader can understand not only your ideas but also those of the author to whom you are responding. As you can see, critical reading and writing require that you use all of the skills you have been studying in this book. You must be able to identify or draw conclusions about main ideas, summarize those ideas for your reader, and then clearly express your own ideas.

Below are some guidelines for critical reading and writing:

1. Read the selection carefully, underlining the main ideas and key words and phrases.

2. Summarize the selection (be as brief but as clear as possible), stating the author's purpose, main idea, and major supporting points.

3. Evaluate the main ideas in the selection and decide whether you agree with the author.

4. Write a critical evaluation of the selection, making sure that you
   a. summarize the main idea of the author
   b. state whether you agree or disagree
   c. state your reasons for agreeing or disagreeing
   d. state the strengths and weaknesses of the selection
   e. evaluate how well the author achieves the purpose of the selection

5. Read your paragraph carefully to be sure it is clear, well organized, and adequately developed. Rewrite the paragraph, making changes and corrections where they are needed.

These guidelines should be useful to you in any assignment that requires critical reading and writing. However, the skill of reading and writing critically is one that is developed slowly as you gain experience with reading and writing. There is no formula or set of rules that can automatically give you these complex skills. Most of all, critical reading and writing require *thinking*—a skill that cannot be acquired instantly. The more you think seriously about what you read and write, the more accomplished you will become as a critical reader and writer.

Guided Practice

To illustrate how you might use these guidelines, we have included below a brief essay, which we have annotated (underlined the important ideas), summarized, and evaluated.

1 BALTIMORE MARYLAND. I was waiting for breakfast in a coffee shop the other morning and reading the paper. The paper had sixty-six pages. The waitress brought a paper place mat and a paper napkin and took my order, and I paged through the paper.

2 The headline said, "House Panel Studies a Bill Allowing Clear-Cutting in U.S. Forests."

3 I put the paper napkin in my lap, spread the paper out on the paper place mat, and read on: "The House Agriculture Committee," it said, "is looking over legislation that would once again open national forests to the clear-cutting of trees by private companies under government permits."

4 The waitress brought the coffee. I opened a paper sugar envelope and tore open a little paper cup of cream and went on reading the paper: "The Senate voted without dissent yesterday to allow clear-cutting," the paper said. "Critics have said clear-cutting in the national forests can lead to erosion and destruction of wildlife habitats. Forest Service and industry spokesmen said a flat ban on clear-cutting would bring paralysis to the

lumber industry." And to the paper industry, I thought. Clear-cutting a forest is one way to get a lot of paper, and we sure seem to need a lot of paper.

5   The waitress brought the toast. I looked for the butter. It came on a little paper tray with a covering of paper. I opened a paper package of marmalade and read on: "Senator Jennings Randolph, Democrat of West Virginia, urged his colleagues to take a more restrictive view and permit clear-cutting only under specific guidelines for certain types of forest. But neither he nor anyone else voted against the bill, which was sent to the House on a 90 to 0 vote."

6   The eggs came, with little paper packages of salt and pepper. I finished breakfast, put the paper under my arm, and left the table with its used and useless paper napkin, paper place mat, paper salt and pepper packages, paper butter and marmalade wrappings, paper sugar envelope, and paper cream holder, and I walked out into the morning wondering how our national forests can ever survive our breakfasts.

Charles Kuralt, "Down with the Forests," in *Dateline America*

The first paragraph of the following response summarizes Kuralt's essay, identifying his thesis and his two major points. The second paragraph gives the reader's reasons for agreeing with Kuralt's stand but points out an omission or weakness in the essay.

SUMMARY/EVALUATION

Main idea
In his essay "Down with the Forests," Charles Kuralt points out that *our widespread use of paper products is a serious threat to our national forests.* He argues that Americans use huge, and probably unnecessary, quantities of paper products; he also argues that this dependence on paper is one reason the government is reluctant to pass laws that prohibit the destruction of entire forests. Kuralt not only implicitly argues against legislation that allows "clear-cutting" in U.S. forests but also indirectly blames American consumers for the thoughtless overuse of paper.

Agreement
I agree with Kuralt's basic argument that our forests are in danger and with his implied argument that Americans use too many paper products. By describing in detail how much paper we use in a typical breakfast served in a

Reasons for agreement	restaurant, Kuralt dramatically illustrates how we waste paper. Because my own experience confirms that of Kuralt, I too realize that we use a lot of paper products—probably more than we need. Moreover, since paper is made from forests, it is obvious that our extravagant use of paper is directly related to the destruction of forests and perhaps specifically to the loss of our
Overall strength/weakness	national forests. However, although Kuralt's essay does identify a potentially serious problem, it does not go beyond identification to suggest possible solutions.

EXERCISE 8.6

Using the guidelines provided on pages 204–205, read the following selection and then write a paragraph in which you evaluate the author's ideas. Be sure that your paragraph includes a summary of the author's main ideas, a statement of whether or not you agree, and the reasons for your opinion.

I think it likely that the passion for the new in the way of teaching-hardware not only does not contribute to higher education achievement but may well serve as a temporary means to evade the real and hard tasks of teaching— which really require almost no hardware at all, besides textbooks, blackboard, and chalk. Admittedly, when one comes to high-school science, something more is called for. And yet our tendency is to always find cover behind new hardware. It's *fun* to get new audio-visual equipment, new rooms equipped with them in which all kinds of things can be done by flicking a switch or twisting a dial, or, as is now the case, to decide what kind of personal computers and software are necessary for a good educational program. Once again, foreign experience can be enlightening. When Japanese education was already well ahead of American, most Japanese schools were in prewar wooden buildings. (They are now as up-to-date as ours, but neither their age nor up-to-dateness has much to do with their good record of achievement.) Resisting the appeal of new hardware not only saves money, and provides less in the way of saleable goods to burglarize, but it also prevents distraction from the principal tasks of reading, writing, and calculating. When it turns out that computers and new software are shown to do a better job at these key tasks—I am skeptical as to whether this will ever be the case—there will be time enough to splurge on new equipment. The teacher, alone, up front, explaining, encouraging, guiding, is the heart of the matter—the rest is fun, and very helpful to corporate income, and gives an inflated headquarters staff something new to do. But students will have time enough to learn about computers when they get to college, and getting there will depend almost not at all on what they can do with computers, but how well they understand words and sentences, and how well they do at simple mathematics.

Nathan Glazer, "Some Very Modest Proposals for the Improvement of American Education"

READING/WRITING ASSIGNMENT 8A

THE GREAT CRASH AND THE GREAT DEPRESSION
Mary Beth Norton et al.

Pre-Reading/Writing Exercise

In your first reading/writing assignment you learned that you can prepare for reading by *surveying* the selection and by *questioning* yourself before you read. Next, you learned that *responding* while reading increases your interest, comprehension, and retention. Finally, you learned that your reading task is not successfully completed without *reciting* and *reviewing* what you have read.

"The Great Crash and the Great Depression" is a passage from a college history textbook. To prepare to read this passage, first survey, or skim through it, reading the title, introductory paragraph, main headings, the first sentence of each paragraph, and the concluding paragraph. As you survey, think about how you can turn the title and main headings into questions as you read. As you form your questions, keep in mind the reporter's questions of *when, where, who, what, why,* and *how*. For example, for the first heading, "Wall Street Crash," you might ask yourself, "When did Wall Street crash?" or "Why did it crash?" or "What effects did the crash have?"

Reading Exercise

After you have completed your preparation, read the entire passage. Read actively to answer the questions you formed in your mind and to discover the author's main points about the crash and the depression. Remember to respond by underlining main ideas, by numbering major points, and by writing your comments in the margins.

1   The gloom and economic woe that people in mining towns, textile mills, and agricultural communities suffered at the end of the 1920s hardly penetrated the elegant offices of Wall Street. There, all seemed magical; glamour stocks such as General Electric, International Harvester, and Radio Corporation of America soared in value. By late 1928 one share of RCA cost $400, the equivalent of several months' income for many people. The bull market attracted millions of buyers, many of whom joined the speculative binge by buying their shares on margin (paying only a portion of the cost in cash and borrowing the rest) or investing their savings. By October 1929 brokers' loans to stock purchasers amounted to a staggering $8.5 billion. John J. Raskob, a member of General Motors' board of directors as well as chairman of the

Democratic party, was so enthusiastic about the boom that he proclaimed that "anyone not only can be rich, but ought to be rich" by speculating in the stock market.

Wall Street Crash

2   The get-rich-quick mentality was jolted in September and early October when stock prices dropped. Analysts attributed the dip to "shaking out the lunatic fringe." But on October 24, Black Thursday, a record number of shares was traded; many stocks sold at low prices, and some could find no takers. Stunned crowds gathered outside the frantic New York Stock Exchange, buzzing about the apparent seriousness of the decline. At noon, banking leaders met at the headquarters of J. P. Morgan and Company to halt the skid and restore confidence. They put up $20 million, told everybody about it, and ceremoniously began by buying ten thousand shares of United States Steel. The mood changed and some stocks rallied. The bankers, it seemed, had preserved the dream of success.

3   But the nation gradually succumbed to panic. News of Black Thursday spread across the country, and trouble ("sell!") ricocheted back to New York via telephone. Another bolt struck on Black Tuesday (October 29) when stock prices plunged again. The market settled into a grim pattern of declines and weak rallies. Hoover, who had never approved of what he called the "fever of speculation," assured Americans that the economy was sound. He shared the popular assumption that the stock market's ills could be quarantined from a generally healthy economy. Businesspeople, schooled in the credo of progress, comforted themselves with the thought that the stock market would soon right itself. Although their boosterism seems terribly misguided or deceptive today, it was sincerely, if blindly, believed at the time. Anyway, said the secretary of labor, "one doesn't improve the condition of a sick man by constantly telling him how ill he is."

Economic Weaknesses

4   The crash ultimately helped to unleash a devastating depression. The economic downturn did not come suddenly; it was more like a leak in a punctured tire than a blowout. There were several interrelated causes of the Great Depression. The first was the increasing weakness of the economy in the 1920s. Had the economy of the new era been strong, it would have stood a better chance of weathering the crash on Wall Street. In fact, some historians suggest that the stock market collapse merely moved an ongoing recession into depression. Throughout the 1920s the agricultural sector was plagued with overproduction, declining prices for farm products, mounting debts, bankruptcies, and small bank failures. Some industries, like coal, railroads, and textiles, were in distress long before 1929, and two mainstays of economic growth, autos and construction, also declined early. . . . What all these weaknesses meant by 1929 was that major sectors of the economy were not expanding; businesspeople were not investing funds to build new plants, hire more workers, and produce more goods. Indeed, the opposite was true: unsold inventories were stacking up in warehouses, investments were shrinking, laborers were being sent home, and consumer purchases were dropping off.

Underconsumption

5   Second and related, the onset and severity of the depression can be attributed to underconsumption. That is, production (supply) had outstripped consumption (demand). Wages and mass purchasing power had lagged behind the industrial surge of the 1920s; the workers who produced the new consumer products ultimately could not afford to buy them. Why did purchasing decline? Laborers and farmers constituted the great majority of consumers. Yet, as we have seen, farmers suffered economic distress and had to trim their purchases. And as industries like coal, autos, and construction declined, they laid off men and women who then lacked the money to sustain buying. Other laborers lost their jobs because machines displaced them. In Hartford and New Haven in 1929, for example, the installation of more efficient machinery threw 1,190 rubber workers out of their jobs. And 35,000 orchestra musicians were unemployed in mid-1929 because "machine music" had been installed in the nation's theaters. Overall, then, a sizable nonconsuming group had grown in America before the Great Depression hit.

Unequal Distribution of Wealth

6   Another important aspect of underconsumption was the unequal distribution of income. In the 1920s the rich got much richer while others made only modest gains. Average per capita disposable income (income after taxes) rose about 9 percent from 1920 to 1929, but the income of the wealthiest 1 percent rose 75 percent. In 1929 experts estimated that about 60 percent of America's families lived on or below the subsistence level ($2,000 a year), despite a 29 percent increase in the number of employed married women over the decade. The Federal Trade Commission reported that 1 percent of the American people owned 59 percent of the country's wealth; 87 percent owned only 10 percent. Income and wealth, in other words, were concentrated at the top of America's economic ladder. Why did this uneven distribution contribute to underconsumption and depression? Because much of the accumulating income was put into luxuries, savings, investments, and stock-market speculation instead of being spent on consumer goods. Put another way, more money in the hands of workers and farmers and less money building up in the vaults of the wealthy would probably have meant more consumption and hence more stable economic growth.

Large Corporations

7   Third, the American business system was shaky, for a few large corporations in each industry—oligopolies—unbalanced it. In 1929 the top two hundred nonfinancial corporations controlled 49 percent of corporate wealth. The old cliché "The bigger they are, the harder they fall" was literally true. Many companies speculated dangerously on the stock market and built pyramidlike businesses based on shady, if legal, manipulation of assets through holding companies. If one part of the edifice collapsed, the entire structure crumbled. Such was the case with Samuel Insull's mighty electrical empire based in Chicago. Insull built a utilities network that produced one-eighth of America's electrical power and operated in thirty-nine states. Within this vast system one company held the stock of another company, which held the stock of another company, and so on. Sometimes Insull's various companies bought stock from one another, each showing an artificially high profit

from the transactions. Even Insull admitted that he was not sure how it all worked; his sixty-five chairmanships, eighty-five directorships, and seven presidencies confused him as much as anybody else. When his interlocking network collapsed in 1932, he fled to Europe to escape arrest for fraud. Found in Turkey, he returned to the United States, hired advertising agencies to improve his public image, and in 1934 was acquitted.

Speculation on the Stock Market

8   The depression derived, fourth, from pell-mell, largely unregulated, speculation on the stock market. Corporations and banks invested large sums in stocks; some speculated in their own issues. Brokers sold stocks to buyers who put up little cash, borrowed in order to purchase, and then used the stocks they bought as collateral for their loans. When the stocks came tumbling down, so did brokers, bankers, and companies. Brokers called up buyers to ask for more cash. Some buyers drained their savings from banks, but when others could not come up with the money, the brokers sold the stock for the little it would command. Bankers, meanwhile, were calling up brokers and other speculators, searching for cash. The domino effect was crushing, and the whole economic system tottered as obligations went unmet. From 1930 to 1933 stock-market losses climbed to $85 billion. A new byword circulated: "Trust God, not stocks."

International Economic Troubles

9   International economic troubles constitute a fifth explanation for the coming of the depression. As the world's leading creditor and trader, the United States was deeply involved with the world economy. Billions of dollars in loans had flowed to Europe during the First World War and then during postwar reconstruction. Yet in the late 1920s American investors were beginning to keep their money at home, to invest it in the more exciting and lucrative stock market. Europeans, unable to borrow more funds and unable to sell their goods easily in the American market because of high tariffs, began to buy less from America and to default on their debts. Pinched at home, they raised their own tariffs, further crippling international commerce, and withdrew their investments from America. It was Hoover's view that "the European disease had contaminated the United States." He would have been more accurate had he said that the European and American illnesses were mutually infectious.

The Failure of Federal Policies

10   Finally, government policies and practices contributed to the crash and depression. The federal government failed to regulate the wild speculation, contenting itself with occasional scoldings of bankers and businesspeople. It neither checked corporate power nor raised income taxes to encourage a more equitable distribution of income. Indeed, it lowered taxes, thus promoting the uneven distribution. And the Federal Reserve Board pursued easy-credit policies, charging low discount rates, or interest rates, on its loans to member banks, even though it knew the easy money was paying for the speculative binge. The "Fed" blundered again after the crash, in 1931. This time the board drastically raised the rate, tightening the money market at a time when just the opposite was needed: loosening to spur borrowing and spending.

11   Today, in an era of computerized data, daily economic forecasts, and the watchdog Council of Economic Advisers . . . it is difficult to recall that in 1929 the state of economic analysis and statistics-gathering was comparatively primitive. The several explanations for the onset of depression were not easily grasped in 1929, especially while people were absorbed in a headlong rush to make as much money as possible as fast as possible. And the conventional wisdom, based on the experience of previous depressions, was that little could be done to correct economic problems. So in 1929 people waited for the deflation to bottom out.

Mary Beth Norton et al., *A People and a Nation: A History of the United States*

1. Write in your own words the main idea, or thesis, of "The Great Crash and the Great Depression."

_____

_____

_____

2. To present their information as clearly as possible, authors of textbooks often employ clearly stated topic sentences and common methods of development. For example, paragraphs 1 and 2 about the 1929 stock market crash are developed primarily by

_____

Paragraphs 4–10, which discuss why the depression occurred, are developed primarily by

_____

3. The stock market crash of 1929 was the immediate trigger of the Great Depression, but the underlying causes of the depression were much deeper. What were these causes as discussed by Norton?

a. _____

_____

_____

b. _____

_____

_____

c. _____

d. _____

_____

_____

e. _____

_____

_____

f. _____

_____

_____

_____

4. Each subject, or discipline—such as chemistry, computer science, political science, and history—contains a number of vocabulary words that are basic to that discipline. Thus, for a chemistry class you must understand the discipline-specific meanings of *compounds* and *elements,* for a computer science class you must know the meanings of *hardware* and *software,* for a political science class you must understand the difference between *social-ism* and *communism,* and for an economics or history class you must understand the concepts of *depression* and *inflation.* The history selection for this assignment contains not only the words *depression* and *inflation* but also the related terms *recession* and *deflation.* Using the following definitions of certain prefixes, roots, and suffixes as well as the context of your reading, define the economic terms listed below:

Prefixes	**Roots**	**Suffixes**
de- = down	cess = to go	-ion = act of
in- = in	flar(t)e = to blow	
	press = to press	

a. deflation _____

_____

b. depression _____

_____

    c. inflation _____

_____

    d. recession _____

_____

    5. Textbook writers often make their readers' task easier by defining in context new words that are essential to an understanding of content. Write below the contextual definition for each word or phrase listed:

    a. buying shares on margin _____

_____

    b. speculation _____

_____

    c. underconsumption _____

_____

    d. disposable income _____

_____

    e. oligopolies _____

_____

Discussion Questions

    1. Do you think another depression could ever occur in the United States? Why or why not?

    2. What should the government and the people of the United States and of other countries do to prevent a worldwide depression?

Writing Exercise

Below are three options for writing about the passage you have just read. For these assignments, you may find it helpful to refer back to the questions you have just answered as well as to the passage itself.

    1. With yourself as your audience, prepare an informal study outline from the reading passage.

    2. Write a one-paragraph summary of the passage. Your purpose may be to prepare a study aid for yourself or to demonstrate your understanding of the passage to an instructor.

3. Pretend for a few minutes that you are a history professor preparing an essay examination on the passage you have just read. What are some questions you might ask your students? The following explanations of different types of essay questions may help you think of some possible questions.

Analyze. Discuss the various elements of an issue or an event, as in analyzing causes or effects.

Compare. Examine specific events, beliefs, individuals, qualities, or problems to show similarities (differences may also be mentioned).

Contrast. Examine specific events, beliefs, individuals, qualities, or problems to show differences.

Discuss. Examine and analyze in detail a specific issue or problem, considering all sides of the issue.

Enumerate. Although you may answer this type of question in paragraph form, you should answer concisely, listing items instead of discussing them thoroughly. Some instructors prefer items listed and numbered in columns.

Explain. Clarify and interpret fully, showing how and why a certain event occurred or a certain belief developed. Often this requires a discussion of causes and effects, as in the question, "Explain the causes . . ."

Illustrate. Present a clear, complete example to clarify your answer.

Relate. Show connections and relationships among ideas, individuals, or events.

Summarize. Present the main ideas in concise, summary form.

Trace (narrate). Describe the progress, sequence, or development of events or ideas.

Write below two essay questions your professor might ask you about "The Great Crash and the Great Depression."

1. _____

2. _____

Now, switch roles to become the student who must answer these questions. As a student, how do you react to essay examinations? Many students are needlessly terrified by such examinations. If you have followed the suggestions in *Contexts* for reading and reviewing your assignments, you should be able to master the content on which you are to be tested. However, you must also know how to take an essay examination. The following strategies can help you perform more successfully on essay examinations:

1. **Read through the entire examination.** Pay close attention to the directions and note whether you are to answer all questions or only a specified number. Reading through the entire test gives you an overview of

the information to be covered and may prevent unnecessary and time-consuming overlapping in your answers. As you read each question, you may want to jot ideas and examples in the margin so you will not forget them later.

2. **Budget your time.** After reading through all of the questions, determine the total time for the test, the total number of questions to be answered, and the point value for each question. Then quickly plan how you will use your time, allowing a short planning period and a review period but saving the bulk of your time for actually answering the questions. Considering the point value of each question, divide your total time into blocks. Below is an illustration of how you might budget your time for a one-hour examination with four test questions, each of different point values:

FIGURE 32

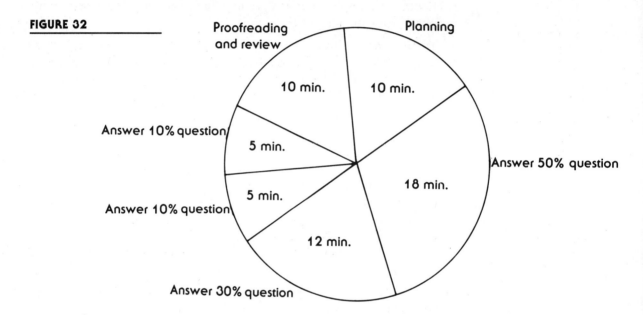

3. **Analyze the question carefully.** Circle or underline key words such as *compare, explain,* or *summarize,* and be sure you understand what each key word requires of you. Also be sure to notice whether the question contains more than one part.

4. **Follow directions.** Be sure you understand the directions, and then follow them closely. If you have been asked to list, don't discuss; if you have been asked to discuss, don't list.

5. **Plan your answer to each question.** Use scratch paper or the inside cover of your test booklet to make a rough outline of the ideas you intend to discuss.

6. **Answer each question clearly, directly, and completely.** Give your thesis or main idea in the first sentence. If there are two or more subpoints to your answer, you may indicate this in your thesis (Example: The Indians of North and South America differed in their civilizations, their governments, their religions, and their property concepts). As you develop your thesis, include specific and thorough support, but don't ramble. In a

short essay question, your thesis can probably be developed in a paragraph; a longer essay question may require a short essay of three or more paragraphs. In either case, pay close attention to transition and include a concluding statement.

7. **If you don't remember the answer to a question, leave a blank space for it.** Return to it after you have finished the other questions. You might remember the answer before you finish the exam (sometimes there are clues in other questions). It is also a good idea to leave wide margins and blocks of blank space after each answer so you can add information you remember later.

8. **Proofread your answers.** Rereading your answers will give you a chance to catch careless mistakes in spelling and punctuation. Reviewing your answers may also jog your memory and help you think of points that did not occur to you earlier. If so, you will be glad you left extra time and space to add to your answers.

Keep these suggestions in mind as you answer the essay question below about "The Great Crash and the Great Depression." Remember that your audience is your history professor and that your purpose is to make as good a grade as possible!

Question: In addition to the stock market crash, there were "several interrelated causes of the Great Depression." In a brief essay, identify these causes and discuss how each was related to the depression.

Rewriting Exercise

Reread your outline, paragraph, or essay carefully and evaluate it individually or in groups.

1. Is your main idea (thesis or topic sentence) clear? What is your main idea?
2. What are your major supporting points? Are they clear, effective, and complete?
3. Are relationships among the supporting points clear?
4. What is your conclusion? Is it effective?
5. Have you edited carefully? (This stage is especially important if your audience is someone other than yourself, but even study aids need to be edited for clarity.)
6. Does your draft fulfill your purpose and communicate to your audience?

If necessary, rewrite your draft, making any necessary additions, deletions, or other changes. Proofread this final draft carefully.

> # RICHARD RODRIGUEZ
> ## Public vs. Private Language

Pre-Reading/Writing Exercise

Language is not only a means of communication but also a source of public and private identity. As part of their different identities, people alter their language in speaking as well as in writing to suit different purposes and different audiences. Children and teenagers often know instinctively how to speak to different audiences to achieve their purposes. As you read the three statements below, determine the audience for each: a close friend, a parent, or a teacher.

> **Example A:** I cut poli-sci today!
>
> **Example B:** I didn't make it to my political science class because my alarm didn't go off.
>
> **Example C:** I was unable to attend your 8:30 Political Science 221 class this morning, but I would like to submit my homework.

Directed to a peer, the first statement is *colloquial,* intended only for informal speech. The second statement, directed to a parent, is appropriate for *informal* speaking or writing. The third statement, appropriate for more *formal* speaking or writing, was directed to a teacher (an authority figure).

As these examples illustrate, we all have different kinds of language for different purposes and audiences. We might even generalize and say that the first two statements given above are part of our "private language" whereas the third statement represents our "public language."

Our language options can be further complicated and enriched when they include not only different kinds of one language but also different languages, such as English, Spanish, French, and Chinese. For a few minutes, think about the various problems and rewards that can arise when a child or an adult is learning a new language or even a new dialect (a variety of language spoken in a particular place or by a particular group):

1. Is learning an additional language or dialect difficult or easy? If you know a language other than your native language, how old were you when you learned this language? Is it easier to learn another language as a child or as an adult?

2. Have you known a child or an adult who was expected to use one kind of language, or even a different language, at home and another at school or at work? Have you had such an experience? What are the difficulties in such a situation?

3. Do you speak one or more languages in addition to your native language? Do you read and write a language other than your native one? Which is the more difficult to learn—the spoken language or the written language?

4. How important is it in today's world to know languages of other countries and cultures?

Now, keeping one or more of these questions in mind, freewrite in your journal for ten minutes about learning and using a language (or dialect) other than your native language. Do not try to answer all of the above questions. Just write about the idea that interests you most. As usual with your freewriting, do not be concerned with form or correctness; just get your ideas down on paper.

Reading Exercise

In the following passage, Richard Rodriguez describes his childhood experience of learning to speak English. Read this passage carefully and critically. Determine not only Rodriguez's main idea but also his primary purpose and his probable audience. Finally, decide whether or not you agree with Rodriguez's thesis and why you feel as you do.

1   Supporters of bilingual education imply today that students like me miss a great deal by not being taught in their family's language. What they seem not to recognize is that, as a socially disadvantaged child, I regarded Spanish as a private language. It was a ghetto language that deepened and strengthened my feeling of public separateness. What I needed to learn in school was that I had the right, and the obligation, to speak the public language. The odd truth is that my first-grade classmates could have become bilingual, in the conventional sense of the word, more easily than I. Had they been taught early (as upper middle-class children often are taught) a "second language" like Spanish or French, they could have regarded it simply as another public language. In my case, such bilingualism could not have been so quickly achieved. What I did not believe was that I could speak a single public language.

2   Without question, it would have pleased me to have heard my teachers address me in Spanish when I entered the classroom. I would have felt much less afraid. I would have imagined that my instructors were somehow "related" to me; I would indeed have heard their Spanish as my family's language. I would have trusted them and responded with ease. But I would have delayed—postponed for how long?—having to learn the language of public society. I would have evaded—and for how long?—learning the great lesson of school: that I had a public identity.

3   Fortunately, my teachers were unsentimental about their responsibility. What they understood was that I needed to speak public English. So their voices would search me out, asking me questions. Each time I heard them I'd look up in surprise to see a nun's face frowning at me. I'd mumble, not really meaning to answer. The nun would persist. "Richard, stand up. Don't look at the floor. Speak up. Speak to the entire class, not just to me!" But I couldn't

believe English could be my language to use. (In part, I did not want to believe it.) I continued to mumble. I resisted the teacher's demands. (Did I somehow suspect that once I learned this public language my family life would be changed?) Silent, waiting for the bell to sound, I remained dazed, diffident, afraid.

4   Because I wrongly imagined that English was intrinsically a public language and Spanish was intrinsically private, I easily noted the difference between classroom language and the language at home. At school, words were directed to a general audience of listeners. ("Boys and girls . . .") Words were meaningfully ordered. And the point was not self-expression alone, but to make oneself understood by many others. The teacher quizzed: "Boys and girls, why do we use that word in this sentence? Could we think of a better word to use there? Would the sentence change its meaning if the words were differently arranged? Isn't there a better way of saying much the same thing?" (I couldn't say. I wouldn't try to say.)

5   Three months passed. Five. A half year. Unsmiling, ever watchful, my teachers noted my silence. They began to connect my behavior with the slow progress my brother and sisters were making. Until, one Saturday morning, three nuns arrived at the house to talk to our parents. Stiffly they sat on the blue living-room sofa. From the doorway of another room, spying on the visitors, I noted the incongruity, the clash of two worlds, the faces and voices of school intruding upon the familiar setting of home. I overheard one voice gently wondering, "Do your children speak only Spanish at home, Mrs. Rodriguez?" While another voice added, "That Richard especially seems so timid and shy."

6   *That Rich-heard!*

7   With great tact, the visitors continued, "Is it possible for you and your husband to encourage your children to practice their English when they are home?" Of course my parents complied. What would they not do for their children's well-being? And how could they question the Church's authority which those women represented? In an instant they agreed to give up the language (the sounds) which had revealed and accentuated our family's closeness. The moment after the visitors left, the change was observed. "*Ahora,* speak to us only *en inglés,*" my father and mother told us.

8   At first, it seemed a kind of game. After dinner each night, the family gathered together to practice "our" English. It was still then *inglés,* a language foreign to us, so we felt drawn to it as strangers. Laughing, we would try to define words we could not pronounce. We played with strange English sounds, often over-anglicizing our pronunciations. And we filled the smiling gaps of our sentences with familiar Spanish sounds. But that was cheating, somebody shouted, and everyone laughed.

9   In school, meanwhile, like my brother and sisters, I was required to attend a daily tutoring session. I needed a full year of this special work. I also needed my teachers to keep my attention from straying in class by calling out, "*Rich-heard*"—their English voices slowly loosening the ties to my other name, with its three notes, *Ri-car-do.* Most of all, I needed to hear my mother and father speak to me in a moment of seriousness in "broken"—suddenly heartbreaking—English. This scene was inevitable. One Saturday morning I entered the kitchen where my parents were talking, but I did not realize that they were talking in Spanish until, the moment they saw me, their voices

changed and they began speaking English. The gringo sounds they uttered startled me. Pushed me away. In that moment of trivial misunderstanding and profound insight, I felt my throat twisted by unsounded grief. I simply turned and left the room. But I had no place to escape to where I could grieve in Spanish. My brother and sisters were speaking English in another part of the house.

10   Again and again in the days following, as I grew increasingly angry, I was obliged to hear my mother and father encouraging me: "Speak to us *en inglés.*" Only then did I determine to learn classroom English. Thus, sometime afterward it happened: one day in school, I raised my hand to volunteer an answer to a question. I spoke out in a loud voice and I did not think it remarkable when the entire class understood. That day I moved very far from being the disadvantaged child I had been only days earlier. Taken hold at last was the belief, the calming assurance, that I *belonged* in public.

11   Shortly after, I stopped hearing the high, troubling sounds of *los gringos.* A more and more confident speaker of English, I didn't listen to how strangers sounded when they talked to me. With so many English-speaking people around me, I no longer heard American accents. Conversations quickened. Listening to persons whose voices sounded eccentrically pitched, I might note their sounds for a few seconds, but then I'd concentrate on what they were saying. Now when I heard someone's tone of voice—angry or questioning or sarcastic or happy or sad—I didn't distinguish it from the words it expressed. Sound and word were thus tightly wedded. At the end of each day I was often bemused, and always relieved, to realize how "soundless," though crowded with words, my day in public had been. An eight-year-old boy, I finally came to accept what had been technically true since my birth: I was an American citizen.

12   But diminished by then was the special feeling of closeness at home. Gone was the desperate, urgent, intense feeling of being at home among those with whom I felt intimate. Our family remained a loving family, but one greatly changed. We were no longer so close, no longer bound tightly together by the knowledge of our separateness from *los gringos.* Neither my older brother nor my sisters rushed home after school any more. Nor did I. When I arrived home, often there would be neighborhood kids in the house. Or the house would be empty of sounds.

13   Bilingual educators say today that children lose a degree of "individuality" by becoming assimilated into public society. (Bilingual schooling is a program popularized in the seventies, that decade when middle-class "ethnics" began to resist the process of assimilation—the "American melting pot.") But the bilingualists oversimplify when they scorn the value and necessity of assimilation. They do not seem to realize that a person is individualized in two ways. So they do not realize that, while one suffers a diminished sense of *private* individuality by being assimilated into public society, such assimilation makes possible the achievement of *public* individuality.

14   If I rehearse here the changes in my private life after my Americanization, it is finally to emphasize a public gain. The loss implies the gain. The house I returned to each afternoon was quiet. Intimate sounds no longer greeted me at the door. Inside there were other noises. The telephone rang. Neighborhood kids ran past the door of the bedroom where I was reading my schoolbooks—covered with brown shopping-bag paper. Once I learned

the public language, it would never again be easy for me to hear intimate family voices. More and more of my day was spent hearing words, not sounds. But that may only be a way of saying that on the day I raised my hand in class and spoke loudly to an entire roomful of faces, my childhood started to end.

Richard Rodriguez, "Aria: A Memoir of a Bilingual Childhood"

1. Although Rodriguez's main idea, or thesis, is not completely stated in a single sentence within the passage, the thesis is partially stated and clearly implied in paragraphs 1, 13, and 14. Write his thesis in your own words.

_____

_____

_____

2. In your opinion, what audience is Rodriguez writing for?

_____

_____

3. Is Rodriguez's purpose in this selection to entertain his audience, to inform his audience, or to persuade his audience to believe as he believes and perhaps to act accordingly?

_____

_____

4. What method(s) of development does Rodriguez use to present his support?

_____

_____

_____

5. A knowledge of the term *bilingual* is essential to an understanding of Rodriguez's purpose. What is the most general meaning of the term?

_____

Rodriguez speaks specifically of *bilingual education*. What does he mean by this term?

_____

6. What did Rodriguez gain from his educational experiences?

What did he lose? _____

7. Sometimes you can use similar but more familiar words to help you define a term. For example, you can use the words *similar* and *assimilate* (to make similar) to help you define *assimilation* as the process in which one group or person becomes similar to another, and usually larger, group. Other words from Rodriguez's passage that can be defined in this way are *intrinsically* and *incongruity*. The related words *intrinsic* (inner, essential) and *congruent* (harmonious) can help you define these words. You may also use the context and, if necessary, a dictionary for your definitions.

   a. intrinsically _____

   b. incongruity _____

8. Rodriguez uses his childhood educational experiences to draw a conclusion about bilingual education. What is that conclusion?

Discussion Questions

1. Should public school classes in the United States be taught in English even if English is not the students' native language? Why or why not?

2. Do you think that children who speak a nonstandard English dialect at home should be forced to speak standard English in elementary school? middle school? high school? Why or why not?

Writing Exercise

From his own experiences, Rodriguez concludes that the advantages of his English public education outweigh the disadvantages. He further concludes that students whose native language is not English benefit more by being taught in the *public* language of English rather than in their own *private* languages. Thus, he disagrees with educators who urge that children be taught in their native languages.

Write a paragraph or essay in which you agree or disagree with Rodriguez about bilingual education. Your general purpose is to persuade your audience—parents, teachers, or school board members—to accept your position. Look back at your freewriting and underline any ideas that relate to this topic. If you wish, freewrite for another five or ten minutes on this subject. Then select a specific subject from your freewriting and determine your main idea and method(s) of development. If necessary, make an informal planning outline of your major supporting details.

You may use ideas or quotations from Rodriguez's essay, but be sure that your paper is not just a summary of his ideas. If you do quote from Rodriguez, be sure to quote accurately and to include the quoted material within quotation marks. Keeping in mind the audience and general purpose specified above, write the first draft of your composition.

Rewriting Exercise

Reread your paragraph or essay carefully and then answer the following questions, either independently or in groups.

1. What is your primary purpose?
2. Who is your audience?
3. What is your main idea (your topic sentence or thesis statement)?
4. What is your primary method of development?
5. What major supporting details have you used? What additional details can you include? Do all of your supporting details develop your main idea? (You can check the unity of your composition by turning your thesis or topic sentence into a question and then checking each supporting sentence or paragraph to see if it answers that question.) Which details, if any, should you omit?
6. How have you arranged your supporting points? Is this arrangement logical? How can it be improved?
7. What types of transitions have you used? What additional transitions can you add?
8. Have you used the most effective type of conclusion for your purpose and audience?

After you have revised your paragraph or essay, edit it to correct any errors in sentence structure, punctuation, spelling, and word choice that you see. Then write your final draft and proofread it carefully.

Part Two

THE SENTENCE

Each year in school you have studied the sentence—its structure, its elements, even its definition. But you may suspect that, in spite of your extensive knowledge of sentences, you still need to know more about them. You may have realized that speaking and listening to sentences are not the same as reading and writing sentences. At times, as you read and write, you need to be able to *analyze* a certain sentence—to take it apart, understand how it works, and put it back together again. The ability to analyze sentences enables you to be a better reader and writer. It also enables you to distinguish between "correct" and "incorrect" sentences—a skill that is much less important than other reading and writing skills, but one that is ultimately important to you and to those with whom you communicate.

A knowledge of sentence structure, then, is valuable because it enables you to be a good editor. We have discussed the importance of revising what you write so that the content and organization accurately reflect your ideas and communicate clearly to your readers. But experienced writers also *edit* their work to make it more readable and to eliminate distracting errors. The chapters that follow, therefore, will emphasize not only reading and writing sentences but also editing sentences—making them more readable, more interesting, more graceful, and ultimately more correct.

In this part of the book you will learn how sentences work, how to increase your comprehension of sentences, how to make choices about sentences, and how to edit sentences. You will be asked to read and write sentences and to work with them in exercises that increase your knowledge of sentence structure and reinforce your understanding of paragraphs.

Chapter 9

Read p. 226-246
Read & do p. 247-249
p. 251-260

THE SIMPLE SENTENCE

Although we usually speak in sentences, at times we use phrases or even single words to communicate. For example, the following conversation would be perfectly clear to the two people involved:

"Going?"

"Yeah."

"Where?"

"Home."

"Okay, see you."

However, reading and writing differ from speaking and listening in that our audience is not usually present. When we communicate in writing, therefore, we usually use complete sentences—groups of words that make a statement or ask a question. Thus, in order to read and write effectively, we need to understand how sentences are constructed.

ESSENTIAL ELEMENTS OF THE SENTENCE

It is possible for a native speaker of English to generate an almost endless variety of sentences. But every complete sentence, regardless of how it varies from other sentences, has two essential parts: a *subject* and a *verb*. The subject of a sentence is what you are writing about, and the verb makes a statement or asks a question about the subject. Although a sentence may have other elements, it must have a subject and verb. The sentence below has only these two essential elements.

S   V

Mary smiled.

Most sentences, however, are longer and more detailed. Notice in the sentence pairs below that the essential elements (subject and verb) remain the same even though more details have been added.

226

EXAMPLES

Mirror hung.

The cracked <u>mirror</u> <u><u>hung</u></u> crookedly on the faded wallpaper.

Several stood.

<u>Several</u> of the construction workers <u><u>stood</u></u> with their backs to us.

Wind blew.

The hot, dry <u>wind</u> constantly <u><u>blew</u></u> the fine sand into our faces.

The sentences above are all examples of *simple sentences.* That is, they all have a single subject/verb relationship: the verb of each sentence makes a statement about the subject of the sentence. Even in a sentence in which the subject or verb is compounded (composed of two or more parts), the sentence is still considered a simple sentence if both the verbs are making the same statement about both of the subjects.

EXAMPLES

Mary *smiled and winked.* (compound verb)

Mary and John smiled. (compound subject)

Mary and John smiled and winked. (compound subject and compound verb)

All three examples are still simple sentences because they have only one subject/verb relationship. But if we change the sentence so that it expresses two subject/verb relationships (*Mary smiled,* and *John winked*), the sentence is no longer a simple sentence.

Note: See Chapter 11 for a more extensive discussion of compound elements.

EXERCISE 9.1

Write five *simple* sentences, including at least one with a compound subject or verb. Underline the subject once and the verb twice.

1. _____

2. _____

3. _____

4. _____

5. _____

Subjects

Since your subject is what you are talking about, it is often a word that names someone or something. We call such words *nouns.* Look at the following list of nouns:

1. arrangement
2. warning
3. receptionist
4. politicians
5. monkey
6. actress
7. Fred
8. pride
9. writers
10. mechanic

EXERCISE 9.2

Each of the nouns listed above can function as the subject of a sentence. Write ten simple sentences using each of these nouns as a subject.

1. _____

2. _____

3. _____

4. _____

5. _____

6. _____

7. _____

8. _____

9. _____

10. _____

Pronouns are words that refer to nouns. Like nouns, a pronoun can function as the subject of a sentence. For example, the following pronouns could refer to the nouns listed above.

1. arrangement—it
2. warning—it
3. receptionist—he
4. politicians—they
5. monkey—it
6. actress—she
7. Fred—he
8. pride—it
9. writers—they
10. mechanic—she

EXERCISE 9.3

Rewrite five of the sentences you wrote in the previous exercise, using an appropriate pronoun as the subject of each sentence.

1. _____

2. _____

3. _____

4. _____

5. _____

EXERCISE 9.4

Many of the subject nouns and pronouns have been deleted from the passage below. Replace the blanks with appropriate nouns or pronouns so that each sentence has a subject that makes sense. Any word that makes sense in the context is acceptable. You should therefore study the context carefully, and then fill in the blanks with words that make sense. Do not worry about right answers or wrong answers. If the word you choose is appropriate for the context, it is "right."

He was raised by this aunt and uncle, who was his father's brother.

_____ had been staying with them when his parents died, and
(1)

he simply stayed on. _____ slept in a narrow bed in a small
(2)

and dingy room. They lived in a sunless ground-floor apartment in an old

five-story red-brick building where his uncle collected the rents for the owner

no one ever saw. The _____ was the talk of their Brooklyn neigh-
(3)

borhood. There was something wrong with it; _____ had gone
(4)

awry from the very beginning. The _____ was whimsical and
(5)

tended to die when it was most needed; valves stuck, _____
(6)

leaked, faucets gushed unevenly when turned on, or gave off explosions of

air; electrical _____ shorted mysteriously; _____
(7)   (8)

of brick worked loose and tumbled to the sidewalk; the tar covering of the

roof, no matter how recently replaced, became warped, then buckled and cracked. But the rents were low, the _____ were always filled,
(9)
and his uncle, who earned an erratic livelihood from the badly organized and decrepit Hebrew bookstore he operated in the neighborhood, was kept very busy. Often his _____ himself fired up the furnace, on
(10)
those early winter mornings when the janitor was in a drunken stupor from which he could not be roused. _____ came and went. His
(11)
uncle's _____ was not an easy one.
(12)

Adapted from Chaim Potok, *The Book of Lights*

Verbs

In addition to a subject, each complete sentence must have a verb—a word or phrase that makes a statement or asks a question about the subject. The verb of a sentence may be a single word (such as *drink*) or a verb phrase (such as *will be drinking*). Each verb has many different forms. The form of a verb changes most often to indicate tense—the time at which the stated action or being takes place. Look at the following examples of the different tenses of the verb *dance:*

> I *dance* each day to keep in shape. (present)
> I *danced* for several hours last night. (past)
> I *will dance* with you later. (future)
> I *have danced* with her before. (present perfect)
> I *had danced* for hours. (past perfect)
> I *will have danced* every dance. (future perfect)
> I *am dancing* too much. (present progressive)
> I *was dancing* energetically. (past progressive)
> I *will be dancing* in the chorus. (future progressive)
> I *have been dancing* with him. (present perfect progressive)
> I *had been dancing* for many years. (past perfect progressive)
> I *will have been dancing* for twenty years next month. (future perfect progressive)

Most speakers of English do not have to think consciously about using the appropriate tense—the one that communicates the intended relationship between the time of the action expressed in the sentence and the actual time at which the sentence is written or spoken. However, choosing the appropriate verb form is part of a writer's responsibility. Within the range of what is considered correct are many choices, but each different choice conveys a different meaning.

EXAMPLES

I danced all night. (past tense, occurring in the past at a specified time)

I have danced to that song before. (present perfect, occurring at some time in the past)

I am dancing too much. (present progressive, occurring at the present time)

Writers also use auxiliaries (such as *should, would, could, might, may, can, must,* and *do* or *did*) to make other distinctions about verbs. Readers use these auxiliaries as clues to interpret a writer's meaning.

EXAMPLES

I may dance.
I might dance. } possibility

I must dance.
I should dance. } obligation

I can dance.
I could dance. } ability

I would dance. —— condition

I do dance.
I did dance. } emphasis

EXERCISE 9.5

Below are four sentences that have no main verb. Using the clues that are provided in each sentence, fill in as many appropriate forms of the verb *speak* as you can:

1. Every day as he walks to work, Gary _____ to her.

   _____

   _____

   _____

   _____

2. Yesterday, as he walked to work, Gary _____ to her.

   _____

_____

_____

_____

3. Tomorrow, as he walks to work, Gary _____ to her.

_____

_____

_____

_____

4. By then, Gary _____ to her.

_____

_____

EXERCISE 9.6

The main verbs have been deleted from each of the sentences in the following passage. Supply a verb for each sentence. Be sure you choose a verb that reflects the appropriate tense and that the resulting paragraph makes sense.

In March there _____ a death on the island. Like most deaths
(1)

on Yamacraw, it _____ with unforeshadowed swiftness; there
(2)

was no lingering or gradual wasting away or bedside farewells. A heart

attack _____ Blossom Smith on a Saturday, an islander raced to
(3)

Ted Stone's house, and Stone immediately _____ for a rescue
(4)

helicopter from Savannah. Blossom was _____ to an open
(5)

field near the nightclub, where half the island gathered around her wailing

and praying. The helicopter appeared, _____ rapidly and effi-
(6)

ciently, received the motionless Blossom into the dark angel with the rotating

wings, _____ into the sky in a maelstrom of debris and air, and
(7)

then _____ over the top of trees. It _____ all
　　　　　　(8)　　　　　　　　　　　　　　　　　　　　(9)

very quick, very impressive, and very futile. Blossom _____ that
　　　　　　　　　　　　　　　　　　　　　　　　　　　　(10)

night in Savannah surrounded by strangers and the ammonia smells of a

death ward.

Pat Conroy, The Water Is Wide

EXERCISE 9.7

Below are two lists of verbs. One consists of five present-tense verbs, and the other consists of the same verbs in the past tense. Use each of the verbs in a sentence that provides the appropriate context for the tense:

Present-Tense Verbs	Past-Tense Verbs
walks	walked
is singing	was singing
has eaten	had eaten
can study	could study
does believe	did believe

BASIC PATTERNS OF THE SIMPLE SENTENCE

All English sentences are derived from three basic patterns. A knowledge of these three patterns will enable you to analyze the structure of any sentence you read or write.

Pattern One:　Subject-Verb (S-V)

Pattern Two:　Subject-Verb-Object (S-V-O)

Pattern Three: Subject—Linking Verb—Complement (S-LV-C)

Pattern One: Subject-Verb (S-V)

This pattern has only the two essential elements of a sentence: a *subject* and a *verb*. However, it may also have modifying words and phrases that describe and/or limit either the subject or the verb. Remember also that the verb of a sentence may be a verb phrase.

EXAMPLES

Students study. (S-V)

Students will be studying. (S-V phrase)

Many students in Dr. Goff's chemistry class study together in the evening. (S-V plus modifying words and phrases)

Although the subject and verb in this pattern usually occur in the order shown above (subject preceding verb), the order may be inverted without affecting the pattern.

EXAMPLES

In the stacks, on the top floor of the library, study the most industrious, dedicated students. (The subject of this sentence is students, and the verb is study. Even though the word order has been inverted, the pattern is still S-V.)

Did the biology students study for their test? (Because this sentence is a question, the word order is inverted: the subject students comes between the auxiliary verb did and the main verb study.)

Sentences with inverted word order offer writers additional options for subtle differences in meaning. "The moon we could not see" is not the same as "We could not see the moon." As a writer, you need to be aware of the options that inversion of word order offers. As a reader, you need to be aware of the problems such sentences present, for they are more difficult to read than sentences in which the elements follow normal word order. A knowledge of basic sentence patterns will help you analyze and understand such sentences.

EXERCISE 9.8

Write five sentences that follow the subject-verb pattern. Include at least one sentence that has inverted word order.

1. _____

   _____

2. _____

   _____

3. _____

   _____

4. _____

   _____

5. _____

   _____

Pattern Two: Subject-Verb-Object (S-V-O)

This pattern has a third major element—an *object* (often called a *direct object*)—in addition to the essential subject and verb. An object completes and receives the action expressed by the verb. Like a subject, an object is a noun or a noun substitute.

EXAMPLES

The husband washed the dishes. (S-V-O)

The husband was washing the dishes. (S–V phrase–O)

Efficiently, the husband washed the dirty dishes. (S-V-O plus modifiers)

The elements in this pattern, like those in the S-V pattern, usually occur in normal order (S-V-O); however, the word order can also be inverted.

EXAMPLES

    O   **S**   **V**

That book he had not read.

    O   **S**   **V**

This solution she had not considered.

PRONOUNS AS OBJECTS

The object form of a personal pronoun should be used when the pronoun is functioning as the object of a verb. Compare the contrasting examples of subject and object forms given below:

EXAMPLES

He caught the frisbee. (personal pronoun as subject)

The frisbee hit *him.* (personal pronoun as object)

I met Chris at the party. (personal pronoun as subject)

Chris met *me* at the party. (personal pronoun as object)

She sent her accountant an invitation. (personal pronoun as subject)

Her accountant sent *her* to the bank. (personal pronoun as object)

They visited their friends. (personal pronoun as subject)

Their friends visited *them.* (personal pronoun as object)

In the first example, the subject form of the pronoun (*he*) is used because the pronoun is functioning as the subject of the sentence. But in the second example, the object form (*him*) is used because the pronoun is functioning as the object of the sentence. Below is a chart that lists both the subject and object forms of the personal pronouns.

	Subject Form	Object Form
First-person singular	I	me
Second-person singular	you	you
Third-person singular	he, she, it	him, her, it
First-person plural	we	us
Second-person plural	you	you
Third-person plural	they	them

Be sure to use the subject form of the pronoun if you are using it as a subject and the object form if you are using it as an object.

EXERCISE 9.9

Write five sentences that follow the S-V-O pattern. Use a pronoun as the object of two of your sentences.

1. _____

   _____

2. _____

   _____

3. _____

   _____

4. _____

   _____

5. _____

   _____

Pattern Three: Subject—Linking Verb—Complement (S-LV-C)

Like the S-V-O pattern, this one also has three elements: *subject, linking verb,* and *complement.* A complement, like an object, completes the meaning of the verb. However, in this pattern the verb is a linking verb, and the complement refers back to the subject. In fact, the complement is often called a *subject complement.* It can be either a noun or pronoun that renames the subject or an adjective that describes the subject.

EXAMPLES

John is my friend. (S-LV-C)

(noun)

John is friendly. (S-LV-C)

(adjective)

Both of the sentences above follow the S-LV-C pattern, but the first has a noun complement (*friend* renames *John,* telling who he is), and the second has an adjective complement (*friendly* describes John, telling something about him). Both complements refer back to the subject *John* even though they are part of the verb. A complement, in fact, is necessary to complete the meaning of the linking verb.

LINKING VERBS

A linking verb connects the subject to the noun or adjective complement. The verb *to be* (*am, is, are, was,* and *were*) is the most frequently used linking verb. (Because it is a highly irregular verb, we have listed its main forms on page 241.)

The following verbs may also function as linking verbs. Notice that each of these verbs could be replaced by some form of the verb *to be.*

Verb	Example of Verb in Sentence
act	The dog *acts* sick. (is sick)
appear	The plants *appear* healthy. (are healthy)
become	They *became* unhappy. (are unhappy)
fall	The gorilla *fell* ill. (is ill)
feel	I *feel* great. (am great)
get	My aunt is *getting* old. (is old)
go	The dog *went* crazy. (was crazy)
grow	The child *grew* sleepy. (was sleepy)
keep	My mother *keeps* healthy. (is healthy)
look	The winner *looked* happy. (was happy)
prove	That decision *will prove* a mistake. (will be a mistake)
remain	The mockingbird *remained* quiet. (was quiet)
run	That river *runs* deep. (is deep)
seem	You *seem* sad. (are sad)
smell	That onion *smells* terrible. (is terrible)
sound	The piano *sounds* off-key. (is off-key)
stay	That door *stays* open. (is open)
taste	The apple *tastes* sour. (is sour)
turn	The leaves *were turning* brown. (were brown)

Although each of these verbs could be replaced by a form of the verb *to be,* they are essential to good writing because they are more specific, concrete ways of expressing the overused verb *to be.*

PRONOUNS AS COMPLEMENTS

Personal pronouns as well as nouns can function as complements. When a personal pronoun is used as a complement, it takes the subject form rather than the object form.

EXAMPLES

She has become an experienced musician. (personal pronoun as subject)

The Department of Music rewarded *her.* (personal pronoun as object)

In fact, the winner of the annual music contest was *she.* (personal pronoun as complement)

EXERCISE 9.10

Write five sentences that follow the S-LV-C pattern. Be sure to include linking verbs other than the verb *to be* in some of your sentences and to use at least one personal pronoun as a complement.

1. _____

   _____

2. _____

   _____

3. _____

   _____

4. _____

   _____

5. _____

   _____

EXERCISE 9.11

All of the objects and complements in the following passage have been deleted. Replace each blank with an appropriate noun, pronoun, or adjective that could function as the object or complement of the verb in the sentence. Be sure to use the appropriate form of any personal pronouns you insert.

He was not interested in the snow. When he got off the freight, one early evening during the depression, Sargeant never even noticed the _____(1)_____. But he must have felt _____(2)_____ seeping down his neck, cold, wet, sopping in his shoes. But if you had asked _____(3)_____, he wouldn't have known it was snowing. Sargeant didn't see the _____(4)_____, not even under the bright lights of the main street, falling white and flaky against the night. He was too _____(5)_____, too _____(6)_____, and too _____(7)_____.

The Reverend Mr. Dorset, however, saw the _____(8)_____ when he switched on his porch _____(9)_____, opened the front _____(10)_____ of his parsonage, and found standing there before him a big black _____(11)_____ with snow on his face, a human piece of night with snow on his face—obviously unemployed.

Langston Hughes, *Something in Common*

EDITING THE SIMPLE SENTENCE

The terms *revising, editing,* and *proofreading* are often used interchangeably and inaccurately. Yet each refers to a distinct part of the rewriting process. We talked in earlier chapters about the need to revise, to see what you have written from your reader's point of view and, if necessary, to make significant changes in the content and organization of what you have written. Revising often means adding new material, getting rid of unnecessary material, substituting, changing, and even starting over. As part of writing as well as rewriting, revision occurs throughout the composing process. You may think of an idea and discard it before you even begin to write. This too is revision.

Editing, in contrast, involves correcting, making more readable, and polishing what you have written. Good editors are concerned with their readers. They want to eliminate distracting errors, awkward constructions, and unclear, difficult-to-read passages—generally to refine and improve what they have written so that the reader can read it with understanding and even pleasure. Whereas revising is concerned with the essay or paragraph as a whole, editing is concerned with sentences and words.

Proofreading is the final step of the rewriting process. Only after a writer has revised and edited a paper should he or she be concerned with proofreading, which is essentially manuscript preparation. Proofreading is that final reading in which you try to alter your normal reading process so that you look at each word and mark of punctuation. It is an essential step in the composing process, for it eliminates small errors that can be distracting to a reader, but it should not be confused with revising and editing and should not occur until both have taken place.

Our concern in this section is primarily with editing. In order to be a good editor, a writer must understand sentences and how they are constructed well enough to identify errors in sentence structure, usage, and punctuation. In the pages that follow, we will discuss briefly some of the most common errors. You may not need to do all of the exercises in this editing section, but you will probably need to review the errors so that you can recognize them should they occur in your own writing.

Subject-Verb Agreement

The subject and verb of a sentence must agree in number. That is, if the subject is singular, the verb must be singular; if the subject is plural, the verb must be plural.

> He is an actor. (singular subject *he* and singular verb *is*)
>
> They are pals. (plural subject *they* and plural verb *are*)

This grammatical rule sounds simple enough to follow, and in most instances it is. In fact, with the exception of the verb *to be,* verbs do not change their forms to indicate number except in the present tense. In the past tense, for example, a verb has the same form in the singular and the plural.

> He walked home. (singular subject and verb)
>
> They walked home. (plural subject and verb)

Therefore, in order to master subject-verb agreement, you need primarily to study the present tense. Begin by looking carefully at the chart below, which gives you the different present-tense forms of a typical regular verb.

PRESENT TENSE OF *TO WALK*

Singular	**Plural**
First person: I walk	First person: we walk
Second person: you walk	Second person: you walk
Third person: he, she, it walks	Third person: they walk

Notice that an *s* is added to the third-person singular form.

Note: Adding an *s* or *es* to a noun makes the noun plural. However, an *s* ending on a verb indicates that the verb is singular.

> The boy walk*s* to school each day. (singular verb)
> The three boy*s* walk to school each day. (plural noun)

EXERCISE 9.12

Supply the correct third-person singular, present-tense form of the verbs indicated in the sentences below. Be sure that all of your verbs end in an *s*.

1. In the evening he always _____ at home.
    to eat

2. She _____ at the library on weekends.
    to work

3. Here he _____ now, late as usual.
    to come

4. He _____ at that corner for the bus each morning.
    to wait

5. She _____ in the chair by the window, watching for his
    to sit
    return.

Now examine carefully the present-tense forms of the three irregular verbs given below. Note especially the third-person singular, present-tense form of each of the verbs.

PRESENT TENSE OF *TO BE*

Singular	**Plural**
First person: I am	First person: we are
Second person: you are	Second person: you are
Third person: he, she, it is	Third person: they are

PRESENT TENSE OF *TO HAVE*

Singular	**Plural**
First person: I have	First person: we have
Second person: you have	Second person: you have
Third person: he, she, it has	Third person: they have

PRESENT TENSE OF *TO DO*

Singular	**Plural**
First person: I do	First person: we do
Second person: you do	Second person: you do
Third person: he, she, it does	Third person: they do

Notice that of these examples (*to be, to have, to do*) the verb *to be* is the most irregular. The other two verbs change their forms only in the third-person singular. Notice that these irregular verbs also end in *s* in the third-person singular. In fact, the only exceptions to this pattern are the auxiliaries *can, shall, may, will, ought,* and *must.* All other verbs end in *s* in the third-person singular present tense.

EXERCISE 9.13

Supply the correct present-tense form of the irregular verbs indicated in the sentences below. Refer to the charts given earlier if you are in doubt.

1. You _____ in a difficult situation.

_to be_

2. _____ she live in the dorm?

_To do_

3. They _____ several reasons for voting as they did.

to have

4. She _____ a friend of mine.

_to be_

5. In the morning, we _____ an appointment with the

to have

   dean.

6. It _____ not matter where you park your car.

_to do_

7. They _____ remaining on campus during vacation.

_to be_

8. _____ he been there before?

To have

9. She _____ the dishes by herself each evening.

_to do_

10. _____ they at home?

_To be_

Thus far you have been given sentences with pronouns as subjects. Look now at the following sentences, which all have noun subjects.

Joe has a tough schedule this semester.

Jogging is a popular form of exercise.

Children play in the park around the corner.

Now fill in the blanks in the sentences below, substituting the appropriate pronoun subjects for the deleted noun subjects.

_____ has a tough schedule this semester.

_____ is a popular form of exercise.

_____ play in the park around the corner.

The pronoun *he* can replace the noun *Joe* in the first sentence; the pronoun *it* can be substituted for the noun *jogging* in the second sentence; and the pronoun *they* can be used instead of the noun *children* as the subject of the third sentence. All of these pronouns are third-person singular or plural.

If your noun subject is third-person singular, your verb must also be singular. And if you are using a present-tense verb, be sure that the verb has an *s* ending. When you are in doubt about subject-verb agreement, substitute a pronoun for the noun subject; you are more likely to recognize errors in subject-verb agreement if the subject is a pronoun.

EXERCISE 9.14

In the sentences below some of the subjects are nouns and some are pronouns. Supply the correct *present-tense* form of the verbs indicated. If you are in doubt about the correct verb form, change the noun subject to a pronoun.

1. A few students _____ in honors courses each
   to enroll

   semester.

2. He _____ like his father.
   to look

3. Smoking _____ not allowed in this building.
   to be

4. The men _____ after the women leave.
   to enter

5. There _____ three new students in our class.
   to be

6. The chest _____ three drawers and a mirror.
   to have

7. My room _____ as if a storm hit it.
   to look

8. Mother _____ me each Friday.
   to visit

9. John, Sam, and Richard _____ new cars.
   to have

10. My sister _____ on the eight o'clock flight.
    to arrive

EXERCISE 9.15

The following sentences have plural subjects and plural verbs. In the space provided under each sentence, rewrite the sentence, changing the subject and verb so that both are singular.

EXAMPLE

My *children like* chocolate cake.

My *child likes* chocolate cake.

1. They have a major problem to solve at the office.

   _____

   _____

2. The streets badly need repairing.

   _____

   _____

3. The books have many illustrations.

   _____

   _____

4. Crossword puzzles are fun to work.

   _____

   _____

5. The phones ring almost constantly.

   _____

   _____

6. The secretaries take a break each morning.

   _____

   _____

7. His letters arrive promptly each morning.

   _____

   _____

8. The planes depart on time.

_____

_____

9. They often volunteer to work in the hospital.

_____

_____

10. Machines always break down at awkward moments.

_____

_____

EXERCISE 9.16

Errors in subject-verb agreement are more difficult to identify when they occur in the context of a paragraph. Read the following paragraph carefully. In it are ten subject-verb agreement errors. Edit the paragraph by underlining the ten verbs that do not agree with their subjects in number. Then correct the errors you identified.

Colleges and universities were once mainly attended by young, middle-class students who had just graduated from high school. Today campuses across the United States are populated with a variety of different types of students, many of whom are neither young, middle-class, or even American. Some of these new students come from lower socioeconomic backgrounds. Government loans enables them to attend college when once they would have been forced to get a job. In addition to students from lower economic backgrounds, U.S. colleges are also accepting increasing numbers of foreign students. A student do not have to be an American citizen to attend a college or a university in this country. One class may have students from several different foreign countries. Students today is also not necessarily young. If an older person decide to start college, he may discover that many of his classmates are also middle-aged or even older. Some of these students have been out of high school for ten to twenty years. Others never completed high school. Yet they seems capable of competing successfully with the young students. In fact, an older student often have an advantage over the young people in his classes because he have more experience and often are more highly motivated. These new students who are poorer, older, or not native Americans add variety and interest to our campuses. Although the new student have not replaced the traditional young high school graduate, he bring a new dimension to higher education in this country.

SPECIAL PROBLEMS WITH SUBJECT-VERB AGREEMENT

A subject and a verb must always agree in number, but in some cases the rule is difficult to apply. Some specific problems with subject-verb agreement are discussed below.

Indefinite Pronoun Subjects

Some indefinite pronouns take a singular verb even though they appear to be plural in meaning. Below is a list of indefinite pronouns that are singular.

anybody	nobody	neither
anyone	none	someone
anything	nothing	somebody
each	one	something
everybody	another	much
everyone	either	
everything		

The following sentences have singular indefinite pronouns as subjects. Notice that the verb in each of the sentences is singular to agree with the singular subject.

EXAMPLES

Everybody *studies* more than he does.

Someone *cares* about what happens to him.

Neither of them *is* invited.

Much of the information *comes* from Washington.

None of the students *listens* to the teacher.

Other indefinite pronouns, such as *few, many, both,* and *several,* are plural and, therefore, take plural verbs.

EXAMPLES

All of them *are* my friends.

Several *attend* the special study sessions.

Many *need* additional help.

A few of the indefinite pronouns can be either singular or plural, depending on their meaning. For example, *all* and *some* are usually considered plural, but if they refer to a mass instead of individual units, they are singular.

All of the cake *has* icing on it. (singular)

All of the puzzle pieces *are* missing. (plural)

Some of the snow *is* melting. (singular)

Some of the students *are* bored. (plural)

In addition, the indefinite pronoun *none* is frequently considered plural even though it means *no one.* Usage appears to be changing regarding this pronoun, and many educated speakers and writers now use *none* as a plural as well as a singular pronoun.

None of the cookies *are* left in the box.

EXERCISE 9.17

The following sentences have subjects that are indefinite pronouns. Provide the appropriate present-tense verbs.

1. Each of us _____wants_____ the same teacher.

to want

2. Few really _____like_____ them.

to like

3. Some of the new Chinese restaurants _____serves_____ hot,

to serve

   spicy food.

4. Nothing _____upsets_____ my boss more than my being late.

to upset

5. Somebody _____locks_____ the building at six o'clock each

to lock

   night.

Intervening Phrases

If a subject and a verb are separated by a phrase, the agreement between them is often difficult to determine.

> One *of the boys* dates a computer science major.

The subject of this sentence is *one;* therefore, the verb *dates* is singular. In this type of sentence, it is important to distinguish between the subject of the main verb and any nouns or pronouns that may be part of the phrase that occurs between the subject and verb.

EXERCISE 9.18

Supply the correct present-tense verb in the following sentences.

1. Marie, rejecting the offers of both Ann and Joan,

   _____*rides*_____ to class with John.

to ride

2. Another of my friends _____*has*_____ a new car.

to have

3. That student, in spite of his teacher's warnings,

   _____*is*_____ absent again.

to be

4. One of our new neighbors _____*comes*_____ from Micronesia.

to come

5. The noise of the airplanes _____*causes*_____ the residents

to cause

   much concern.

Compound Subjects

A compound subject is one in which two or more nouns or pronouns are joined by coordinating conjunctions (*and, or, nor*). Subjects joined by *and* are usually plural.

> The table and chair *are* both for sale.

Subjects joined by *nor* and *or* are usually singular.

> The coach or the trainer *is* with the injured player.
> Neither Mary nor Sue *plans* to graduate this semester.

However, if both the subjects joined by *or* or *nor* are plural, then a plural verb should be used.

> Tapes or records *are* available.

If *or* or *nor* joins one singular subject and one plural subject, the verb agrees with the nearer subject.

The teacher or the students *are* always unhappy.

The students or the teacher *is* always unhappy.

EXERCISE 9.19

Choose the correct present-tense form of the verb indicated in the sentences below.

1. Both my uncle and my aunt _____*plan*_____ to come to the

to plan

   wedding.

2. The choir members and their director _____*travel*_____ to Rus-

to travel

   sia each summer.

3. The mare and colt _____*seem*_____ healthy.

to seem

4. Neither my fears nor my anger _____*is*_____ justified.

to be

5. The veterinarian or his assistants _____*check*_____ on the ani-

to check

   mals each evening.

Inverted Sentence Order

Sentences in which the subject does *not* come before the verb also present special problems with subject-verb agreement.

EXAMPLES

Where are the vegetables you cooked? (vegetables *are*)

Where is the shirt you ironed? (shirt *is*)

In the door flies a bright yellow canary. (canary *flies*)

In the door fly several small birds. (birds *fly*)

There are three reasons I can't go. (reasons *are*)

There is a good reason for his not coming. (reason *is*)

EXERCISE 9.20

In each of the following sentences, locate the subject and underline it. Then choose the correct present-tense form of the verb indicated.

1. There _____*are*_____ several reasons why the plan failed.

to be

2. Under the bed _____sleeps_____ an enormous cat.
   to sleep

3. _____Have_____ the computers been installed?
   to have

4. _____Does_____ the captain always obey his orders?
   to do

5. Here _____comes_____ the bus.
   to come

EXERCISE 9.21

The following paragraph contains ten errors in subject-verb agreement. Edit the paragraph by underlining the incorrect verb forms and then writing the correct verb forms above them.

Science fiction shows on television provides a look into the future. These programs take a writer's dreams about the future and makes them seem real to the television viewers. The remarkable thing about these shows is that what the television audience considered science fiction twenty or thirty years ago is science reality today. In the fifties and sixties, for example, robots and computers began to appear on television. Now everyone consider these marvels of technology rather commonplace. Industry, as well as our homes, are increasingly dependent upon computers. And even robots are fairly commonplace in our complex society. They may not look like the ones on the early science fiction shows, but they can do basically the same things. Early television also showed man in space years before he actually accomplished this remarkable feat. Neither television nor its viewers was aware that within a few years our astronauts would actually be able to orbit the earth in space ships. Today movies on television often portrays man moving across the galaxies, visiting various planets. There is several reasons to expect that this fantasy too will come true in the near future. It will not be long before our technology, together with our talented scientists, have us to the point that we are ready to undertake these types of space voyages. Not all the science fiction shows on television becomes a reality, but many of them seem to be a reliable prediction of what the future hold.

Bill McRee, student

Pronoun Reference and Agreement

Since a pronoun is a noun substitute, it must always refer specifically to some noun. The noun to which a pronoun refers is called the *antecedent*. A pronoun must always agree with its antecedent in number (singular or plural), gender (masculine, feminine, or neuter), and person (first, second, or third).

EXERCISE 9.22

Correct any pronoun agreement errors in the following sentences.

1. A person will have to learn a lot if ~~you~~ *he* expect to graduate from college.

_____

_____

2. A good student learns to ignore stress and just ~~enjoy themselves.~~ *enjoys himself*

_____

_____

3. Most people have met someone who is at their low when they are free of pressure.

_____

_____

4. Homesickness, a worry that affects everyone at some time or another in ~~their lives,~~ *his life* is especially prevalent among college students.

_____

_____

5. The student is away from the security of friends at home and has to make it socially on their own.

_____

_____

_____

INDEFINITE PRONOUNS

Indefinite pronouns are always third person and have only one form, but problems sometimes arise in using these pronouns if the writer does not know which are singular and which are plural.

SINGULAR INDEFINITE PRONOUNS

everybody	one
everyone	someone
each	somebody
anyone	nobody
anybody	everything
neither	nothing
none	

PLURAL INDEFINITE PRONOUNS

all	any
some	both
few	none
several	

If an indefinite pronoun functions as the antecedent of another pronoun, that pronoun must agree with it in number.

> *Everyone* left *his* shoes outside the door. (singular pronouns)
> *All* of them left *their* shoes outside the door. (plural pronouns)

EXERCISE 9.23

In the following sentences, correct the pronoun agreement errors.

1. Both must apply for his own parking ticket. *their*

_____

_____

2. Does anybody know their Spanish well enough to translate this joke?

(his)

3. Each of the routes has their advantages.

(its)

4. How can anyone enjoy themselves in this miserable place?

(himself)

5. The teacher wants everybody to furnish their own paper and pencil.

(his)

RELATIVE AND DEMONSTRATIVE PRONOUNS

The problem in using demonstrative (*this, that, these,* and *those*) and relative pronouns (*who, whom, which, what,* and *that*) is that a writer sometimes fails to have a clear antecedent for these pronouns.

I had to wait two hours *which* made me angry.

Two hours is not the antecedent of the pronoun *which;* rather the "waiting" made the writer angry. But because the pronoun does not have a clear antecedent, the sentence is unclear and awkward. The sentence can be rewritten to express the same idea more clearly by eliminating the unclear pronoun *which.*

Because I had to wait two hours, I was angry.

The reason I was angry is that I had to wait two hours.

Note: In using relative pronouns, it is also important to remember that *who* refers only to people, *which* refers only to animals and inanimate objects, and *that* refers to people, animals, or objects.

EXERCISE 9.24

Correct the pronoun reference errors in the following sentences.

1. We found the gun in his car which suggests he is guilty.

_____

_____

2. The person which called failed to give his name.

_____

_____

3. Jim told Tom a lie. This caused a lot of trouble.

_____

_____

4. I frequently called home long distance, which annoyed my father.

_____

_____

5. My friend often works in her garden, which is obvious.

_____

_____

Using Nonsexist Pronouns

Since pronouns frequently indicate gender, a writer is often faced with a decision about which gender to choose if the sex of the antecedent is not apparent. Traditionally, masculine pronouns were used when the sex of the antecedent was not stated.

A *teacher* should motivate *his* students.

However, this solution is increasingly considered unacceptable. A fairer practice is to alternate masculine and feminine pronouns.

A *teacher* should motivate *her* students.

Or you can use both the masculine and feminine pronouns.

A *teacher* should motivate *his* or *her* students.

Using both pronouns is perhaps fairer, but the result is somewhat awkward and wordy. Another way to solve this problem is to use the plural form of the noun and thus avoid the dilemma completely.

Teachers should motivate *their* students.

Consistency in Point of View

The most frequently used pronouns are the personal pronouns, which have various forms to indicate number, gender, and person.

	Singular	**Plural**
First person	I (me, my)	we (us, our)
Second person	you (your)	you (your)
Third person	he, she, it (him, his, her, its)	they (them)

First-person pronouns (*I* and *we*) always refer to the person who is speaking or writing. The second person (*you*), which is the same in the singular and plural, refers to the person spoken to or addressed (the audience). The third-person pronouns (*he, she, it,* and *they*) refer to a person or thing spoken or written about.

EXAMPLES

I need to exercise each day because I feel better when I am active. (first-person point of view)

You need to exercise each day because you feel better when you are active. (second-person point of view)

People need to exercise each day because they feel better when they are active. (third-person point of view)

When you are writing, it is important to be consistent in your point of view. If you choose to write from the first-person point of view (*I* or *we*), you must use this point of view throughout your paper. Avoid shifting casually from one point of view to another unless there is a good reason for doing so. In some types of formal writing, first- and second-person points of view are not often used. In fact, it is usually best to avoid using a second-person point of view (you) unless you are giving directions or explaining a process.

Revise the following sentences to eliminate unnecessary shifts in point of view.

1. I like math because it is easy for me, and you can grasp it on your own.

   _____

   _____

2. When we had received our sheets and blankets, we were shown how to make one's bed according to army regulations.

   _____

   _____

3. I need to improve my writing skills. To be able to express yourself in writing is of great importance.

   _____

   _____

4. Graduation, to me, marks the beginning of a new life, a demanding life, from which a person can expect to receive only as much as you give.

   _____

   _____

   _____

5. I want to learn all the rules you need to know in order to stay out of trouble with the authorities.

   _____

   _____

EXERCISE 9.26

Correct the following paragraph using the third-person plural point of view consistently.

Every teacher needs a broad liberal arts education as well as training in a special area of study. You must be prepared to face a variety of challenges in a classroom for which a narrow, specialized education is inadequate. For example, if you are a teacher of social studies, you also need to know something about literature, art, and music. I think that I will use the courses I have had in my general studies program as much as I will those that I have taken in my major. A teacher cannot be too well prepared. The students whom they teach will depend on you to answer a variety of questions and to be knowledgeable about the world in general.

Consistency in Tense

When you are writing, you should be consistent in your use of tense (i.e., the time at which the stated action or being takes place). If you start a paragraph or essay in the present tense, you should keep it in the present; if you start in the past tense, you should keep it in the past. Generally, you should avoid a shift in tense unless a shift is supported by the context of your material. Unnecessary and awkward shifts in tense, such as those in the following example, can confuse your reader:

> The plumber installs the new faucets, will repair the drain, and connected the disposal.

This sentence is confusing because the writer shifts needlessly from the present tense (*installs*) to the future tense (*will repair*) to the past tense (*connected*). Since these actions occurred at approximately the same time, the tense of all three verbs should be the same, as illustrated in the edited sentences below.

> The plumber installs the new faucets, repairs the drain, and connects the disposal. (present tense)
>
> The plumber installed the new faucets, repaired the drain, and connected the disposal. (past tense)
>
> The plumber will install the new faucet, repair the drain, and connect the disposal. (future tense)

However, as the following example shows, changing tenses is permissible if the context indicates that the events or actions occurred at different times.

> The plumber installed the new faucets yesterday, is repairing the drain today, and will connect the disposal tomorrow. (present, past, and future tense)

Do not confuse your readers by changing tenses unless a shift is clearly justified.

EXERCISE 9.27

Underline any needless shifts in tense that you find in the following sentences. Rewrite the sentences correctly.

1. The war was horrible, and anyone who goes through it had to endure great hardships.

   _____

   _____

2. The plane passes over the highway and barely missed the tower.

   _____

   _____

3. The concert started at 8:00 P.M., will last two hours, and ends at 10:00 P.M.

   _____

   _____

   _____

4. Out of the jungle creeps a large spotted leopard, which turned suddenly when he sees the hunters on the other side of the river.

   _____

   _____

   _____

5. The planning committee met every Wednesday for three weeks and decides on the projected goals for the next year.

   _____

   _____

EXERCISE 9.28

The following paragraph is in the present tense. Correct it by changing it to the past tense. Be sure your use of tense is consistent.

The peoples of North Africa gain independence after World War II. For Algeria in particular the struggle is long and bitter. The independent countries introduce programs of modernization, but their approaches differ. Tunisia and Morocco develop trade ties with Western Europe and the United States. Both gain considerable income from tourists. Algeria adopts some features of socialism; most of its industry is taken over by the state. It benefits from rich deposits of natural gas. The Algerian government invests in education with good results.

Adapted from Marvin Perry, *Unfinished Journey: A World History*

READING/WRITING ASSIGNMENT 9A

ELVIS IS DEAD
Lewis Grizzard

Pre-Reading/Writing Exercise

For each of us, certain events in our lives stand out as being especially significant. Some of these events, like Maya Angelou's graduation (Reading/Writing Assignment 2A), represent an important change in our personal lives. Others, however, affect not only each of us personally but also those around us. For example, the death of a relative can affect an entire family, and events such as the bombing of Pearl Harbor, the death of Martin Luther King, Jr., or the explosion of the space shuttle *Challenger* can influence the lives of an entire generation. Brainstorm for a few minutes about events that have affected not only you but also those around you.

Discuss your brainstorming, comparing your ideas with those of the other members of your class. Then freewrite, or write a journal entry, about the importance one of these events had for you and those around you—your friends, your family, or your entire generation.

Reading Exercise

In the narrative passage below, Lewis Grizzard writes about hearing of Elvis Presley's death while visiting with friends on the beach. As you read, think about the effect that Elvis's life and death had on Grizzard and his generation.

1 I remember distinctly that it was Franklin who went back to the condo to get more beer. I also remember distinctly that the month was August and the year was 1977. We had the radio playing. It was a country station.

2 Franklin was gone thirty minutes. When he came back, he had another twelve-pack. He also had a troubled look on his face.

3 "What took you so long?" Price asked him. "You didn't call Sweet Thing back home, did you?"

4 "You're not going to believe what I just heard on television," he answered.

5 I had just taken the first pull on my fresh beer when I heard him utter three incredible words.

6 "Elvis is dead," he said.

7 *Elvis is dead.* The words didn't fit somehow. The queen of England is dead. There has been a revolution in South America and the dictator is dead. Some rock singer has been found in his hotel room with a needle in his arm and he is dead. All that made sense, but not *Elvis is dead.*

8 "They figure he had a heart attack," said the bad news bearer.

9 A heart attack? Elvis Presley couldn't have a heart attack. He was too young to have a heart attack. He was too young to have anything like that. Elvis Presley was my idol when I was a kid. Elvis changed my life. Elvis turned on my entire generation. I saw *Love Me Tender* three times. He died in *Love Me Tender,* but that was just a movie.

10 I figured this was some sort of joke. Right, Elvis Presley had a heart attack. And where did they find the body? In Heartbreak Hotel, of course.

11 The music had stopped on the radio. A man was talking.

12 "Elvis Presley is dead," said the voice. "He was forty-two."

13 Forty-two? That had to be wrong, too. How could he be that old? Elvis had to be younger than that. He was one of us, wasn't he? If he was forty-two, maybe he could have had a heart attack. If he was over forty, that meant he probably had wrinkles and maybe his hair had already fallen out and he had been wearing a wig.

14 But if Elvis Presley was forty-two and old enough to die, what did that say about me and the generation he had captured? He had been what separated us from our parents. He had been our liberator. He played the background music while we grew up.

15 *Elvis is dead.* Suddenly, I didn't feel so good myself.

Lewis Grizzard, *Elvis Is Dead And I Don't Feel So Good Myself*

1. Because narratives are stories, they may be written primarily to entertain and may not include a stated main idea, or thesis. However, a narrative is often used to support a stated or implied thesis. Is Grizzard's purpose to entertain or to make a point?

If Grizzard's purpose is to make a point, is his thesis stated or implied?

_____

_____

What is his thesis? _____

_____

2. Notice how Grizzard uses details to make his narrative realistic. Write below some particularly effective factual and sensory details from the passage.

a. Factual details: _____

_____

b. Sensory details: _____

_____

3. Notice that Grizzard records the dialogue, or conversations, of his characters. What effect does this use of dialogue have on the narrative?

_____

_____

Notice, too, how the dialogue is punctuated. Each statement is enclosed in quotation marks with commas, periods, and question marks placed within the quotation marks.

Examples: "What took you so long?" Price asked him.

"You're not going to believe what I just heard on television," he answered.

4. When you have an informal discussion with your friends, your language is informal. For example, you discuss your "dorm room" rather than your "dormitory room," and you complain about going to "chem lab" rather than "the chemistry laboratory." Similarly, Grizzard's language recreates the informal atmosphere of the afternoon with his friends. List several informal words or phrases Grizzard uses:

_____

5. Grizzard uses a series of short, simple sentences to record his immediate thoughts after he hears about Elvis's death. These short sentences are effective because they suggest that Grizzard was shocked—unable to con-

nect his thoughts into more complex statements. In addition, Grizzard uses a short, simple sentence to emphasize the high point, or climax, of the narrative. What is this sentence?

_____

6. At what point does Grizzard accept the reality of Elvis's death?

_____

What does Elvis's death make Grizzard realize about himself and his generation?

_____

7. What effect has Elvis's life and death had on Grizzard and his friends?

_____

_____

_____

Discussion Questions

1. Can you think of a well-known person—perhaps a singer like Elvis—who has influenced the lives of you and your friends as Elvis did Grizzard and his friends?

2. What important events have influenced you and your generation?

Writing Exercise

Write a narrative paragraph or essay about an event that had a significant effect not only on your life but also on the lives of those around you—your friends, your family, or your entire generation. The event may have directly influenced your lives, or, as in Grizzard's essay, it may have made you more aware of changes that had already taken place in your lives. Your purpose is to explain the significance of the event through your narrative. You may state your thesis at the beginning of your narrative, or you may lead into your thesis as Grizzard does.

For this assignment, you should specify your audience. For example, if you have been in an accident involving a drunk driver, you might write to a driver education class to illustrate the dangers of drunk driving. Or, if you are old enough to remember the assassination of John F. Kennedy or Martin Luther King, you might narrate one of these events to today's youth to illustrate the significance the event had on you and your generation. After you have decided on your specific purpose, thesis, and audience, write your rough draft.

Rewriting Exercise

Reread your draft carefully to see whether you have achieved your purpose and communicated to your audience. Answer the following questions independently or in a peer review group.

1. What is your primary purpose?

2. Who is your audience?

3. What is your main idea (topic sentence or thesis)? Is it effectively stated or implied?

4. What are the major supporting details in your narrative? Do you include both factual and sensory details? If your narrative needs more support, what other details can you add? Are all of the details of your narrative related to your thesis? Which, if any, should be deleted?

5. How are your details arranged? (The most common narrative arrangement is *chronological*—the order in which the events occurred—but you may use a "flashback" arrangement if you wish.) If the arrangement is confusing, how can it be improved?

6. What types of transition have you used? What transition, if any, should you add?

7. Does your narrative contain dialogue? If so, is it punctuated properly? If not, what dialogue can you add to improve your narrative?

8. What kind of conclusion does your narrative have?

After you have made the major revisions needed in your draft, edit it carefully. As you edit, consider the following questions. (You may want to read your composition aloud to help you *hear* your mistakes.)

1. Is each sentence a complete sentence, with a subject and a verb?

2. Do you have any errors in subject-verb agreement?

3. Do you have any errors in pronoun reference or agreement?

4. What tense have you used? Is your use of tense consistent?

5. What point of view have you used (first person, second person, third person)? Is your point of view consistent?

6. Is your level of usage (formal or informal) appropriate to your purpose and audience?

7. Do you have any misspelled words?

8. Do you have any additional errors in capitalization, punctuation, grammar, or usage?

After you have edited your narrative, write your final draft and proofread it carefully.

TELEVISION FANTASIES
Peggy Charren and Martin W. Sandler

Pre-Reading/Writing Exercise

Think for a few minutes about the influence of television on your life and the lives of others. How much time do you spend watching television each week? Do you watch television more or less than the average viewer? What kinds of shows do you watch? How is life represented by these shows? How is life represented by television commercials? By news programs? As one idea generates another, map your ideas on a blank sheet of paper (see Reading/Writing Assignment 4A for a review of mapping).

Writing Exercise

Peggy Charren and Martin Sandler suggest that television presents an unrealistic picture of life, a fantasy world. Read the passage below to discover what aspects of life, according to the authors, are misrepresented or oversimplified by television.

1   The world according to television is a world of extremes. There are very few shades of gray in TV's world of fantastic feats, crucial moments, and urgent emotions. Most television characters are either beautiful or ugly, benevolent or ruthless. In TV's world neither the people nor the situations are average, for average is dull and dull doesn't draw ratings.

2   For people who watch a lot of TV, programs set up expectations that life and the process of everyday living resemble what they see on their sets. When our day-to-day existence turns out to be not as simple, not as neatly packaged, not as happy, as that portrayed on TV, frustration and tension are often the result. When the real world doesn't mesh with expectations set by watching TV, we believe there is something wrong with us. This is particularly true for those who have limited life experiences. For these viewers, television provides almost all of the information they receive about people with life-styles different from their own.

3   The world of television is one in which, according to a study by George Gerbner, policemen, doctors, lawyers, judges and law-breakers outnumber all other working people combined. On TV there are almost no clerical workers, salespeople, artists, or engineers. And blue collar workers, the largest segment of the working force in the real world, are nearly invisible. The result is that heavy TV-watchers and children come to know more about spies, coroners, and small-town sheriffs than they do about those who carry out the basic tasks in American society.

4   In the world of television, police and private detectives alike fill their days with devil-may-care car chases, shoot-ups, and amorous adventures.

The real world is far less glamorous: police handle plenty of traffic violations and domestic problems, and private detectives chase debtors, look for missing people, and shadow straying husbands and wives. Television's private eyes regularly solve crimes and bring criminals to justice; most real private detectives have little to do with the actual solving of major crimes.

5   And, of course, TV's men in blue always get their man, with a speed unprecedented in the annals of real life, since loose ends must be neatly tied by the close of the thirty- or sixty-minute segment. What of the long hours, mundane tasks, and many frustrations that plague real-life law enforcers, what of the bad guys who never get caught? Where are they on TV? . . .

6   The typical action-adventure shows that feature private detectives, police, or other law enforcement agencies are put together by highly skilled writers, producers, and technicians. Actual police or FBI buildings are shown. Locales around the world are used and identifiable landmarks are featured. Official badges and uniforms are commonplace. Often we are told that the episode is based on some actual case (only the names have been changed to protect the innocent), and at the end of some of these programs we are even informed as to what sentence was given to the "actual criminals." All of this gives an air of authenticity to these series, increasing problems for viewers who have difficulty distinguishing between the truth and the fantasy world of TV.

7   These misconceptions cause trouble in the real world of lawyer's offices and courtrooms. Lawyers around the country report increased difficulty conveying to clients just what they as lawyers can and cannot accomplish. If Perry Mason can wrap up a case successfully in an hour, why can't they? And many legal officials are concerned that jurors will expect clearcut resolutions of cases as a result of TV lawyers' freeing their clients by breaking down witnesses on the stand and then pointing to the actual criminal before the startled eyes of judge and jury.

Peggy Charren and Martin W. Sandler, *Changing Channels: Living (Sensibly) with Television*

1. What is Charren and Sandler's thesis? _____

_____

_____

Is it stated or implied? _____

2. "Television Fantasies" explains how unrealistic television shows (causes) produce unrealistic expectations (effects) in the viewers. The primary method of development in the essay, then, is cause and effect. In the spaces below, list the method(s) of development used in each separate paragraph:

Paragraph 1 _____

Paragraph 2 _____

Paragraph 3 _____

Paragraph 4 _____

Paragraph 5 _____

Paragraph 6 _____

Paragraph 7 _____

3. According to the authors, what specific aspects of life are misrepresented or oversimplified by television?

_____

_____

_____

_____

4. Use the following word parts to help you figure out the meanings of the words listed below (remember that a prefix changes the meaning of a root word, whereas a suffix affects the word's function or part of speech):

Prefixes	Root	Suffix
bene = good, well	*amor* = love	*-ed* = past tense (v.)
con- = with, together	*ced* = go	*-ous* = full of (adj.)
	cep = take	*-tion* = act of (n.)
mis- = bad	*vol* = wish	*-ent* = characterized
pre- = before		by (adj.)
un- = not		

a. benevolent _____

_____

b. amorous _____

_____

c. misconception _____

_____

d. unprecedented _____

_____

Discussion Questions

1. An *addict* is someone who has a habitual and compulsive attraction to a particular substance or activity. We usually use this word to refer to drug addicts or alcoholics, but television can also be addicting. Are you addicted to television, or do you know someone who is? Does the television addict you know watch only certain types of shows or just whatever happens to be on at the time? What are the immediate effects of television addiction? What are the long-range effects?

2. The authors state that problems appear to be easily resolved on television because "loose ends must be neatly tied by the close of the thirty- or sixty-minute segment." What effect does this apparently easy resolution have on the viewer's—especially the young viewer's—perception of life? Do some shows give a more realistic picture of life? Give examples.

3. The authors argue that television programs present an unrealistic view of life. What about television commercials? Do they contribute to an unrealistic and even stereotyped view of life? Give examples.

4. Do news reports always give the news accurately and completely? Give examples.

5. The authors of this passage focus on the negative aspects of television programming. What are some positive aspects of television?

Writing Exercise

Look back at your mapping and at your reading exercise on television. Then select two or three issues about television that particularly interest you and write them below:

_____

_____

_____

Your assignment is to try to convince the programming director of your local television station or of a national network to agree with you about a particular programming decision. For your specific purpose, you might try to persuade the director to return to the air a program that has been cancelled, you might try to get another program or commercial cut, you might try to get the number of situation comedies or Saturday morning cartoons reduced, or you might attempt to influence the choice of topics for feature stories on your local news.

Whatever your purpose, be sure to state your thesis clearly and directly and to support it with good reasons or examples arranged in a logical order—perhaps in order of importance (see Chapter 6). After you have decided on your purpose, write in paragraph or essay form the rough draft of your "letter." Because of the education and prestige of the person to whom you are writing, use a relatively formal level of usage, both in word choice and in sentence style.

Rewriting Exercise

Reread your draft considering the following questions.

1. What is your purpose?
2. Who is your audience?
3. What is your main idea (topic sentence or thesis statement)? Is it clearly stated or implied?
4. What method(s) of development have you used?
5. What are your major supporting points? What additional support can you include? Which supporting points, if any, should be deleted?
6. How have you arranged your supporting points (time order, space order, order of importance)?
7. What types of transition have you used? What additional transitions should you include?
8. Are your word choices and sentence style appropriate for your audience, a well-educated director of programming? (Remember that a busy director will have little patience with unnecessary or inappropriate words or with a dull, unvaried sentence style.) How can you improve your word choice and sentence style?
9. What kind of conclusion did you use? How can you improve it?
10. Does your letter achieve its purpose? That is, will it persuade the director to consider your request seriously? If not, how can you improve it?

After you have made the major revisions needed in your draft, edit it carefully. As you edit, consider the following questions. (You may want to reread your composition for each question, thus keeping only one editing task in mind at a time.)

1. Is each sentence a complete sentence, with a subject and a verb?
2. Do you have any errors in subject-verb agreement?
3. Do you have any errors in pronoun reference or agreement?
4. What tense have you used? Is your use of tense consistent?
5. What point of view have you used (first person, second person, third person)? Is your point of view consistent?
6. Is your level of usage formal enough for your purpose and audience?
7. Do you have any misspelled words?
8. Do you have any additional errors in capitalization, punctuation, grammar, or usage?

After you have finished editing, write your final draft, and proofread it carefully.

Chapter 10

MODIFICATION: EXPANDING THE SIMPLE SENTENCE

One of the most important ways we expand the basic elements of a simple sentence is by using modifiers—words and phrases that describe, limit, point out, identify, and make more specific the words they modify. Although modifiers are not an essential part of a sentence, they add information to the basic elements of the sentence. Without modifiers we could communicate only general ideas.

EXAMPLES

Armadillos dig. (basic elements unmodified)

Two large armadillos dig ruthlessly in my yard every night. (basic elements modified)

Adding modifiers to the basic elements in the second example makes the sentence much more specific and vivid. We now know *how many* armadillos, the *size* of the armadillos, and *how, where,* and *when* they dig.

ADJECTIVES

Adjectives are modifiers of nouns or noun substitutes and can be divided into several types.

1. *Indefinite adjectives* limit the nouns they modify, usually by restricting the amount or number. Look at the following list of frequently used indefinite adjectives:

some	every	much
many	each	most
other	all	another
few	any	several

Notice in the following sentences how the indefinite adjectives limit in some way the nouns they modify.

269

EXAMPLES

Some restaurants stay open *all* night.

Several photographers and a *few* reporters were seen at *each* meeting.

Few, if *any,* policemen were at the *other* riot.

Notice also that an indefinite adjective always comes before the noun it modifies.

2. *Demonstrative adjectives* identify or point out. There are only four demonstrative adjectives—*this, that, these,* and *those*—and they too occur before the noun they modify.

EXAMPLES

This class is as boring as *that* one.

These sandwiches are stale and soggy.

He selected *those* roses for his garden.

3. *Descriptive adjectives,* as their name implies, describe the nouns they modify. They usually occur before the noun but may occur in a variety of positions.

EXAMPLES

The *sleek, shiny antique* car was *spotless.*

Sleek and *shiny,* the *antique* car was *spotless.*

The *antique* car, *sleek* and *shiny,* was *spotless.*

Spotless was the *sleek, shiny antique* car.

As a writer, you should be aware of the options you have in placing descriptive adjectives. Try to vary your basic sentence patterns by placing descriptive adjectives in different positions. Notice, as in the examples above, that the meaning, rhythm, and emphasis of each sentence are altered slightly by the changes in the placement of the adjectives.

4. *Participles* are verb forms used as adjectives. For example, the verb *shake* has a present participle form, *shaking,* and a past participle form, *shaken.* Both of the participle forms can be used as part of a verb phrase that functions as the main verb of a sentence.

EXAMPLES

The old man *is shaking* his fist at us.

The medicine *was shaken* thoroughly.

They can also be used as adjectives.

EXAMPLES

The *shaking* child ran to her mother's waiting arms.

The child, *shaking,* ran to her mother.

Shaking and crying, the child ran to her mother.

The old man, pale and *shaken,* sat down carefully

Shaken by the accident, the woman began to cry.

Notice in these examples the different positions that a participle may take in relation to the word it modifies. In your own writing, try to vary the position of the participles you use.

In the following example and in Exercise 10.1, you are given a series of short simple sentences. Using the first sentence as your basic sentence pattern, reduce the sentences that follow to modifiers that can be used to expand the basic sentence.

EXAMPLE

The wall stretched for miles.

The wall was granite.

The granite was gray.

The wall was thick.

The miles were endless.

Combinations: The thick, gray granite wall stretched for endless miles.

focus

Thick and gray, the granite wall stretched for endless miles.

The granite wall, thick and gray, stretched for endless miles.

Notice that several combinations are possible. There is no single correct combination. Try to think of as many different combinations as you can, and then choose the one you like best. You may want to say some of the combinations aloud before deciding on your choice. Try to vary the positions of your adjectives so they do not all come before the nouns they modify.

Punctuation Note: Notice that adjectives that do not come before the nouns they modify are set off by commas.

The quilt, torn and ragged, lay on the bed.

Notice also that if a series of adjectives precedes a noun, a comma is inserted between the adjectives if they are coordinate (equal). Test for coordination by inserting the word *and* between the adjectives. If the resulting construction makes sense, then you should insert a comma.

The torn and ragged quilt lay on the bed.

This construction makes sense; therefore, you can omit the *and* and use a comma between the adjectives.

The torn, ragged quilt lay on the bed.

But notice what happens if we insert *and* between the two adjectives in the following sentence.

The careless and young man failed to signal as he turned.

In this sentence, *careless* and *young* are not coordinate; a comma is therefore not necessary.

The careless young man failed to signal as he turned.

EXERCISE 10.1

Combine the following sentences; discuss punctuation possibilities with your instructor or classmates.

1. The girl slept in the bed.
    The girl was young.
    The girl was pretty.
    The bed was old.
    The bed was ugly.

    The (pretty young) girl slept in the old, ugly bed

    The girl, young and pretty, slept in the old, ugly be

2. The groundhog peeked out of his hole.
    The groundhog was shy.
    The groundhog was shaggy.
    The hole was private.

    The groundhog, shy and shaggy, peeked out of his
    private house

    The shy, shaggy groundhog peeked out of his private hol

3. The dancers kept time to the music.
    The dancers were moving energetically.
    The music was loud.
    The music was pulsating.

    The loud, pulsating music

    The energetically dancers were moving to the loud pulsating
    kept time   music

    The dancers, energitically, kept time to the load, pulsating music

4. The candle went out.
   The candle was sputtering.
   The candle was hissing.

   The sputtering hissing candle went out

   The candle, sputtering and hissing, went out

   Sputtering and hissing, the candle went out

5. The woman was visiting her aunt.
   The aunt was her favorite.
   The woman was middle-aged.
   The woman was dutiful.

   The middle-aged dutiful woman was visiting her aunt

6. He finished the book.
   The book was long.
   The book was boring.

7. My laundry is piling up again.
   My laundry is dirty.
   My laundry is stinking.
   My laundry is inconsiderate.

8. The child looked into the box.
   The child was curious.
   The box was tiny.
   The box was carved.
   The box was wooden.

_____

_____

9. The bull rider shot out of the chute.
   The rider was shouting.
   The rider was waving his hat.
   The chute was open.

_____

_____

_____

10. The nurse checked his watch.
    The nurse was sniffing.
    The nurse was clucking.
    The nurse was starched.
    The nurse was efficient.
    The watch was large.
    The watch was waterproof.

_____

_____

_____

EXERCISE 10.2

Adjectives have been deleted from the following passage. Replace the blanks with appropriate adjectives.

It was a beautiful college. The buildings were _____ and
                                                    (1)
covered with vines and the roads gracefully winding, lined with hedges
and wild roses that dazzled the eyes in the _____ sun. Honey-
                                                  (2)
suckle and _____ wisteria hung heavy from the trees
                  (3)
and _____ magnolias mixed with their scents in the
          (4)
_____ air. I've recalled it often, here in my hole: How the grass
     (5)
turned _____ in the springtime and how the mockingbirds flut-
              (6)
tered their tails and sang, how the moon shone down on the buildings, how

the bell in the chapel tower rang out the precious short-lived hours; how the girls in _____ (7) summer dresses promenaded the _____ (8) lawn. Many times, here at night, I've closed my eyes and walked along the _____ (9) road that winds past the girls' dormitories, past the hall with the clock in the tower, its windows warmly _____ (10), on down past the _____ (11) white Home Economics practice cottage, whiter still in the moonlight, and on down the road with its sloping and turning, paralleling the _____ (12) power-house with its engines droning earth-shaking rhythms in the dark, its windows _____ (13) from the glow of the furnace, on to where the road became a bridge over a _____ (14) riverbed, tangled with brush and _____ (15) vines; the bridge of rustic logs, made for trysting, but virginal and untested by lovers; on up the road, past the buildings, with the _____ (16) verandas half-a-city-block long, to the sudden forking, barren of buildings, birds, or grass, where the road turned off to the insane asylum.

Ralph Ellison, *Invisible Man*

ADVERBS

Another way of expanding basic sentence patterns is by using adverbs to modify the verb of the sentence. Although adverbs can also modify other modifiers or even entire sentences, they usually give additional information about the verb of a sentence. Adverbs that modify verbs tell *how* (in what manner), *when*, or *where*.

The student entered the classroom *late*. (when)
They went *home* after the party. (where)
The moon rose *slowly* and *majestically*. (how)

Adverbs do not necessarily occur either immediately before or after the verbs they modify, although they may occur in these positions. Notice that in the third example, the adverbs *slowly* and *majestically* occur after the verb *rose.* However, these adverbs could be shifted to the beginning of the sentence.

> *Slowly* and *majestically,* the moon rose.

Adverbs, especially those that end in -*ly,* can be shifted from one position in the sentence to another. However, when adverbs are placed at the beginning of the sentence rather than in their normal position after the verb, they are usually followed by a comma.

EXERCISE 10.3

Following is a series of short simple sentences. Using the first sentence as your basic pattern, reduce the other sentences to adverbs and use them to expand the basic sentence. Remember to vary the placement of your adverbs.

1. The walrus waddled.
    The waddling was comical (ly).
    The waddling was clumsy (ly).
    The waddling was backward.

    _____

    _____

    _____

2. The guitarist played.
    The playing was soft (ly).
    The playing was steady (ly).
    The playing was all evening.

    _____

    _____

    _____

3. The plant grew.
    The growing was unexpected (ly).
    The growing was sudden (ly).

    _____

    _____

    _____

4. The president spoke to the press.
   The press was eager.
   The speaking was serious (ly).
   The speaking was unpretentious (ly).

   _____

   _____

   _____

5. Alice rode the motorcycle.
   The riding was fearless (ly).
   The riding was natural (ly).
   The riding was along the trail.

   _____

   _____

   _____

6. The wind blew.
   The blowing was constant (ly).
   The blowing was relentless (ly). *without pity*
   The blowing was day and night.

   Day and night, the wind blew constantly and relentlessly

   Constantly and relentlessly, the wind blew day and night

   The wind, constantly and relentlessly, blew day and night

7. Professor Scott peered at his class.
   The peering was uneasy (ly).
   The peering was this morning.

   Uneasily, professor Scott peered at his class this morning

   This morning professor Scott peered at his class uneasily

   Professor Scott, uneasily peered at his class this morning

8. Their mother explained the rules.
   The explaining was clear (ly).
   The explaining was emphatic (ly).

   Clearly and emphatically, their mother explained the rules

Their mother explained the rules clearly and emphaticly

9. The bank teller whispered to the guard.
The whispering was urgent (ly).
The guard was at the door.

Urgently, the bank teller whispered to the guard at the door

At the door, the bank teller whispered urgently to the guard

The bank teller urgently whispered to the guard at the door

10. We will start for home.
The starting will be this morning.
The starting will be later.

Later this morning we will start for home

This morning we start late for home

Late, we start for home this morning

we start, this morning, late for home

EXERCISE 10.4

The adverbs have been deleted from the following passage. Replace each blank with an appropriate adverb.

The stern of the vessel shot by, dropping, as it did so, into a hollow between

the waves; and I caught a glimpse of a man standing at the wheel, and of

another man who seemed to be doing little else than smoke a cigar. I saw

the smoke issuing from his lips as he _____ turned his head and glanced
(1)

_____ over the water in my direction. It was a careless, unpremeditated
(2)

glance, one of those haphazard things men do when they have no immedi-

ate call to do anything in particular, but act because they are alive and must

do something.

But life and death were in that glance. I could see the vessel being

swallowed _____ in the fog; I saw the back of the man at the wheel, and
(3)

the head of the other man turning, _____ turning, as his gaze struck the
                                    (4)
water and _____ lifted along it _____ me. His face wore an
          (5)   (6)
absent expression, as of deep thought, and I became afraid that if his eyes
did light upon me he would nevertheless not see me. But his eyes did light
upon me, and looked _____ into mine; and he did see me, for he
                      (7)
sprang to the wheel, thrusting the other man _____, and whirled it round
                                              (8)
and _____, hand over hand, at the same time shouting orders of some
     (9)
sort. The vessel seemed to go _____ at a tangent to its former course and
                               (10)
leapt almost _____, from view into the fog.
             (11)

   I felt myself slipping into unconsciousness, and tried with all the power
of my will to fight above the suffocating blankness and darkness that was
rising around me. A little _____ I heard the stroke of oars, growing nearer
                          (12)
and _____, and the calls of a man. When he was _____ near I heard
     (13)   (14)
him crying, in vexed fashion, "Why in hell don't you sing out?" This meant me,
I thought, and _____ the blankness and darkness rose over me.
               (15)
                                                    Jack London, *The Sea Wolf*

PREPOSITIONAL PHRASES

Prepositional phrases provide a third way to expand basic sentences. Prepositional phrases consist of a preposition and its object (a noun or noun substitute). The prepositional phrase itself may be expanded by the addition of adjectives that modify the object of the preposition.

EXAMPLES

The clown smiled *at the child.*
The clown smiled *at the small, timid child.*

The fighter *in the corner* looked mean.
The fighter *in the far corner* looked mean.

We caught the bus *at the station.*
We caught the bus *at the central station.*

The following words are commonly used as prepositions:

aboard	behind	from	throughout
about	below	in	to
above	beneath	into	toward
across	beside	like	under
after	between	near	underneath
against	beyond	of	until
along	but (except)	off	unto
amid	by	on	up
among	down	over	upon
around	during	past	with
at	except (but)	since	within
before	for	through	without

Examples of compound prepositions follow:

according to	due to	instead of
along with	in addition to	on account of
because of	in place of	out of
contrary to	in spite of	

Function

Prepositional phrases function in a sentence as either adjectives or adverbs, depending on whether they modify a noun or a verb. Those that function as adverbs give information (where, how, when, or why) about a verb.

EXAMPLES

The party was held *at the beach.* (where)

The stunned man wandered about *in a daze.* (how)

They arrived early *in the morning.* (when)

They came *for the homecoming party.* (why)

Prepositional phrases that function as adjectives modify a noun by telling *which one(s).*

EXAMPLES

The girl *in the red dress* raised her hand.

That book *of mine* caused a lot of trouble.

The room *on the second floor* is vacant.

In the examples above, the prepositional phrases function as adjectives be-cause they modify nouns; they tell us which girl, which book, and which room; in other words, they identify as well as describe the nouns they modify.

Placement

Most prepositional phrases that function as adverbs can be moved about freely.

EXAMPLE

During the morning, the rain fell steadily.

The rain fell steadily *during the morning.*

Notice the slight difference in emphasis and style that results from the shift in the position of the prepositional phrase. The placement of adverbial prepositional phrases is another option that a writer has. However, prepositional phrases that function as adjectives are placed *immediately after* the noun or pronoun they modify.

EXERCISE 10.5

In the following sentence-combining exercise, use the first sentence as your basic sentence pattern and reduce the others to prepositional phrases that modify a noun or verb in the main sentence. Remember to vary the placement of your adverb phrases but be sure that each adjective phrase follows immediately the word that it modifies.

1. The wilting fern sat.
   The sitting was in a dusty corner.
   The corner was of the waiting room.

   _____

   _____

   _____

2. Jeff swept the dirt.
   The sweeping was in a hurry.
   The sweeping was under his bed.

   _____

   _____

   _____

3. The picture hung crookedly.
   The picture was of my grandfather.

My grandfather was on my mother's side.
The hanging was in the dark hall.
The hall was of the old family home.

_____

_____

_____

4. The banker parked his car.
   The parking was in a no-parking zone.
   The no-parking zone was near a fire hydrant.

_____

_____

_____

5. The father placed the small child.
   The placing was in her crib.
   The crib was beside the big bed.
   The placing was at night.

_____

_____

_____

6. The senator spoke to the crowd.
   The senator was from Wisconsin.
   The crowd was of retired citizens.
   The speaking was with great enthusiasm.

With great enthusiasm, the senator of Wisconsin spoke to the crowd
                                        retired citizens.
The senator from Wisconsin spoke to the crowd of retired citizens with great enthusiasm

_____

7. Georgia rode.
   The riding was in a canoe.
   The canoe was of light aluminum.
   The riding was over the rapids.
   The rapids were of the White River.

Over the rapids of the White River,
        Georgia rode in a canoe of light aluminum

_____

_____

8. The window faced a brick wall.
   The window was in his bedroom.
   The brick wall was across the alley.
   The alley was narrow.

In his bedroom, the window faced a brick wall across the narrow alley

The window in his bedroom faced a brick wall across the narrow alley

_____

9. The baby laughed.
   The baby was in the swing.
   The laughing was with joy.
   The laughing was sudden.

The baby in the swing laughed suddenly with joy

Suddenly, the baby in the swing laughed with joy

_____

10. The teacher announced the name.
    The name was of the winner.
    The announcement was to the class.
    The announcement was loud.
    The announcement was clear.

Loudly and clearly, the teacher announced the name of the winner to the class

The teacher announced loudly and clearly the name of the winner to the class

The teacher, loudly and clearly, announced the name of the winner to the class

EXERCISE 10.6

Prepositions have been deleted from the following passages. Write appropriate prepositions in the blanks.

PASSAGE A

The distance _____ the earth _____ the moon changes
                    (1)   (2)

every day, even _____ minute _____ minute, because
                      (3)   (4)

both the earth and the moon travel _____(5)_____ oval orbits. Since the moon's orbit is not circular, but oval-shaped, the moon is closer _____(6)_____ the earth _____(7)_____ some times and farther away _____(8)_____ other times. _____(9)_____ the nearest approach to the earth, the moon is 360,000 km away. _____(10)_____ its farthest point, the moon is 404,800 km away. . . .

The moon does not actually change shape. It is the pattern _____(11)_____ reflected light that changes. The moon does not give off light _____(12)_____ its own. It receives light _____(13)_____ the sun, just as the earth and other planets do. The moon's barren surface reflects much _____(14)_____ the light into space and some _____(15)_____ that light reaches the earth. One half of the moon is always lighted _____(16)_____ the sun and one half is always dark, just as the earth is. But the same half _____(17)_____ the moon is not lighted all _____(18)_____ the time because the moon is traveling _____(19)_____ an orbit _____(20)_____ the earth while the earth travels around the sun.

William H Matthews, III, et al., *Investigating the Earth*

PASSAGE B

Democratic people applauded Castro's overthrow _____(1)_____ Batista's dictatorship. Some in the United States gave guarded approval _____(2)_____ the first steps Castro was taking to improve conditions _____(3)_____ poor Cubans. As 1960 wore on, however, the United States grew alarmed _____(4)_____ Castro's growing ties _____(5)_____ the Soviet Union. _____(6)_____ January 1961, the United States broke diplomatic

relations _____ Cuba, and _____ the end _____
           (7)   (8)   (9)

that year Castro made his position clear. "I am a Marxist," he proclaimed.

Marvin Perry, *Unfinished Journey: A World History*

APPOSITIVES *is interchangable, but the adjective is not*

A final way that basic sentence patterns can be expanded is by use of appositives. An appositive is a noun or noun phrase (noun plus modifiers) that gives additional information about another noun. Unlike adjectives—which describe, limit, or identify nouns—an appositive explains or defines a noun.

EXAMPLES

The picture, *a pastel watercolor,* was for sale.

They served my favorite dessert, *raspberry sherbet.*

An energetic person, Ms. Smith is always up before dawn.

In the first two examples, the appositives follow the nouns they explain. This is by far the most common position for an appositive. In the third sentence, however, the appositive comes before the noun it explains. In either case, whether the appositive comes before or after the noun it explains, it must be immediately adjacent to it. Appositives cannot be shifted about in the sentence pattern as freely as can adjectives and adverbs.

Punctuation

An appositive is usually set off by commas. In instances in which the appositive is essential to identify the noun it explains (e.g., *my friend Dale*), commas may be omitted. But most of the time—in fact, any time the appositive could be omitted from the sentence without changing the meaning of the sentence—it is set off by commas.

EXERCISE 10.7

Combine each sentence pair into one sentence by making one of the sentences an appositive that explains a noun in the other sentence.

EXAMPLE

The swing hung from a tree.

The tree was an old live oak with low, gnarled branches.

Combination: The swing hung from a tree, an old live oak with low, gnarled branches.

1. Dr. Morris performed the delicate operation.
    Dr. Morris is a renowned heart surgeon.

    _____

    _____

    _____

2. The plants were set in large clay pots around the patio.
    The plants were geraniums and periwinkles.

    _____

    _____

    _____

3. They liked the other car.
    The other car was a small foreign model.

    _____

    _____

    _____

4. An aardvark was the main attraction at the zoo.
    An aardvark is one of the strangest looking animals in existence.

    _____

    _____

    _____

5. I chose a new color for my bedroom walls.
    The new color was a pale, cheerful yellow.

    _____

    _____

    _____

6. Ms. Johnson will be the party's nominee.
    Ms. Johnson is a former college president.

    Ms. Johnson, a former college president, will be the party's
    nominee.

A former college president, Ms. Johnson, will be the party's nominee

7. The movie was a disappointment.
   The movie was an adaptation of a novel.

An adaption of a novel, the movie was a disappointment

The movie, an adaption of a novel, was a disappointment

8. He sent his aunt a description of his new home.
   His aunt is an interior decorator.

He sent his aunt, an interior decorator, a description of his new home

9. The school was closed for repairs.
   The school was an old red-brick structure.

10. He introduced her to his friends.
    His friends were John, Chris, and Bob.

EXERCISE 10.8

This sentence-combining exercise contains a series of sentence groups that can be combined in various ways. Using the first sentence as your basic sentence pattern, reduce the sentences that follow to modifiers (adjectives, adverbs, or prepositional phrases) or appositives that can be used to expand the basic sentence. Try to vary the position of the modifiers. If you are unsure of the correct punctuation, discuss the sentence with your instructor or classmates.

1. The cat stretched.
   The cat was fat.
   The cat was sleek.
   The cat was a Burmese.
   The stretching was lazy (ly).

   _____

   _____

   _____

2. The car rolled.
   The car was a Mercedes.
   The car was expensive.
   The rolling was slow (ly).
   The rolling was arrogant (ly).
   The rolling was to a stop.

   _____

   _____

   _____

3. I read the book.
   The reading was reluctant.
   The book was silly.
   The book was repetitious.
   The reading was to my son.

   _____

   _____

   _____

4. The dancer twirled.
   The dancer was holding his arms up.
   The dancer was lifting his head high.
   The twirling was rapid (ly).
   The twirling was for several moments.

   _____

   _____

   _____

5. The salesperson took the money.
   The salesperson was a young girl.
   The young girl was shy.
   The money was the customer's.
   The customer was complaining.

   _____

   _____

   _____

6. The hotel sat.
   The hotel was brick.
   The brick was whitewashed.
   The sitting was on a hill.
   The hill was overlooking a cliff.
   The sitting was precarious (ly).

   _____

   _____

   _____

7. The man wore a hat.
   The man was dignified.
   The man was otherwise well dressed.
   The hat was ridiculous.
   The hat was a derby.
   The derby was old.
   The derby was black.
   The wearing was unexpected (ly).

   _____

   _____

   _____

8. The child cried.
   The child was small.
   The child was hiding.
   The hiding was under the sheets.
   The sheets were on his bed.
   The crying was uncontrollable (ly).

   _____

_____

_____

9. Albert Norris voted.
   Norris was the senator from Wyoming.
   The voting was for the bill.
   The bill was controversial.
   The bill was about water conservation.

_____

_____

_____

10. The dishes were stacked.
    The dishes were dirty.
    The stacking was high.
    The high was dangerous (ly).
    The stacking was in the sink.
    The sink was enamel.
    The enamel was chipped.

_____

_____

_____

EXERCISE 10.9

Combine the following sentences. Then rewrite the sentences in paragraph form.

1. Sante Fe is a town.
   The town has a past.

_____

_____

_____

2. It seems to belong.
   The belonging is to another time.
   The belonging is to another place.

It is located in the hills.
The hills rise to meet the mountains.

_____

_____

_____

3. One immediately notices.
   What one notices is the age.
   The age is of the town.
   The age is obvious.
   One leaves the highway.
   The highway is modern.
   The highway is four-lane.
   The highway leads to Sante Fe.

_____

_____

_____

4. Some buildings date.
   The dating is back.
   The dating is to the 1600s.

_____

_____

_____

5. Even the buildings are designed.
   The buildings are new.
   The designing is to look old.

_____

_____

_____

6. Everything is built.
   The everything is new.
   The everything is old.
   The building is adobe.
   The adobe is pink.

_____

_____

_____

7. Streets are narrow.
   Streets are unpaved.
   The unpaving is frequent (ly).

_____

_____

_____

8. Dogs wander.
   The wandering is free (ly).
   The wandering is about the plaza.
   The plaza is central.
   The dogs ignore the traffic.
   The dogs ignore the tourists.

_____

_____

_____

9. Women peddle their wares.
   The women are Indian.
   The women are wrapped.
   The wrapping is in shawls.
   The shawls are hand-woven.
   The peddling is along the sidewalks.
   The sidewalks encircle the plaza.

_____

_____

_____

10. They too ignore the traffic.
    They too ignore the tourists.

_____

11. People are dressed.
    The people are few.
    The dressing is in styles.
    The styles are current.

    _____

    _____

    _____

12. The Indians cling.
    The clinging is to their clothing.
    The clothing is traditional.

    _____

    _____

    _____

13. The artists continue to wear clothes.
    The students continue to wear clothes.
    The artists and students are local.
    The clothes are unconventional.
    The clothes are comfortable.
    The clothes are of the 1960s.

    _____

    _____

    _____

14. Even the tourists have sense.
    The sense is enough.
    The sense is to leave their shirts.
    The sense is to leave their bags.
    The shirts are Polo.
    The bags are Gucci.
    The leaving is in their hotel rooms.

    _____

    _____

    _____

15. The town disdains anything.
    The anything is new.
    The town reveres anything.
    The anything is old.
    The anything is with a past.

    _____

    _____

    _____

16. And it wears its past.
    The past is its own.
    The wearing is with pride.
    The wearing is with dignity.
    The dignity is crumbling.

    _____

    _____

    _____

EDITING THE EXPANDED SENTENCE

Adjective or Adverb?

Adjectives modify nouns, and adverbs modify verbs or other modifiers (adjectives and adverbs). This rule usually presents few problems. It's easy to remember that you shouldn't use an adverb to modify a noun. You are not likely to say or write a sentence such as the following:

He is an *unhappily* person.

But it's more difficult to remember not to use an adjective to modify a verb, as in the following sentence:

The patient is breathing *normal* again. (should be *normally*)

It is also sometimes difficult to decide whether to use an adjective or adverb following the verb *to be.* The verb *to be* should always be followed by an adjective, since it modifies, not the verb, but the subject.

The new teacher was *nervous.* (not *nervously*)

The same rule applies when the verb is a "sense" verb (a verb such as *feel, taste, smell, sound,* and *look*) that is followed by a modifier describing the subject.

> That pizza tastes *awful.* (not *awfully*)
>
> He feels *bad.* (not *badly*)

The following adjectives and adverbs are especially tricky:

bad/badly	You feel *bad.* (adjective)
	You slept *badly.* (adverb)
good/well	You feel *good.* (adjective) ~feel well = healthy~
	You slept *well.* (adverb)
sure/surely	You are *sure.* (adjective)
	You are *surely* ready. (adverb)
real/really	You sound *real.* (adjective)
	You sound *really* angry. (adverb)

EXERCISE 10.10

Choose the adjective or adverb that is correct in each sentence below.

1. The steak was burned (bad, badly).
2. I slept (real, really) (good, well) last night.
3. She walked very (graceful, gracefully) into the room.
4. Her walk was (graceful, gracefully).
5. Are you (sure, surely) that she is (real, really) angry?
6. The infection made her feel (bad, badly).

Misplaced and Dangling Modifiers

Although a writer has options in placing modifiers in a sentence, sometimes a misplaced or dangling modifier can confuse a reader.

MISPLACED MODIFIERS

Most modifiers need to be as near as possible to the word they modify. Otherwise, the meaning of the sentence may not be clear.

> The clown entertained the children wearing baggy pants and an old top hat.

In the example above, it is not clear who is wearing the baggy pants and old top hat. If it is the clown who is dressed in this way, then that phrase should be placed immediately before or after the word *clown.*

Wearing baggy pants and an old top hat, the clown entertained the children.

The clown, wearing baggy pants and an old top hat, entertained the children.

EXERCISE 10.11

Rewrite the following sentences so that the misplaced modifiers are appropriately placed.

1. The children watched the television show *eating sandwiches.*

   _____

   _____

   _____

2. As we continued to tease him, the child was ready to *almost* cry.

   _____

   _____

   _____

3. She found a scorpion *on the floor doing exercises.*

   _____

   _____

   _____

4. Because of increasing inflation, she asked to have her salary adjusted *yearly.*

   _____

   _____

   _____

5. Their mother cautioned the children *carefully* to carry the dishes.

   _____

_____

_____

6. The teachers advised the students *regularly* to go to the Writing
   Center.

   ꞏ_____

   _____

   _____

7. The governess told the children *properly* to eat their dinner.

   _____

   _____

   _____

3/5/90

DANGLING MODIFIERS

Sometimes modifiers are not just misplaced but occur in a sentence in which
there is no word for them to modify. We call such modifiers *dangling
modifiers.*

> *Sweeping the porch with a straw broom,* the dust filled the air.

In the example above, the modifying phrase *sweeping the porch with a
straw broom* is dangling because there is no word in the sentence that it
modifies. We need to know *who* is doing the sweeping.

> *Sweeping the porch with a straw broom,* the old woman filled the
> air with dust.

In the corrected example above, the modifying phrase describes the old
woman.

Participles

Most dangling modifiers are participial phrases that occur at the beginning of
a sentence. Since participles are modifiers that derive from verbs (*sweeping*
is the present participle of the verb *to sweep*), they must modify a word that
is capable of performing the action implied by the verb. Usually the subject
of the sentence is the word modified by the participial phrase. The subject must, therefore, be the person or thing that is performing the action
implied.

Rewrite the following sentences, correcting the dangling modifier in each one.

1. Using brainwashing techniques, the captives began to weaken in their resolve.

    _____

    _____

    _____

2. Rowing frantically, the boat began to sink.

    _____

    _____

    _____

3. Arriving by ship, Los Angeles looked like an enormous city.

    _____

    _____

    _____

4. By reading late that night, the examination was passed.

    _____

    _____

    _____

5. Hanging on a hook in the hall closet, my sister found her lost umbrella.

    _____

    _____

    _____

Fragments 03/5/90

A fragment is a separated sentence part that does not express a complete thought. To decide whether a group of words is a sentence, ask yourself these two questions: (1) Does it have a verb *and* a subject? (2) Does it express a complete thought? If the answer to either question is "no," the group of words is not a sentence but a part of a sentence—a fragment.

Three of the sentence elements that are commonly mistaken for complete sentences are (1) participial phrases, (2) appositive phrases, and (3) prepositional phrases.

PARTICIPIAL PHRASE SENTENCE FRAGMENTS

A participle is a word formed from a verb but used as an adjective. As illustrated in the example below, present participles (*-ing* form of verbs) are frequently mistaken for main verbs, and the phrases in which they appear are frequently mistaken for complete sentences.

Reading comic books all the time.

Although the participle *reading* is a verb form, it is not a verb since it cannot be used with a subject (I reading, you reading, he reading, etc.). Only when accompanied by a form of the verb *to be* (*am, is, are, was, were, been, being*) can a participle be used as a main verb (I am reading, you are reading, etc.).

A participial phrase most frequently functions as an adjective, modifying the subject of the main verb in the independent clause to which it is attached.

Reading comic books all the time, Jim lived in a world of fantasy.

Jim, reading comic books all the time, lived in a world of fantasy.

Jim lived in a world of fantasy, reading comic books all the time.

Notice that the participial phrase in the examples above is separated from the independent clause by a comma or commas.

EXERCISE 10.13

Below are six participial phrases incorrectly written as sentences. Write six complete sentences by adding an independent clause to each of the phrases. Be sure the phrase modifies the subject of your independent clause.

1. Waiting alone.

_____

_____

MODIFICATION: EXPANDING THE SIMPLE SENTENCE ■ CHAPTER 10   299

2. Seeing the exit sign ahead.

_____

_____

3. Expecting guests soon.

_____

_____

4. Sitting on a bus all day.

_____

_____

5. Working on the project for weeks.

_____

_____

6. Seeing no way out.

_____

_____

APPOSITIVE PHRASE SENTENCE FRAGMENTS

An appositive phrase explains the noun or pronoun it follows. As shown below, neither an appositive nor an appositive phrase can stand alone as a sentence.

> The eighteen sailors rowed 3,618 miles to Timor. An island near Java.

An island near Java is an appositive phrase explaining *Timor*, and should be joined to the preceding sentence.

> The eighteen sailors rowed 3,618 miles to Timor, an island near Java.

Notice that the appositive phrase is set off from the rest of the sentence by a comma or, as in the sentence below, by commas.

> Jim, one of my best friends, has left for college.

EXERCISE 10.14

Combine the following sentences and appositive phrases, attaching the appositive phrases to the nouns from which they have been incorrectly separated. Change punctuation and capitalization whenever necessary.

1. We enjoy playing Parcheesi. A game from India.

    _____

    _____

    _____

2. The entrance to the Mediterranean is guarded by a rocky peninsula. Gibraltar.

    _____

    _____

    _____

3. Astronomers have recently photographed Saturn. The planet encircled by rings.

    _____

    _____

    _____

4. Thursday was named for Thor. The Norse god of thunder.

    _____

    _____

    _____

5. We went to a double feature. A mystery and a western.

    _____

    _____

    _____

6. *The Twilight Zone* was made into a movie. A successful television series.

_____

_____

_____

7. The Battle of Marathon was won by the Greeks. One of the famous battles in the history of the world.

_____

_____

_____

8. The telephone can be both a blessing and a curse. An invention that has changed our lives.

_____

_____

_____

9. The water in Cypress Gardens near Charleston, South Carolina, is black because it contains tannic acid. A secretion of the cypress trees.

_____

_____

_____

10. Confucius said, "Learning without thought is labor lost." A famous Chinese philosopher of the fifth century B.C.

_____

_____

_____

PREPOSITIONAL PHRASE SENTENCE FRAGMENTS

Less frequently, but occasionally, a very long prepositional phrase or series of prepositional phrases will be mistaken for a sentence. Sometimes such phrases are attached to an element that could be part of a complete sentence.

The example below is a fragment because even though it has a word that could function as its subject (*dancer*), there is no verb—only a series of prepositional phrases.

> The dancer in the short, pink skirt with the orange ribbon in her hair and purple scarf in her hand.

The next example is a fragment also because it begins with a word (*day*) that could either be a subject or an adverb but is followed only by a long series of prepositional phrases.

> The other day on the plane to Miami with my new luggage from Bloomingdale's on the seat beside me.

The example below has only prepositional phrases: *in the summer, around the old swimming pool, in the field,* and *behind our house.* There is no subject or verb.

> In the summer around the old swimming pool in the field behind our house.

We could correct this fragment by supplying a subject and verb so that a statement is made.

> In the summer *we meet* around the old swimming pool in the field behind our house.

EXERCISE 10.15

Supply the fragments below with the essential elements they need in order to be complete sentences.

1. Without looking in the direction of the traffic on the street.

   _____

   _____

   _____

2. My broker at the respected firm of Jones, Jones, and Jones.

   _____

   _____

   _____

3. Out of the bushes to the right of the large oak tree.

_____

_____

_____

4. Occasionally in the morning after a night out with my friends.

_____

_____

_____

5. The fly in my cup of lukewarm coffee on the table before me.

_____

_____

_____

EXERCISE 10.16

The following paragraphs contain six fragments. Rewrite the paragraphs, joining the fragments to independent clauses so that they become part of complete sentences.

The American frontier, if we are to believe the tales that have been handed down, was populated with some amazing personalities. The men about whom we hear were always at least six feet tall and often reached the height of giants. Not only were these men large; they were also strong and clever. Eating enormous amounts of food, performing astounding feats of strength and courage, inventing miraculous methods of accomplishing difficult tasks, and doing an amazing amount of work. These heroes could out-run, out-jump, out-brag, out-drink, out-shoot, and out-fight anyone foolish enough to challenge them. These giants among men were our folk heroes. Super humans created to populate and tame the rugged, often dangerous frontier.

These folk heroes tell us something about the people who created them. Faced with countless dangers and constant weariness. The frontiersmen created mythical men who were capable of facing dangers and doing work in unusual and often humorous ways. Many of these supermen, such as Paul Bunyan and Pecos Bill, were entirely the products of the frontiersmen's imagination. However, sometimes the early Americans glorified actual men. For example, Davy Crockett and John Henry. In an effort to transform them into larger-than-life heroes. Whether based on fact or fancy, these heroes were projections of the men who created them. Ordinary mortals needing to be superhuman in order to tame the frontier.

READING/WRITING ASSIGNMENT 10A

A LESSON IN LIFE
James Herriot

Pre-Reading/Writing Exercise

You have spent most of your life attending school and studying books. On the left side of a blank sheet of paper, brainstorm for a few minutes about what you have learned about life from school. When you finish, look back at your brainstorming and think about how the things you listed helped or didn't help you prepare for life after school.

Next, think about some of your experiences outside of school. Then brainstorm, using the right side of the paper, about what you have learned about life from these experiences. Finally, compare your two brainstorming exercises and discuss them in class. Have you learned more about life in school or out of school? Have your classmates learned more about life from school or from experiences outside of school?

Reading Exercise

According to a well-known expression, "Experience is the best teacher." As you read the following passage by Herriot, decide whether or not he would agree with this statement.

1   They didn't say anything about this in the books, I thought, as the snow blew in through the gaping doorway and settled on my naked back.

2   I lay face down on the cobbled floor in a pool of nameless muck, my arm deep inside the straining cow, my feet scrabbling for a toe hold between the stones. I was stripped to the waist and the snow mingled with the dirt and the dried blood on my body. I could see nothing outside the circle of flickering light thrown by the smoky oil lamp which the farmer held over me.

3   No, there wasn't a word in the books about searching for your ropes and instruments in the shadows; about trying to keep clean in a half bucket of tepid water; about the cobbles digging into your chest. Nor about the slow numbing of the arms, the creeping paralysis of the muscles as the fingers tried to work against the cow's powerful expulsive efforts.

4   There was no mention anywhere of the gradual exhaustion, the feeling of futility and the little far-off voice of panic.

5   My mind went back to that picture in the obstetrics book. A cow standing in the middle of a gleaming floor while a sleek veterinary surgeon in a spotless parturition overall inserted his arm to a polite distance. He was relaxed and smiling, the farmer and his helpers were smiling, even the cow was smiling. There was no dirt or blood or sweat anywhere.

6   That man in the picture had just finished an excellent lunch and had moved next door to do a bit of calving just for the sheer pleasure of it, as a kind of dessert. He hadn't crawled shivering from his bed at two o'clock in the morning and bumped over twelve miles of frozen snow, staring sleepily ahead till the lonely farm showed in the headlights. He hadn't climbed half a mile of white fell-side to the doorless barn where his patient lay.

James Herriot, *All Creatures Great and Small*

  1. Write Herriot's thesis in your own words.

_____

_____

_____

Would Herriot agree or disagree with the saying, "Experience is the best teacher"?

_____

  2. Herriot uses a personal experience to illustrate his thesis. Summarize his experience in your own words.

_____

_____

_____

_____

_____

  3. Herriot uses several sensory details in this passage. What are two of the most effective?

_____

_____

_____

4. Professional writers sometimes use sentence fragments intentionally for a special effect. In "Getting 'em Ready for Darrell," for example, Larry King uses fragments to portray conversation realistically, as when Bradley's father says, "Way to *go*, Bradley." What is a fragment that Herriot uses in paragraph 5?

_____

_____

_____

What effect does this fragment create?

_____

How could this fragment be changed to a complete sentence?

_____

_____

Would a complete sentence be equally effective?

_____

5. Herriot uses numerous modifiers to recreate the scene inside the barn. To illustrate the effectiveness of these modifiers, rewrite the second paragraph of the passage *leaving out all modifiers.* Then compare the effectiveness of the two versions.

_____

_____

6. In Herriot's passage, -ed and -ing endings may indicate a verb, as in "*settled*" or "*was smiling*," a noun, as in "about *searching*," or an adjective, as in "*gaping* doorway" and "*cobbled* floor." What are three additional -ing words used as adjectives?

_____

7. Using the context and your dictionary, define the words below:
a. obstetrics

_____

b. parturition

_____

Writing Exercise

Write a paragraph or essay in which you show which educational experiences have been more valuable to you, those lessons you received from books and school or those you learned from your own experiences. After you decide on your purpose, draft your topic sentence or thesis statement and determine the best method of development for your composition. You may use a descriptive narrative like Herriot's, an extended illustration, or a comparison of what you have learned from your own experience and from school. Whatever method(s) of development you choose, however, use ample specific support. For this assignment, you should specify your audience—perhaps former schoolteachers or prospective employers. After you have determined your purpose, thesis, and audience, write your rough draft.

Rewriting Exercise

Reread your draft carefully to see that you have achieved your purpose and communicated to your audience. Answer the following questions independently or in a peer review group.

1. What is your purpose?
2. Who is your audience?
3. What is your main idea (topic sentence or thesis statement)? Is it clearly stated or implied?
4. What method(s) of development have you used?
5. What are your major supporting points? Does each major point develop your main idea?
6. How have you arranged your supporting points (time order, space order, order of importance, etc.)?
7. What types of transition have you used? What additional transitions should you include?
8. Are your word choices and sentence style appropriate for your audience? How could you improve them?
9. What is your conclusion? How can you improve it?
10. Does your paragraph or essay achieve your purpose and communicate to your audience? Why or why not?

After you have made the major revisions needed in your draft, edit it carefully. As you edit, consider the following questions. (You may want to reread your composition for each question, thus keeping only one editing task in mind at a time.)

1. Is each sentence a complete sentence, with a subject and a verb?
2. Do you have any errors in subject-verb agreement?
3. Do you have any errors in pronoun reference or agreement?

4. What tense have you used? Is your use of tense consistent?

5. What point of view have you used (first person, second person, third person)? Is your point of view consistent?

6. Do you have any misused, misplaced, or dangling modifiers?

7. Do you have any misspelled words?

8. Do you have any additional errors in capitalization, punctuation, or usage?

After you have edited your paragraph or essay, write your final draft, and proofread it carefully.

READING/WRITING ASSIGNMENT 10B

AGING IN THE LAND OF THE YOUNG
Sharon Curtin

Pre-Reading/Writing Exercise

Think about the position elderly people have in our society. What problems do they have? How do young people react to them? How are the elderly depicted in movies? On television? In advertisements? How are they treated by employers and by their own families? What are some of their economic problems? What are some of their health problems? Jot down in list form a number of the specific problems faced by many old people in our society—perhaps by specific old people that you know.

If possible, interview an elderly person (perhaps a relative or neighbor or a resident of a nursing home). Ask questions that will allow the person you are interviewing to discuss some of the problems he or she has experienced because of age, but be sure that you also consider the feelings of the person you are interviewing and allow him or her to talk about some of the positive aspects of aging.

Reading Exercise

In the following selection, Sharon Curtin discusses an attitude toward aging that is often found in our contemporary society. As you read, determine what this attitude is.

1 Old men, old women, almost 20 million of them. They constitute 10 percent of the total population, and the percentage is steadily growing. Some of them, like conspirators, walk all bent over, as if hiding some precious secret, filled with self-protection. The body seems to gather itself around those vital parts, folding shoulders, arms, pelvis like a fading rose. Watch and you see how fragile old people come to think they are.

2   Aging paints every action gray, lies heavy on every movement, imprisons every thought. It governs each decision with a ruthless and single-minded perversity. To age is to learn the feeling of no longer growing, of struggling to do old tasks, to remember familiar actions. The cells of the brain are destroyed with thousands of unfelt tiny strokes, little pockets of clotted blood wiping out memories and abilities without warning. The body seems slowly to give up, randomly stopping, sometimes starting again as if to torture and tease with the memory of lost strength. Hands become clumsy, frail transparencies, held together with knotted blue veins.

3   Sometimes it seems as if the distance between your feet and the floor were constantly changing, as if you were walking on shifting and not quite solid ground. One foot down, slowly, carefully force the other foot forward. Sometimes you are a shuffler, not daring to lift your feet from the uncertain earth but forced to slide hesitantly forward in little whispering movements. Sometimes you are able to "step out," but this effort—in fact the pure exhilaration of easy movement—soon exhausts you.

4   The world becomes narrower as friends and family die or move away. To climb stairs, to ride in a car, to walk to the corner, to talk on the telephone; each action seems to take away from the energy needed to stay alive. Everything is limited by the strength you hoard greedily. Your needs decrease, you require less food, less sleep, and finally less human contact; yet this little bit becomes more and more difficult. You fear that one day you will be reduced to the simple acts of breathing and taking nourishment. This is the ultimate stage you dread, the period of helplessness and hopelessness, when independence will be over.

5   There is nothing to prepare you for the experience of growing old. Living is a process, an irreversible progression toward old age and eventual death. You see men of eighty still vital and straight as oaks; you see men of fifty reduced to gray shadows in the human landscape. The cellular clock differs for each one of us, and is profoundly affected by our own life experiences, our heredity, and perhaps most important, by the concepts of aging encountered in society and in oneself.

6   The aged live with enforced leisure, on fixed incomes, subject to many chronic illnesses, and most of their money goes to keep a roof over their heads. They also live in a culture that worships youth.

7   A kind of cultural attitude makes me bigoted against old people; it make me think young is best; it makes me treat old people like outcasts.

8   Hate that gray? Wash it away!

9   Wrinkle cream.

10   Monkey glands.

11   Face-lifting.

12   Look like a bride again.

13   Don't trust anyone over thirty.

14   I fear growing old.

15   Feel Young Again!

16   I am afraid to grow old—we're all afraid. In fact, the fear of growing old is so great that every aged person is an insult and a threat to the society. They remind us of our own death, that our body won't always remain smooth and responsive, but will someday betray us by aging, wrinkling, faltering,

failing. The ideal way to age would be to grow slowly invisible, gradually disappearing, without causing worry or discomfort to the young. In some ways that does happen. Sitting in a small park across from a nursing home one day, I noticed that the young mothers and their children gathered on one side, and the old people from the home on the other. Whenever a youngster would run over to the "wrong" side, chasing a ball or just trying to cover all the available space, the old people would lean forward and smile. But before any communication could be established, the mother would come over, murmuring embarrassed apologies, and take her child back to the "young" side.

17   Now, it seemed to me that the children didn't feel any particular fear and the old people didn't seem to be threatened by the children. The division of space was drawn by the mothers. And the mothers never looked at the old people who lined the other side of the park like so many pigeons perched on the benches. These well-dressed young matrons had a way of sliding their eyes over, around, through the old people; they never looked at them directly. The old people may as well have been invisible; they had no reality for the youngsters, who were not permitted to speak to them, and they offended the aesthetic eye of the mothers.

18   My early experiences were somewhat different; since I grew up in a small town, my childhood had more of a nineteenth-century flavor. I knew a lot of old people, and considered some of them friends. There was no culturally defined way for me to "relate" to old people, except the rules of courtesy which applied to all adults. My grandparents were an integral and important part of the family and of the community. I sometimes have a dreadful fear that mine will be the last generation to know old people as friends, to have a sense of what growing old means, to respect and understand man's mortality and his courage in the face of death. Mine may be the last generation to have a sense of living history, of stories passed from generation to generation, of identity established by family history.

Sharon R. Curtin, *Nobody Ever Died of Old Age*

1. To emphasize the importance of her subject, Curtin begins her essay with an intentional fragment rather than with a stated thesis. Thus, the thesis, or main idea, of this reading selection is implied rather than directly stated. What is this main idea?

_____

_____

_____

_____

2. What are two or three details in the passage that really give you a sense of what it feels like to grow old physically?

_____

_____

_____

3. Curtin also discusses the mental, social, and economic effects of aging. What are some specific examples she gives of these effects?

_____

_____

_____

_____

_____

4. According to the author, what is the overall attitude expressed by the young toward the old in our society?

_____

_____

What specific details support this attitude?

_____

_____

_____

_____

5. How do you suppose the elderly people in the park felt?

_____

_____

_____

6. Although _old_ and _elderly_ have almost identical denotations (dictionary meanings), they have quite different connotations (associations). What are the connotations of _elderly?_

_____

What are the connotations of *old?*

_____

_____

_____

_____

In this passage Curtin uses the word *old* instead of *elderly.* Why do you suppose she made this choice?

_____

_____

_____

7. Explain the phrase "they offended the aesthetic eye of the mothers." What does *aesthetic* mean?

_____

_____

_____

What attitude toward the mothers does Curtin show in this phrase?

_____

_____

8. Curtin uses modifiers effectively to describe the effects of age. For example, she says that "Aging paints every action gray, lies *heavy* on every movement, imprisons every thought." What are three other modifiers she uses to recreate the feeling of age?

_____

_____

Discussion Questions

1. Curtin points out that the aged "live with enforced leisure, on fixed incomes." Do you know old people who were forced to retire or who live on fixed incomes? What are their lives like?

2. Curtin also mentions that the elderly are "subject to many chronic illnesses." What are some illnesses common to old people? What problems do they have with hospital costs, Medicare, and insurance? What problems are posed for old people and their families by such illnesses as Alzheimer's disease and hardening of the arteries?

Writing Exercise

Look back at your earlier brainstorming and, if you wish, add to it. Study your list and determine which problems are related to one another. Circle and draw lines between related problems.

When you have finished your list of problems of elderly people, study your categories and decide which group of ideas interests you most. Then use the ideas and details in this group as the basis for a paragraph or essay about a particular problem of the elderly in the United States. Your audience might be a group of young people, a nursing home staff, a hospital staff, or even a member of Congress. Try to include, as Curtin did, specific modifiers and details to show your audience what it is like to be an elderly person with the problem you are describing.

Rewriting Exercise

Reread your paragraph or essay to see if you have achieved your purpose and communicated to your audience. Use the questions below to help you revise it.

1. What is your purpose?

2. Who is your audience?

3. What is your main idea (topic sentence or thesis statement)? Is it clearly stated or implied? Have you limited your subject to a particular problem of the elderly in our society and your focus to a particular point about that problem? If necessary, limit your subject and focus further.

4. What method(s) of development have you used?

5. What are your major supporting points? Does each supporting point develop your main idea?

6. How have you arranged your supporting points (time order, space order, order of importance, etc.)?

7. What types of transition have you used? What additional transitions should you include?

8. Are your word choices and sentence style appropriate for your audience?

9. What is your conclusion? How can you improve it?

10. Does your paragraph or essay achieve its purpose and communicate to your audience? Why or why not?

After you have made the major revisions needed in your draft, edit it carefully. As you edit, consider the following questions.

1. Is each sentence a complete sentence, with a subject and verb?

2. Do you have any errors in subject-verb agreement?

3. Do you have any errors in pronoun reference or agreement?

4. What tense have you used? Is your use of tense consistent?

5. What point of view have you used (first person, second person, third person)? Is your point of view consistent?

6. Do you have any misused, dangling, or misplaced modifiers?

7. Do you have any misspelled words?

8. Do you have any additional errors in capitalization, punctuation, or usage?

After you have edited your paragraph or essay, write your final draft and proofread it carefully.

Chapter 11

COORDINATION: THE COMPOUND SENTENCE

Coordination is a concept that we discussed earlier in connection with reading and writing paragraphs. Elements that are coordinate are equal. For example, if a paragraph has three equally important major supporting points, we say that those points are coordinate. Similarly, if a subject is composed of two or more nouns or a complement of two or more adjectives, we say that these elements are coordinate. We can also describe these coordinate elements as *compound*.

Each of the following sentences has a compound element composed of two or more coordinate words or phrases:

1. Compound subject:
    A cup of coffee and *the morning paper* entice me out of bed each morning.
2. Compound verb:
    She *ran to the edge of the cliff* and *looked at the trail far below*.
3. Compound direct object:
    The secretary typed *the long report* and *several letters*.
4. Compound subject complement (adjective):
    The gymnast was *small* but *strong*.
5. Compound modifier (adverb):
    The mayor ended her speech *quickly* but *gracefully*.
6. Compound modifier (prepositional phrase):
    James reached *into the drawer* and *under the papers*.

All of these compound, coordinate elements are connected by *coordinating conjunctions*. The chart below lists the coordinating conjunctions that are used to connect compound, coordinate elements.

ADDITION	CONTRAST	CAUSE AND EFFECT OR CONCLUSION
and	but	for
both . . . and	or	so
	nor	
	yet	
	either . . . or	
	neither . . . nor	

Using the coordinate conjunctions listed above, combine the following pairs of sentences so that the resulting sentence has a compound element.

1. Compound subject:
   The *truck* ran the stop sign.
   The *bus* ran the stop sign.

   _____

   _____

2. Compound verb:
   She *opened* the door.
   She *helped* him from the car.

   _____

   _____

3. Compound modifier (adverb):
   I called him *loudly*
   I called him *urgently*.

   _____

   _____

4. Compound subject complement (adjective):
   The hot dog was *messy*.
   The hot dog was *good*.

   _____

   _____

5. Compound modifier (prepositional phrase):
   She drove *over the steep hill.*
   She drove *across the broken-down bridge*.

   _____

   _____

6. Compound object:
   The painting had *vivid colors.*
   The painting had a *sense of movement.*

7. Compound subject complement (noun):
   I could become an *acrobat*.
   I could become an *accountant*.

_____

_____

8. Compound verb (with modifiers):
   The desk was *cluttered with papers*.
   The desk was *stacked high with books*.

_____

_____

9. Compound object:
   My uncle makes delicious *cakes*.
   My uncle makes delicious *pies*.

_____

_____

10. Compound modifier (participial phrase):
    Dodging traffic, he called to the driver of the car.
    Waving frantically, he called to the driver of the car.

_____

_____

COMPOUND SENTENCES

In Chapter 9 you learned that a simple sentence consists of one subject/verb relationship and makes a single statement or asks a single question. But we do not always speak and write in simple sentences. Often we combine two or more related thoughts in the same sentence. Entire sentences can, therefore, be compound.

EXAMPLES

The taxi driver honked his horn. (simple sentence)

The pedestrian yelled back. (simple sentence)

The taxi driver honked his horn, and the pedestrian yelled back. (compound sentence)

Simple sentences are called independent clauses when they become part of a compound sentence. Therefore, a compound sentence can be described as a combination of two or more independent clauses—groups of words that have a subject and verb and can function as a simple sentence.

Notice that the two independent clauses (simple sentences) in the example above are coordinate. That is, they are equal; each could function as a sentence on its own, each has a subject and verb, and each contributes equally to the meaning of the sentence.

Figure 33

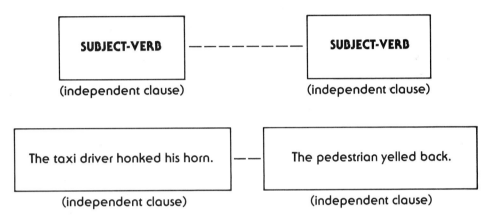

SUBJECT-VERB	SUBJECT-VERB
(independent clause)	(independent clause)

The taxi driver honked his horn.	The pedestrian yelled back.
(independent clause)	(independent clause)

A compound sentence can be diagrammed as shown in Figure 33. In reading and writing compound sentences, you need to understand the relationship that exists between independent clauses. Like other compound elements, independent clauses are often connected by coordinating conjunctions. These coordinating conjunctions indicate the relationship between the elements they connect. For example, the meaning of each of the sentences that follows is completely altered when the coordinating conjunction is changed.

He was defeated, *but* he kept trying.

He was defeated, *or* he kept trying.

He was defeated, *yet* he kept trying.

He was defeated, *and* he kept trying.

He was defeated, *so* he kept trying.

In the compound sentences above, a different relationship is indicated by each coordinating conjunction used. As a reader, you must be alert to these words that signal the relationship between the two thoughts, and as a writer, you must be careful to choose the connecting word that indicates the appropriate relationship.

In addition to being connected by coordinating conjunctions (*and, or, nor, for, but, yet, so*), the independent clauses in a compound sentence can be connected by *conjunctive adverbs*. These connecting words, like coordinating conjunctions, indicate relationships between the independent clauses. The chart below lists some of the most common conjunctive adverbs and indicates the relationships they express.

ADDITION, EMPHASIS, COMPARISON	CONTRAST	CAUSE/EFFECT, CONCLUSION	EXAMPLE	TIME
moreover	however	therefore	for example	then
also	nevertheless	accordingly	for instance	later
too	instead	as a result	to illustrate	next
besides	on the	consequently	that is	first, second,
plus	contrary	hence		third, etc.
furthermore	on the	thus		meanwhile
in addition	other	in conclusion		afterward
indeed	hand	in summary		finally
in fact	otherwise	in other words		
likewise	in contrast	of course		
similarly		then		
certainly				
again				
another				
at the same time				

PUNCTUATING COMPOUND SENTENCES

There are three ways to connect independent clauses and to punctuate correctly the resulting compound sentence.

1. Use a coordinating conjunction and place a comma before the conjunction.

Some students want an education, but others simply want a degree.

2. Use a conjunctive adverb and place a semicolon before the conjunction and a comma after it.

Some students want an education; however, others simply want a degree.

Note: Conjunctive adverbs may appear in a sentence in which they do not introduce an independent clause.

Some students, however, simply want a degree.

When used in this way, the conjunctive adverb is set off by commas but requires no semicolon because it is not introducing a second independent clause.

3. Use no conjunction and place a semicolon between the two independent clauses.

Some students want an education; others simply want a degree.

Notice that the independent clauses in a compound sentence are closely and logically related in thought. If the relationship between them is not apparent, the resulting sentence will be ridiculous.

Some students want an education; teachers should receive higher salaries.

If independent clauses are connected with just a semicolon and no connecting word or phrase that indicates their relationship, the two clauses must be clearly related in meaning. If a coordinating conjunction or a conjunctive adverb is used, the relationship can be less obvious but should, nevertheless, be clearly expressed by the connecting word.

Joan studied hard; _____ she failed the test.

A good choice for the connecting word in the example above would be *however* because the relationship here is one of contrast. If a conjunctive adverb such as *moreover*, indicating addition, or *therefore*, indicating result or conclusion, were used, the sentence would not make sense because the relationship between the two clauses would not be logical.

EXERCISE 11.2

In this exercise, all of the coordinating conjunctions and conjunctive adverbs that connect the independent clauses have been omitted. Write in each blank an appropriate connecting word. In making your choice, consider (1) the relationship between the two clauses and (2) the existing punctuation. Remember that a comma is placed before a coordinating conjunction that connects two independent clauses and a semicolon is placed before a conjunctive adverb that connects two independent clauses.

Many of today's young students have an attention span that has been conditioned by years of watching television. They focus their attention on an issue

for a very few minutes, approximately the length of a television commercial;

_____, they expect something different, _____
      (1)   (2)

they grow bored. As a result, teachers must constantly arrange for a variety of learning activities, _____ they lose the attention
                                                      (3)

of their students. Teachers, in effect, assume the role of entertainers;

_____, students assume the role of audience. One of the
(4)

problems that arises from this situation is that students who perceive themselves as an audience tend to be passive. Learning requires active participa-
tion rather than passivity; _____, these passive students are
(5)

often nonlearners.

EXERCISE 11.3

In this exercise, you are given one independent clause and a connecting
word, either a coordinating conjunction or a conjunctive adverb. Supply a
second independent clause that is related appropriately to the first.

1. The sentimental good-bys were over, and _____

   _____

2. The sentimental good-bys were over; however, _____

   _____

3. The sentimental good-bys were over; therefore, _____

   _____

4. The airplane must land quickly, or _____

   _____

5. The airplane must land quickly, for _____

   _____

6. The airplane must land quickly; consequently, _____

   _____

7. The airplane must land quickly; otherwise, _____

   _____

8. Children often disobey, and _____

   _____

9. Children often disobey; then _____

   _____

10. Children often disobey, yet _____

    _____

11. Children often disobey; for example, _____

    _____

12. Large cars tend to use more fuel, so _____

    _____

13. Large cars tend to use more fuel; in contrast, _____

    _____

14. Large cars tend to use more fuel; in addition, _____

    _____

15. Large cars tend to use more fuel; of course, _____

    _____

Punctuation Review

COORDINATE CONJUNCTION AND COMMA

Independent clause	, coordinate conjunction	independent clause
The wind blew	, and (addition)	the lightning flashed.
The mother called	, but (contrast)	her son didn't come.

CONJUNCTIVE ADVERB AND SEMICOLON

Independent clause	; conjunctive adverb,	independent clause
The wind blew	; moreover, (addition)	the lightning flashed.
The mother called	; however, (contrast)	her son didn't come.

SEMICOLON

Remember also that if two independent clauses are closely and obviously related, you may connect them by using just a semicolon.

Independent clause	;	independent clause

| The wind blew | ; | the lightning flashed. |
| The mother called | ; | her son didn't come. |

EXERCISE 11.4

Read each of the following pairs of independent clauses carefully to determine the relationship between them. Then, noting the punctuation that is given, write in each blank an appropriate connecting word.

1. The price of oil declined; _____, the economy of

   the oil-producing states suffered.

2. The politician spoke longer than she was supposed to;

   _____, her speech was interesting.

3. The money was missing from the cash drawer,

   _____ the valuables had been taken from the safe.

4. The children behaved badly; _____, one refused to

   eat.

5. You may want the pecan pie for dessert, _____ you

   may prefer the cheesecake.

6. His handwriting was barely legible; _____, we could

   make out the words.

7. First, he opened the door carefully; _____ he peered

   inside the dimly lit room.

8. The weather was hot and humid; _____, everyone

   was terribly uncomfortable.

9. The wine tasted sweet and fruity; _____, it went

well with the bread and cheese.

10. Somehow they managed to move the huge chest,

_____ they were not able to get it through the door.

11. Her suit looked soiled and wrinkled; _____, her

shoes were scuffed and unshined.

12. The book lay unopened on her desk for years, _____

she rarely disturbed anything that had belonged to her mother.

13. The grass remained green late into the summer,

_____ the rains had been plentiful and timely.

14. The theater was almost completely dark, _____ the

usher was able to direct them to their seats.

15. Her face became pale and lifeless; _____, her voice

remained strong.

EXERCISE 11.5

Combine the following pairs of independent clauses into compound sentences. Punctuate each sentence appropriately.

1. The yellow Camaro swerved dangerously.
   The driver remained in control of the car.

   _____

   _____

2. The young widow lived alone.
   She was occasionally lonely.

   _____

   _____

3. The rain fell steadily all day.
   By evening the water had risen dangerously.

   _____

   _____

4. The Morris sisters look alike.
   They are not twins.

   _____

   _____

5. Hunting is not permitted in these parks.
   Many animals are killed.

   _____

   _____

6. The television commercial lasted only a few moments.
   It seemed to last forever.

   _____

   _____

7. He must pay in cash.
   He will lose the merchandise.

   _____

   _____

8. This is not the first time.
   It will be the last.

   _____

   _____

9. Rainfall is scarce.
   Water is precious.

   _____

   _____

10. The clouds were thick.
    The eclipse was not visible.

    _____

    _____

11. She looked into the lighted mirror for a long time.
    She sighed and turned away.

    _____

    _____

12. Jim fell asleep almost at once.
    He was exhausted.

    _____

    _____

13. The house is built to be energy efficient.
    The windows all have double-paned glass.

    _____

    _____

14. I want that job.
    I intend to have it.

    _____

    _____

15. The leading man could sing.
    He couldn't act.

    _____

    _____

EXERCISE 11.6

Write the following types of compound sentences, punctuating each appropriately.

1. Three compound sentences in which the two independent clauses are connected by a coordinating conjunction:

a. _____

_____

b. _____

_____

c. _____

_____

   2. Three compound sentences in which the two independent clauses are connected by a conjunctive adverb:

a. _____

_____

b. _____

_____

c. _____

_____

   3. Three compound sentences in which no connecting word is used:

a. _____

_____

b. _____

_____

c. _____

_____

EDITING COMPOUND SENTENCES

Although the compound sentence is an effective way of combining two or more thoughts in the same sentence, a writer must be careful to choose an appropriate method of combining the two independent clauses. A compound sentence that is not punctuated correctly can be awkward and confusing for your reader. The following compound sentences are all incorrectly punctuated:

I like the Nelsons but I'm not inviting them to my party.

Then it dawned on us we were here to work.

The man threw his hat on the floor, then he stomped on it.

In the first example, a coordinating conjunction connects the two independent clauses, but no comma has been placed before it (I like the Nelsons/but I'm not inviting them to my party.). The second example is a run-on sentence because there is no punctuation between the two independent clauses (Then it dawned on us/we were here to work.). The final example is also a run-on sentence because a comma has been incorrectly used to separate two independent clauses connected by the conjunctive adverb *then* (The man threw his hat on the floor/then he stomped on it.).

These sentences could be corrected in the following ways:

1. Write the two independent clauses as two separate simple sentences.

EXAMPLE

I like the Nelsons. But I'm not inviting them to my party.

Then it dawned on us. We were here to work.

The man threw his hat on the floor. Then he stomped on it.

2. Punctuate the two independent clauses correctly as a compound sentence.

EXAMPLE

I like the Nelsons, but I'm not inviting them to my party.

Then it dawned on us; we were here to work.

The man threw his hat on the floor; then he stomped on it.

Note: Remember that *then* is a conjunctive adverb, not a coordinating conjunction. Therefore, if you use *then* to connect two independent clauses, you should place a semicolon before it, but you do not need to place a comma after it.

EXERCISE 11.7

Edit the following sentences carefully by supplying punctuation where it is needed. Some of the sentences are correct.

1. My cousin plays the flute and clarinet and my aunt plays the harp.
2. Every Thanksgiving my grandmother bakes a pumpkin pie and mother cooks the turkey.
3. It was a long, dull, boring lecture and the student at the back went to sleep.

4. He trimmed the shrubbery very carefully for he hoped to keep the hedge alive for the entire summer.

5. Rain is needed now or the plants will die.

6. Today was a holiday he was determined to have a good time.

7. Night falls quickly in the mountains yet the cabin is comfortable and warm.

8. This is the most beautiful part of the river but boats should avoid its treacherous currents.

9. The nets were full of fish but we were too exhausted to haul them in.

10. You must buy that house today; tomorrow will be too late.

11. He did not play football in college he played soccer and tennis.

12. The snow continued to fall, so I remained at the hotel.

13. We ran into heavy snow by the river consequently, we arrived late for the meeting.

14. The little girl held my hand but her brother walked on ahead.

15. There was no moon we could not see.

16. He had lost his key nevertheless, he got into the house by the side door.

17. Shut the door, but do not bang it.

18. The car broke down therefore, he had to walk all the way to the filling station.

19. Several answers appeared likely none was absolutely correct.

20. Don't worry you are not late.

21. My grandmother was a talented gardener she raised a number of exotic plants.

22. They pulled into the driveway then they turned off the motor.

23. I can't eat any more candy it is too fattening.

24. In her lab the chemist tested the product in her office she typed her report.

25. You can come however you can't bring your horse.

EXERCISE 11.8

The following paragraph has ten compound sentences that are incorrectly punctuated. Identify the errors and then rewrite the paragraph correctly.

Yesterday morning I looked up from my hot tea and bagel and noticed an aardvark nibbling on the okra in my back yard. I had no idea where the aardvark had come from and I certainly did not know where it was going. I sat for a moment, munching on my bagel, thinking about what I should do. I could run into the back yard and chase the animal away or I could take it inside and housebreak it. Somehow I must stop it from eating all of my okra for I loved okra. Walking to the back door, I considered other plans. I was leaning toward the idea of buying a muzzle for the aardvark however I wasn't sure that the usual sizes would fit this particular animal. Before stepping into the back yard, I stood watching the aardvark. He, or perhaps she (I couldn't really be sure), finished eating one large okra plant then he went on to a smaller one in the next row. I hesitated to disturb him he seemed so content. But I had my okra to think of so I walked toward him briskly, making friendly noises and trying to look disapproving but gracious. I suggested to him in a helpful way that eating too much okra could be dangerous for his health. He looked up at me and nodded in agreement or perhaps he was just chewing his last bite of the small okra plant. Then an idea hit me I would call the Society for the Prevention of Cruelty to Aardvarks. The aardvark would be taken off my hands furthermore my okra would be saved. It was the perfect solution.

READING/WRITING ASSIGNMENT 11A

THE HUMAN BRAIN AND THE COMPUTER
Isaac Asimov

Pre-Reading/Writing Exercise

Computers are becoming increasingly important in our daily lives. Think for a few minutes about the topic "computers" and then cube this topic, approaching it from the six different points of view listed below:

1. Describe it.
2. Compare it.

3. Associate it.

4. Analyze it.

5. Apply it.

6. Argue for or against it.

Remember that cubing is similar to freewriting, except that you switch points of view as you go, writing without worrying about form or correctness whatever comes into your mind about the topic from each different angle. Spend approximately three minutes writing from each point of view on the topic "computers." (If you need a further review of cubing, see Reading/Writing Assignment 5A.)

Reading Exercise

In the following passage, the scientist and science fiction writer Isaac Asimov compares and contrasts a human brain and a computer. As you read, think about whether you agree or disagree with Asimov's thesis and major supporting statements.

1 The difference between a brain and a computer can be expressed in a single word: complexity.

2 The large mammalian brain is the most complicated thing, for its size, known to us. The human brain weighs three pounds, but in that three pounds are ten billion neurons and a hundred billion smaller cells. These many billions of cells are interconnected in a vastly complicated network that we can't begin to unravel as yet.

3 Even the most complicated computer man has yet built can't compare in intricacy with the brain. Computer switches and components number in the thousands rather than in the billions. What's more, the computer switch is just an on-off device, whereas the brain cell is itself possessed of a tremendously complex inner structure.

4 Can a computer think? That depends on what you mean by "think." If solving a mathematical problem is "thinking," then a computer can "think" and do so much faster than a man. Of course, most mathematical problems can be solved quite mechanically by repeating certain straightforward processes over and over again. Even the simple computers of today can be geared for that.

5 It is frequently said that computers solve problems only because they are "programmed" to do so. They can only do what men have them do. One must remember that human beings also can only do what they are "programmed" to do. Our genes "program" us the instant the fertilized ovum is formed, and our potentialities are limited by that "program."

6 Our "program" is so much more enormously complex, though, that we might like to define "thinking" in terms of the creativity that goes into writing a great play or composing a great symphony, in conceiving a brilliant scientific theory or a profound ethical judgment. In that sense, computers certainly can't think and neither can most humans.

7   Surely, though, if a computer can be made complex enough, it can be as creative as we. If it could be made as complex as a human brain, it could be the equivalent of a human brain and do whatever a human brain can do.

8   To suppose anything else is to suppose that there is more to the human brain than the matter that composes it. The brain is made up of cells in a certain arrangement and the cells are made up of atoms and molecules in certain arrangements. If anything else is there, no signs of it have ever been detected. To duplicate the material complexity of the brain is therefore to duplicate everything about it.

9   But how long will it take to build a computer complex enough to duplicate the human brain? Perhaps not as long as some think. Long before we approach a computer as complex as our brain, we will perhaps build a computer that is at least complex enough to design another computer more complex than itself. This more complex computer could design one still more complex and so on and so on and so on.

10   In other words, once we pass a certain critical point, the computers take over and there is a "complexity explosion." In a very short time thereafter, computers may exist that not only duplicate the human brain—but far surpass it.

11   Then what? Well, mankind is not doing a very good job of running the earth right now. Maybe, when the time comes, we ought to step gracefully aside and hand over the job to someone who can do it better. And if we don't step aside, perhaps Supercomputer will simply move in and push us aside.

Isaac Asimov, *Please Explain*

1. Is Asimov's thesis stated or implied? _____

What is his thesis? _____ _____

_____

2. According to Asimov, what word summarizes the difference between a computer and a brain?

_____

3. What is Asimov's primary method of development?

_____

4. What details does Asimov use in the second and third paragraphs to contrast a computer and a brain?

_____

_____

_____

5. Like a comparison/contrast paragraph, a comparison/contrast essay focuses on the relationships between two items, the likenesses and the differences. A pure comparison essay shows only likenesses, whereas a pure contrast essay shows only differences. Many comparative essays, however, illustrate both likenesses and differences. Does Asimov's essay show likenesses, differences, or both?

_____

Give examples. _____

_____

_____

_____

_____

6. You may recall that a comparison/contrast paragraph can be arranged in either of two basic patterns, the divided pattern or the alternating pattern, as illustrated below:

Divided Pattern

A. Computer
   1. Point 1
   2. Point 2
   3. Point 3
B. Brain
   1. Point 1
   2. Point 2
   3. Point 3

Alternating Pattern

1. Point 1
   A. Computer
   B. Brain
2. Point 2
   A. Computer
   B. Brain
3. Point 3
   A. Computer
   B. Brain

A comparison/contrast essay may also follow either of these patterns. Reread Asimov's essay, carefully examining its structure. Which comparison/contrast pattern does he use: divided or alternating?

_____

7. Asimov de-emphasizes some of the differences that most people believe exist between a computer and a human brain, but he nevertheless associates certain words more directly with computers and other words

more directly with the human brain. For example, he uses *components* in association with computers and *potentialities* in association with human beings. Thus, he uses words connotatively, choosing them for the connotations or associations they communicate to his readers. In the spaces below, write two or three more words that we, as Asimov's readers, associate with computers and two or three more words that we associate with the human brain:

Computers   **Brain**

_____   _____

_____   _____

_____   _____

Discussion Questions

1. Do you agree that "if a computer can be made complex enough, it can be as creative as we"? Why or why not?

2. Asimov believes that the human brain contains only "the matter that composes it." Do you agree? Why or why not?

3. Asimov predicts that someday a computer will exist that duplicates or surpasses the human brain. Do you agree or disagree with his prediction? Why or why not? If Asimov's prediction were to come true, what effects would it have on human life as we know it today?

Writing Exercise

Reread your cubing exercise and the questions about Asimov's essay. Then choose one of the specific assignments below and write a paragraph or essay about some aspect of the topic "computers." (Your instructor may specify one for you.)

1. Compare and contrast a computer with another machine such as a typewriter or an adding machine.

2. Using your own ideas rather than Asimov's, write your own comparison or contrast of a computer and a human brain. Do you see more similarities or differences?

3. What are some of the specific effects of computers on our daily lives? (You may want to limit your essay to one particular effect.) Support your ideas with a narrative illustration, examples, or specific statistics.

4. Do computers have more advantages or more disadvantages? What are the major advantages? What are the major disadvantages? Compare and contrast the advantages and disadvantages, arguing for or against computers. Or you might focus on either the advantages or disadvantages, giving examples.

Whatever topic you write on, determine your purpose and audience. For example, you might compare a word processor and a typewriter to persuade your parents to buy you a word processor for your college work. You might write to persuade your office manager to install computers in your office to perform a particular function, such as figuring payrolls. Or you might write to your college president to inform him or her that computerized record-keeping has depersonalized relationships on campus. After you have narrowed your topic and decided on your purpose, thesis, and audience, determine your method(s) of development and write your rough draft.

Rewriting Exercise

Reread your draft carefully to see whether you have achieved your purpose and communicated to your audience. Answer the following questions independently or in a peer review group.

1. What is your primary purpose?
2. Who is your audience?
3. What is your main idea (topic sentence or thesis)? Is it clearly stated and effectively limited and focused?
4. What primary method of development have you used (comparison/contrast, cause and effect, example, etc.)?
5. What are your major supporting points? What additional evidence, details, examples, and illustrations can you include?
6. Do all of your details support the main idea? If not, which should be deleted?
7. What pattern of arrangement have you used (alternating comparison/contrast, divided comparison/contrast, time order, space order, order of importance, etc.)?
8. What types of transition have you used? What other transitions do you need to add?
9. What is your conclusion? How can you improve it?
10. Does your composition achieve its purpose and communicate to its audience? If not, what revisions do you need to make?

After you have made the major revisions needed in your draft, edit it carefully. As you edit, consider the following questions.

1. Is each sentence a complete sentence with a subject and a verb?
2. Do you have any errors in subject-verb agreement?
3. Do you have any errors in pronoun reference or agreement?
4. What tense have you used? Is your use of tense consistent?
5. What point of view have you used (first person, second person, third person)? Is your point of view consistent?

6. Do you use transitions that indicate appropriate relationships between ideas?
7. Are all of your compound sentences punctuated correctly?
   a. Have you inserted a comma before coordinate conjunctions (*and, or, nor, for, but, yet,* and *so*) connecting independent clauses?
   b. Have you inserted a semicolon before conjunctive adverbs (*then, however, furthermore,* etc.) connecting independent clauses?
   c. Have you inserted a semicolon between independent clauses not connected by a transition word?
8. Do you have any run-on sentences?
9. Have you varied your sentence structure?
10. Is your word choice appropriate? Have you used any unnecessary or repetitious words?
11. Do you have any misspelled words?
12. Do you have any additional errors in capitalization, punctuation, or usage?

After you have edited your composition, write your final draft and proofread it carefully.

READING/WRITING ASSIGNMENT 11B

TYPES OF LONELINESS
William J. Lederer and Don D. Jackson

Pre-Reading/Writing Exercise

Many different relationships exist between married partners. Freewrite for five or ten minutes about the different kinds of marriages you have observed. What makes some marriages different from other marriages? What makes some marriages succeed while others fail?

Reading Exercise

In the following passage Lederer and Jackson classify loneliness in marriage into three different types. As you read, try to identify each of these three types of loneliness and to determine what distinguishes each type from the others.

1   Loneliness is seldom alleviated by marriage. People who marry each other so they will stop being lonely often discover that the most excruciating loneliness of all is shared with another.

2   There are three main types of loneliness. First, there is the loneliness of the individual who simply has not learned how to get along with people. When such lonely people marry each other, each one has high expectations of his spouse. Neither realizes that the other is paralyzed by the same limitations as he is. As a result, both of them wind up lonelier than ever. The TV and movie play *Marty,* where a shy, inarticulate man meets a shy, inarticulate woman and they find happiness together, is about on a par with *Cinderella* when it comes to realism.

3   A second type of loneliness is found in people who are the very opposite of those in the first group. They have bright personalities and well-developed social skills and are obsessed with the desire to be popular at all costs. Such people make good sales and advertising personnel and social leaders. Many of them give the appearance of being "sexy," when in reality they may be sexually unskilled or frigid, even though they may have had a number of affairs with the opposite sex. This type of person finds it difficult to be intimate with anyone whom he does not feel to be his inferior. The fact remains, however, that in marriage—as in relations with people in general—unless one person can deal with another on a basis of equality, he will be lonely, no matter how outgoing and what a good mixer he may appear to be.

4   A third kind of loneliness is seen in the type of person who must be best in whatever it is he does. Many successful people in the arts, industry and business fall into this category. Often they are kind and loving only to those who can be useful to them. People of this sort trust no one to do anything well, suspecting that almost everyone—even their spouses—will stand in the way of their headlong rush toward success. They require virtually everything and everyone to revolve around themselves. If they are glamorous or powerful enough, they may be able to get mates who will put up with this for a while. However, such marriages usually don't last, and they try again and again, drifting from one marriage to another, becoming more and more suspicious and more and more lonely.

Adapted from William J. Lederer and Don D. Jackson,
The Miracles of Marriage

1. Is the authors' thesis stated or implied? _____

What is their thesis? _____

_____

_____

2. What is the primary method of development in the passage?

_____

3. What three kinds of loneliness do the authors discuss?

    a. _____

_____

b. _____

_____

c. _____

_____

4. List three characteristics of the "type of person who must be best" in everything.

a. _____

_____

b. _____

_____

c. _____

_____

5. The words below may be unfamiliar to you. Use the context to help you define these words.

a. alleviated _____

b. excruciating _____

c. inarticulate _____

d. obsessed _____

e. frigid _____

Discussion Questions

1. What are some other causes of loneliness in a relationship?

2. Do you know someone who has a lonely marriage? Does this person fit into one of Lederer and Jackson's types of loneliness or into another category?

3. How does the loneliness that comes *after* a marriage compare with loneliness *in* a marriage? Do you know someone who is divorced or whose spouse has died? What feelings and problems does this person have?

4. What is the difference between *loneliness* and *aloneness* in a relationship? Is *aloneness* sometimes desirable?

Writing Exercise

Look back at your freewriting on different types of marriages. How many types of marriages did you identify? You and your classmates probably used different principles of classification—some of you classifying marriages according to the reasons couples marry, others classifying marriages according to how long they last, and still others classifying marriages by how happy the partners are. Be sure that you use only one method of classification; that is, don't mix methods in the same paper. After you have determined your major categories, decide on your purpose, main idea, and audience. Then write your rough draft of a paragraph or essay explaining the different types of marriages in your classification and providing examples of each type.

Alternate Assignments

1. Write a rough draft of a paragraph or essay about some aspect of loneliness not discussed by Lederer and Jackson. You might describe a person who is lonely; you might try to define loneliness, beginning with a formal definition (see Chapter 5, p. 107) and then supporting your definition with an illustration, a comparison, or several examples; or you might discuss the causes or the effects of loneliness. Determine your purpose and audience, and then use the most appropriate method of development to achieve your purpose and communicate to your audience.

2. Write a rough draft of a paragraph or essay in which you classify friends, sales clerks, waitresses, or some other group of people for a particular audience. Be as original as possible in your classification, and then use specific illustrations and examples to support your categories.

Rewriting Exercise

Reread your draft carefully to see whether you have achieved your purpose and communicated to your audience. Answer the following questions independently or in a peer review group.

1. What is your purpose?
2. Who is your audience?
3. What is your main idea (topic sentence or thesis)? Is it clearly stated and effectively narrowed and focused?
4. What method(s) of development have you used? If you used classification, do all examples of your topic (marriage, friends, waitresses, etc.) fit into one of your categories? Do you need to add a category? Have you confused or mixed categories unnecessarily?
5. Have you supported each point with specific details and examples? What other details can you add?
6. Do all of your details support your main idea? If not, which should be omitted?
7. How have you arranged your supporting points? Is this arrangement logical?

8. What types of transition have you used? What other transitions can you add?

9. What is your conclusion? How can it be improved?

10. Does your composition achieve your purpose and communicate to your audience? Why or why not? What changes should you make?

After you have made the major revisions needed in your draft, edit it carefully. As you edit, consider the following questions.

1. Is each sentence a complete sentence with a subject and a verb?

2. Do you have any errors in subject-verb agreement?

3. Do you have any errors in pronoun reference or agreement?

4. What tense have you used? Is your use of tense consistent?

5. What point of view have you used (first person, second person, third person)? Is your point of view consistent?

6. Do you use transitions that indicate the appropriate relationships between ideas?

7. Are all of your compound sentences punctuated correctly?
   a. Have you inserted a comma before coordinate conjunctions (*and, or, nor, for, but, yet,* and *so*) connecting independent clauses?
   b. Have you inserted a semicolon before conjunctive adverbs (*then, however, furthermore,* etc.) connecting independent clauses?
   c. Have you inserted a semicolon between independent clauses not connected by a transition word?

8. Do you have any run-on sentences?

9. Have you varied your sentence structure?

10. Is your word choice appropriate? Have you used any unnecessary or repetitious words?

11. Do you have any misspelled words?

12. Do you have any additional errors in capitalization, punctuation, or usage?

After you have edited your composition, write your final draft and proofread it carefully.

Chapter 12

SUBORDINATION: THE COMPLEX SENTENCE

Like coordination, subordination is a concept that is essential to reading and writing. We must understand subordination in order to understand relationships between ideas in essays, paragraphs, and sentences. Whereas coordinate elements are equal, a subordinate element is dependent on another element. In an essay, the topic sentences are subordinate to the thesis statement; in a paragraph, major details are subordinate to the topic sentence, and minor details are subordinate to major details; and in sentences, some ideas, clauses, or details are subordinate to others.

In a simple sentence or a compound sentence, modifiers are subordinate to the main idea expressed by the subject and verb. Subordination within sentences most clearly occurs, however, in the complex sentence. A complex sentence consists of an independent clause that contains within it a subordinate, or dependent, clause. Unlike the compound sentence, which consists of two equal (coordinate) independent clauses, the complex sentence is made up of two different types of clauses: an independent clause and a subordinate clause. The independent clause expresses the main idea of the sentence, and the subordinate clause expresses a supporting idea or detail. As shown in Figure 34, the subordinate clause functions as *part of* the independent clause.

FIGURE 34

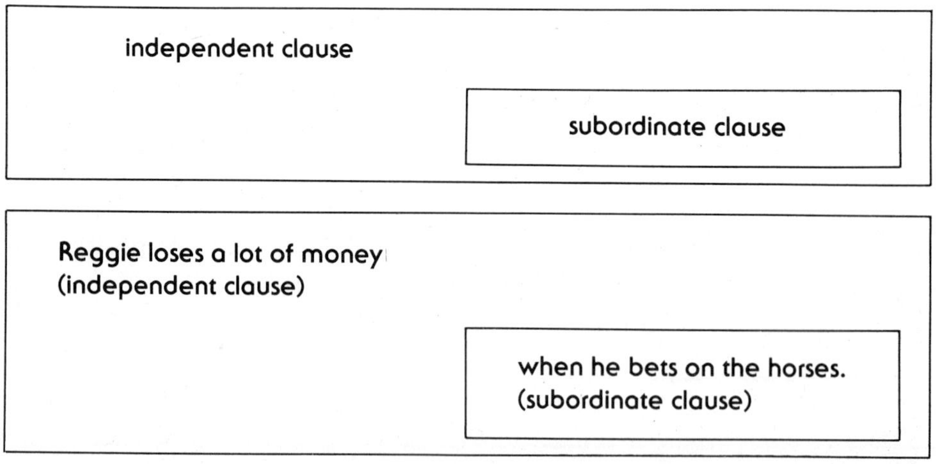

independent clause

subordinate clause

Reggie loses a lot of money (independent clause)

when he bets on the horses. (subordinate clause)

In order to understand subordinate clauses, you must first understand phrases and independent clauses because a subordinate clause has characteristics of both. The chart in Figure 35 summarizes the characteristics of both phrases and clauses.

342

FIGURE 35

Phrase (to the theater)	Does not have a subject and verb	Functions as a unit in a sentence	Cannot stand alone as a sentence
Subordinate clause (when he went to the theater)	Has a subject and a verb	Functions as a unit in a sentence	Cannot stand alone as a sentence
Independent clause (he went to the theater)	Has a subject and a verb	Does not function as a unit in a sentence	Can stand alone as a sentence

As the chart indicates, a subordinate clause, unlike an independent clause, cannot function as a sentence even though it has a subject and a verb. A subordinate clause is like a phrase in that it is part of an independent clause and functions as an adverb, an adjective, or a noun within the independent clause. Thus, the two clauses of a complex sentence are not equal (coordinate) as are the clauses of a compound sentence. In a complex sentence, the subordinate clause is dependent on—or subordinate to—the independent clause.

EXAMPLES

Although the forests are old, much undergrowth is recent. (adverb clause)

The actress *who appeared in the second act* had a shrill voice. (adjective clause)

The jury concluded *that he was guilty of the murder.* (noun clause)

ADVERB CLAUSES

An adverb clause is a subordinate clause that functions as an adverb within the independent clause in which it appears. Adverb clauses usually modify the verb of the independent clause. Listed below are some of the signal words, or subordinate conjunctions, that are commonly used to introduce adverb clauses.

after	as	whereas	so that
before	as if	although	even if
when	as soon as	though	even though
whenever	if	since	where
while	unless	because	wherever
	whether	until	

The following complex sentences contain adverb clauses. Observe how the placement and punctuation of the adverb clause differ in the two sentences.

Adverb clause at the beginning of a sentence:

Unless you save carefully, you will not have enough money for your tuition next semester.

Adverb clause at the end of a sentence:

You will not have enough money for your tuition next semester *unless you save carefully.*

Notice that in the first sentence the adverb clause comes at the beginning of the sentence and is followed by a comma. In the second sentence, the adverb clause comes after the independent clause and is not separated from it by a comma. An introductory adverb clause is always followed by a comma; adverb clauses that occur at the end of a sentence, however, require *no* punctuation.

EXERCISE 12.1

Combine each of the following pairs of sentences into a complex sentence with an adverb clause. Vary the position of your adverb clauses and punctuate appropriately. You may wish to refer to the signal words listed on page 343.

1. The desert is hot and dry.
   Many flowers grow there.

   _____

   _____

   _____

2. Several states are passing stricter driving-while-intoxicated laws.
   The number of traffic deaths connected with drinking may be reduced.

   _____

   _____

   _____

3. In recent years several airlines have suffered record losses.
   The days of low airline rates may be over.

   _____

_____

_____

4. In extremely hot weather elderly people can die from heat stroke.
They stay in an air-conditioned environment.

_____

_____

_____

5. I put my arm out the window of the car.
I came to a stop at the busy intersection.

_____

_____

_____

6. The Ramsays escaped from their burning house.
Their three-year-old son was awakened by the heat.

_____

_____

_____

7. Last evening I was reading the paper.
I noticed a peculiar odor coming from the kitchen.

_____

_____

_____

8. I broke my leg.
I went skiing in Colorado.

_____

_____

_____

9. The room was uncomfortably hot.
   The speaker opened a window.

   _____

   _____

   _____

10. Fifteen spectators were injured in the accident at the racetrack.
    No one was killed.

   _____

   _____

   _____

EXERCISE 12.2

In the spaces below write five complex sentences with adverb clauses. Be
sure to vary the position of the adverb clauses you use. Punctuate your
sentences appropriately.

1. _____

   _____

   _____

2. _____

   _____

   _____

3. _____

   _____

   _____

4. _____

   _____

   _____

5. _____

   _____

   _____

ADJECTIVE CLAUSES

An adjective clause modifies a noun or a noun substitute within the independent clause in which it appears. Signal words used to introduce adjective clauses are listed below:

who	which
whom	where
whose	when
that	why

Both of the following sentences contain adjective clauses. As you read the sentences, notice the difference between them.

Restrictive:

restrictivo

The woman *who married Hitler* committed suicide to prevent capture by the Allies.

Nonrestrictive:

Eva Braun, *who married Hitler,* committed suicide to prevent capture by the Allies.

In the first sentence the word *woman* is identified by the adjective clause *who married Hitler.* Adjective clauses that are needed to identify the words they modify are called *restrictive* clauses and require no punctuation. In the second sentence the adjective clause is not needed to identify Eva Braun; the clause is therefore nonessential, or *nonrestrictive.* Nonrestrictive adjective clauses must be set off by commas.

Note: *That* usually introduces restrictive clauses; *which* usually introduces nonrestrictive clauses.

EXERCISE 12.3

Combine each of the following pairs of sentences into a complex sentence with an adjective clause. Be sure to punctuate each sentence correctly. You may wish to refer to the signal words listed above.

1. The city council supports a rapid-transit plan.
   The plan will reduce freeway traffic.   *which*

   _____

   _____

   _____

   _____

2. The junkyard dealer has been robbed several times.
   He now uses a seven-foot ostrich as a night guard.

   _____

   _____

   _____

   _____

3. The citizens of Buffalo rallied to the defense of the man.
   The man was accused of stabbing his daughter's rapist.

   _____

   _____

   _____

   _____

4. The blue lake mirrored the snow-capped mountains.
   The lake was crescent-shaped.

   _____

   _____

   _____

   _____

5. I shopped at the new mall with my sister Myra.
   Myra lives in Anaheim.

   _____

_____

_____

_____

6. Charles Lindbergh was received in New York with wild enthusiasm.
   He had accomplished a remarkable feat.

_____

_____

_____

_____

7. On a trip to the Rockies last summer I met an interesting old man.
   He claimed to be ninety-nine years old.

_____

_____

_____

_____

8. The student looked surprised but happy.
   The student's paper had received the A.

_____

_____

_____

_____

9. We went to the ballet.
   It was performed by the Royal Canadian Ballet Company.

_____

_____

_____

_____

10. John Kennedy was elected President of the United States in 1959. He was a Roman Catholic.

_____

_____

_____

_____

EXERCISE 12.4

In the spaces below write five complex sentences with adjective clauses. Be sure to include at least one sentence with a restrictive clause and one with a nonrestrictive clause. Punctuate your sentences appropriately.

1. _____

_____

_____

2. _____

_____

_____

3. _____

_____

_____

4. _____

_____

_____

5. _____

_____

_____

NOUN CLAUSES

A noun clause functions as the subject, object, subject complement, or object of a preposition within the independent clause of a complex sentence. Signal words used to introduce noun clauses are listed below.

who	what	whomever	where
whom	that	whichever	wherever
which	whoever	whatever	when
			whenever

Below are four sentences that illustrate the different kinds of noun clauses. Following each sentence is a second sentence in which a simple noun or pronoun has been substituted for the noun clause. By comparing these sentence pairs, you will be able to see more clearly how the noun clause functions within a complex sentence.

1. Noun clause as subject:

   Whoever arrives early can set up the tables and chairs. (*They* can set up the tables and chairs.)

2. Noun clause as direct object:

   He knew *what she wanted to do.* (He knew her *plan.*)

3. Noun clause as subject complement:

   The problem was *that we were already late.* (The problem was our *lateness.*)

4. Noun clause as object of a preposition:

   I will go to the play with *whoever asks me first.* (I will go to the play with *Fran.*)

Note: Since noun clauses function as an essential element within a sentence, they require *no* added punctuation. If you are not sure whether a clause is a noun clause, substitute a noun or pronoun for the clause. If the substitution makes sense, the clause is functioning as a noun.

EXERCISE 12.5

Combine each of the following sentence pairs into a complex sentence with a noun clause. You may wish to use the signal words suggested in parentheses.

1. The patient knew something. (that)
   The operation might be fatal.

   _____

   _____

   _____

2. Please select something. (whichever)
   The dessert is your favorite.

   _____

   _____

   _____

3. Murder was the crime. (for which)
   The prisoner was tried.

   _____

   _____

   _____

4. The winner is someone. (whoever)
   Someone is elected.

   _____

   _____

   _____

5. Please give the package to someone. (whoever)
   Someone answers the door.

   _____

   _____

   _____

6. (that) Amy had not read her assignment.
   Something was apparent to her psychology professor.

   _____

_____

_____

EXERCISE 12.6

In the spaces below write five complex sentences with noun clauses.

1. _____

   _____

   _____

2. _____

   _____

   _____

3. _____

   _____

   _____

4. _____

   _____

   _____

5. _____

   _____

   _____

EXERCISE 12.7

The following groups of sentences can be combined into complex sentences. Combine the sentence groups, being sure to punctuate each new sentence appropriately. Remember to put main ideas in independent clauses and supporting ideas in subordinate clauses. Then rewrite the sentences in paragraph form.

1. Tennessee Williams reveals something.
   The revelation is in *The Glass Menagerie*.
   The something is that dreams are fragile.

   _____

   _____

   _____

   _____

2. Laura Wingfield is extremely shy.
   Laura is physically crippled.
   Laura has retreated from the real world.
   Laura has retreated into a world of Victrola music.
   Laura has retreated into a world of little glass animals.

   _____

   _____

   _____

   _____

3. Her mother is Amanda Wingfield.
   Amanda lives in the past.
   The living is with her girlhood memories.
   The memories are of "gentlemen callers."

   _____

   _____

   _____

   _____

4. Laura's brother is Tom.
   Tom escapes from his job.
   The job is drab.
   The job is at a warehouse.
   The warehouse is for shoes.
   He escapes by going to the movies.
   He escapes by writing poetry.

   _____

   _____

   _____

5. Tom is in a dilemma.
   He feels responsible.
   The responsibility is for his family.
   He needs freedom.
   The freedom is for himself.

   _____

   _____

   _____

   _____

6. The situation is brought to a climax.
   The situation is tense.
   The situation is in the Wingfield household.
   Tom brings home a "gentleman caller."
   The "gentleman caller" is named Jim O'Connor.
   The "gentleman caller" is to meet Laura.

   _____

   _____

   _____

   _____

7. Jim comes home with Tom.
   Jim is kind.
   The kindness is to Laura.

   _____

   _____

   _____

   _____

8. Laura comes out of her world.
   The world is of dreams.
   The coming out is only for a while.
   Laura thinks something.
   The something is that she has found someone.
   The someone is to love her.

_____

_____

_____

_____

9. However, Jim breaks something.
   The breaking is accidental.
   The something is a unicorn.
   The unicorn is little.
   The unicorn is glass.
   The unicorn is Laura's ornament.
   The ornament is her favorite.
   Jim shatters her hopes.
   Jim tells her something.
   The something is that he is already engaged.

_____

_____

_____

_____

10. Jim leaves.
    Laura is left with her dreams.
    Laura is left with her animals.
    The animals are little.
    The animals are glass.
    The dreams comfort her.
    The animals comfort her.

_____

_____

_____

_____

11. Amanda discovers something.
    The something is that Jim is engaged.
    The something is that Laura has no hope.
    The hope is of marrying Jim.
    Amanda accepts reality.

Amanda admits something to herself.
The admission is that Laura is crippled.

_____

_____

_____

_____

12. The play ends.
Tom has joined the merchant marine.
Tom is looking back at his memories.
The memory is of his mother.
The memory is of his sister.

_____

_____

_____

_____

SIGNALING RELATIONSHIPS IN COMPLEX SENTENCES

Good readers and writers are able to determine main ideas and supporting ideas within sentences and to understand the relationships between those ideas. One of the best ways to identify supporting ideas in subordinate clauses is to look for the signal words that introduce them. The signal words also indicate the relationship that exists in a complex sentence between the subordinate clause and the independent clause of which it is a part.

In previous exercises you have used signal words to connect independent and subordinate clauses. The following chart should be helpful to you because it not only lists the most common signal words used to introduce subordinate clauses but also indicates the relationships shown by the signal words. Study the words carefully so that you can use them appropriately to connect independent and subordinate clauses.

Place	Cause, Effect, Conclusion	Example
where	so that	such as
wherever	in order that	as
	because	
	since	

Manner, Condition	**Contrast**	
if	although	until
unless	though	whenever
as, as if	even though	as long as
lest	even if	as soon as
provided	whereas	as often as
provided	than	
that	except	**Agent**
in case	except that	who
just as		whom
whether	**Time**	whose
how	after	which
	before	that
	when	whichever
	while	whoever
		whomever
		whosoever
		whatever
		wherever

EXERCISE 12.8

Read each sentence carefully and then insert in the blank a signal word that shows the proper relationship between the main idea expressed in the independent clause and the supporting idea expressed in the subordinate clause.

EXAMPLE

The concert was canceled *because* rain was forecast.

(The relationship here is one of cause and effect, so either *because* or *since* would be a good choice.)

1. _____ a left-handed child is forced to write with his or her right hand, the child may become confused.

2. The nurse ran into the patient's room _____ he could assist the doctor.

3. Most college students call their parents _____ they run out of money.

4. I wasn't sure _____ had given me the flowers until I read the card.

5. I don't know _____ the test is being given on Tuesday or Thursday.

6. _____ he is no longer a child, a teenager is not an adult.

7. The baby didn't know _____ the stove was hot.

8. _____ the car stopped, I crossed the street.

9. Cats can never be owned; they will live with _____ is kind to them.

10. I hope _____ I have time to eat lunch
    _____ I have to go to my next class.

11. _____ Pam has been jogging, her health is much better.

12. _____ the dog seemed friendly, I was afraid of him.

13. My brother was as happy _____ he could be with his new job.

14. _____ the rain has stopped, we can play golf.

15. Joan tries to take her college classes during the mornings
    _____ her children are in school.

EXERCISE 12.9

In the following paragraph signal words used to introduce subordinate clauses have been omitted. Read the paragraph carefully and write in the blanks appropriate signal words.

Then he was alone in the galley and sure of the look he would see in the

Indian's eyes. The tribes of the villages _____ would form his
                                                    (1)

patrol belonged to a people _____ had never been at war
                                          (2)

with the white man. They lived _____ they had always lived.
                                            (3)

They fished _____ they had always fished, known for their
(4)

intelligence and a culture _____ was perhaps the most highly
(5)

developed of any native band on the continent. In the old days

_____ a chief had given a great feast for his rivals, he let the
(6)

fire _____ burned in the center of his ceremonial house catch
(7)

the roof beams _____ the red hot embers fell, knowing
(8)

that _____ he gave the sign, no guest dared move
(9)

_____ he admit the host's fire had conquered him.
(10)

_____ he served his guests from the great ceremonial dishes,
(11)

he spilt hot grease on their bare arms to see _____ he could
(12)

make them wince. And sometimes he broke his own copper—big as a

shield, its buying power as great as three thousand of the white man's dol-

lars—broke it to show to his guests his disdain for his own wealth. Surely the

look would be one of arrogance.

Margaret Craven, *I Heard the Owl Call My Name*

EXERCISE 12.10

In this exercise, you are given an independent clause and a connecting word.
Supply a dependent clause that fits the relationship indicated by the signal
word.

1. They left the house before _____

   _____

2. They left the house so that _____

   _____

3. They left the house although _____

   _____

4. They left the house because _____

    _____

5. We believe that _____

    _____

6. We believe what _____

    _____

7. We believe whoever _____

    _____

8. We believe whatever _____

    _____

9. Because _____

    the child sleeps peacefully.

10. After _____

    the child sleeps peacefully.

11. Whereas _____

    the child sleeps peacefully.

12. If _____

    the child sleeps peacefully.

13. The man who _____

    is here.

14. The letter, which _____

    is here.

15. The man whose _____

    is here.

16. The package that _____

    is here.

17. Ms. Johnson, who _____

    ate heartily.

18. The black cat, which _____

    ate heartily.

19. Mr. Stokes, whose _____

    ate heartily.

20. The Wells' baby, who _____

    ate heartily.

EDITING COMPLEX SENTENCES

Subordination is a necessary tool for indicating relationships between ideas. Each time you use a subordinate clause in your writing, however, you should be sure (1) that it is punctuated correctly and (2) that it is connected to an independent clause and therefore not a subordinate clause fragment.

Punctuation of Subordinate Clauses

As you have seen earlier in this chapter, different types of subordinate clauses require different punctuation. Review the following punctuation guide:

1. An introductory adverb clause is set off by a comma.

   Because the rain was coming down in torrents, the game was delayed.

2. An adverb clause at the end of a sentence is not set off by a comma.

   The game was delayed *because the rain was coming down in torrents.*

3. A nonrestrictive adjective clause is set off by commas.

   Jim, *who is president of my fraternity,* is my best friend.

4. A restrictive adjective clause is *not* set off by commas.

   The boy *who is president of my fraternity* is my best friend.
5. A noun clause is *not* set off by commas.

   Did you know *that I was here?*

EXERCISE 12.11

Edit the following complex sentences carefully by supplying punctuation where it is needed. Some sentences are correct.

1. When the party is over we'll have our meeting.
2. We took a vacation on Padre Island where there is a good beach.
3. I'll take you to Venice where you can ride in gondolas.
4. You have some very important decisions to make when you graduate.
5. Paul Farrell to whom my sister is engaged graduated from Yale.
6. The girl that the boss hired is very efficient.
7. Mrs. Thomas fired the secretary that Mr. Thomas liked so well.
8. Mr. Crockett who used to be a football player is enormous.
9. When I push this button the motor begins to run.
10. Because it was hot he opened the window.
11. This ball club never won a game until Jack was named manager.
12. When I married Sara she weighed only ninety pounds.
13. His car skidded around the corner because the tires were slick.
14. When I came home late I entered quietly.
15. I bought him a card because it was his birthday.
16. That I lost my library card caused me many problems.
17. I discovered that I was overdrawn when I balanced my checkbook.
18. Although my sister loves to cook she hates to do the dishes.
19. The horse that broke through the fence did not hurt itself.
20. Your roommate wanted to know what time you got home.
21. Since I am a mountain man I like high places.
22. He visits his parents when he can.
23. The flight attendant who spilled my drink apologized profusely.
24. Their club president who was elected by only one vote resigned yesterday.
25. Although missing one class may not be serious missing a week of classes can hurt your grades.

Subordinate Clause Fragments

A subordinate clause has a subject and a verb but does not express a complete thought. It cannot stand by itself as a sentence but must always be attached to an independent clause. The diagrams in Figures 36 and 37 illustrate a subordinate clause that is used correctly as part of an independent clause and incorrectly as a fragment unattached to an independent clause.

FIGURE 36

Subordinate clause as part of an independent clause (correct):

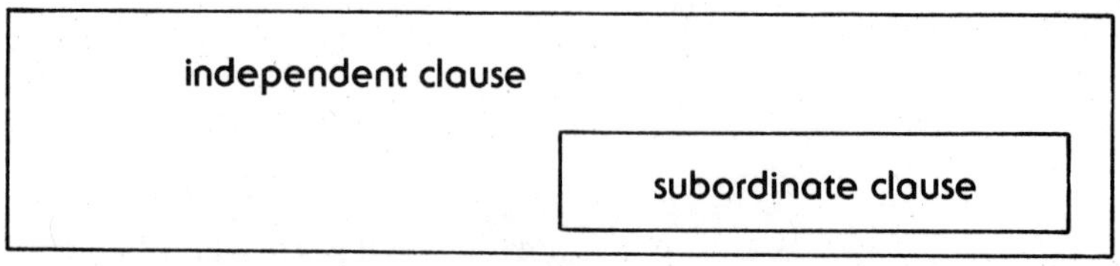

She knew with certainty
that he was the prowler.

FIGURE 37

Subordinate clause as a fragment (incorrect):

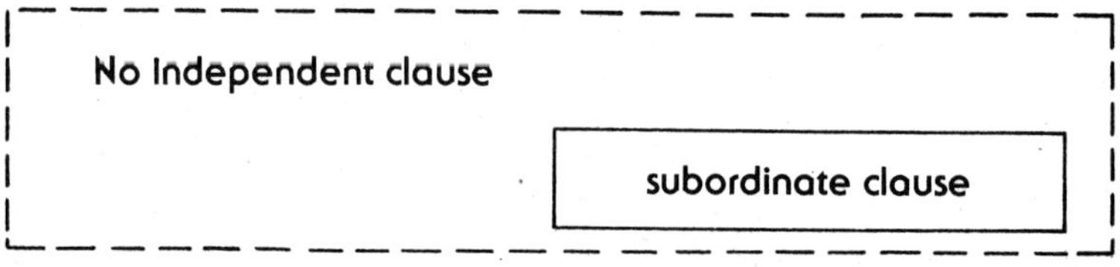

That he was the prowler.

EXERCISE 12.12

Change each of the following fragments into a complete sentence by adding an independent clause to the subordinate clause that is given.

EXAMPLE

Because I missed the bus by seconds. (A subordinate clause—a fragment)

I was twenty minutes late to school because I missed the bus by seconds. (An independent clause modified by a subordinate clause—a complete sentence)

1. who broke her glasses

2. because the lights on the stage went out during the performance

_____

_____

_____

3. while the motor was running

_____

_____

_____

4. after the prowler ran away

_____

_____

_____

5. who is president of the student senate

_____

_____

_____

6. that we had made a mistake

_____

_____

_____

7. if you want to buy a computer

_____

_____

_____

8. which raced across the lake

_____

_____

_____

9. because the library closes at ten o'clock

_____

_____

_____

10. whom I met at your party

_____

_____

_____

EXERCISE 12.13

The following passage contains twelve fragments, each of which is a subordinate clause incorrectly written as a sentence. Rewrite the passage on a separate sheet of paper, connecting each fragment to a related independent clause.

Almost every book on art includes a reproduction of the "Mona Lisa." Which is one of the most famous paintings in the world. The "Mona Lisa" was painted by Leonardo da Vinci. Who worked on it for four years (1503–1506). The painting was never quite finished. After he had worked for several hours. Leonardo would sit down in front of the "Mona Lisa" to quiet his nerves. Some people say. That Leonardo did not finish the painting. Because he wanted an excuse to keep it with him.

On the face of the woman in the painting there is a mysterious smile. Which has intrigued people for centuries. Although no one knows the true explanation of the smile. Several different legends have grown up about it. One story says that the woman was smiling sadly. When she sat for the portrait. Because her child had died. Another story, however, goes on to say that Leonardo hired musicians, flutists and violinists, to play during the sittings. So that he could capture the young woman's rapt expression.

When Leonardo left Italy and moved to France. He took the painting with him. The French king persuaded him to sell the painting. Which now hangs in the Louvre, an art museum in Paris.

THE THROW-AWAY SOCIETY
Alvin Toffler

Pre-Reading/Writing Exercise

Think for a few minutes about your relationships with certain objects that you see and use daily. What are some items that you use and quickly discard? What are other items, or perhaps a particular item, that you use carefully and then preserve for future use? How does your attitude differ toward objects that you discard easily and those that you keep? Do you use and throw away more items today than you did five years ago? Ten years ago? Freewrite for five to ten minutes about your relationship with things you use frequently.

Reading Exercise

In the following excerpt from *Future Shock,* Alvin Toffler discusses man's relationship with things. Read this excerpt to see how, according to Toffler, "man-thing relationships" are changing.

1   Our attitudes toward things reflect basic value judgments. Nothing could be more dramatic than the difference between the new breed of little girls who cheerfully turn in their Barbies for the new improved model and those who, like their mothers and grandmothers before them, clutch lingeringly and lovingly to the same doll until it disintegrates from sheer age. In this difference lies the contrast between past and future, between societies based on permanence, and the new, fast-forming society based on transience.

2   That man-thing relationships are growing more and more temporary may be illustrated by examining the culture surrounding the little girl who trades in her doll. This child soon learns that Barbie dolls are by no means the only physical objects that pass into and out of her young life at a rapid clip. Diapers, bibs, paper napkins, Kleenex, towels, non-returnable soda bottles—all are used up quickly in her home and ruthlessly eliminated. Corn muffins come in baking tins that are thrown away after one use. Spinach is encased in plastic sacks that can be dropped into a pan of boiling water for heating, and then thrown away. TV dinners are cooked and often served on throw-away trays. Her home is a large processing machine through which objects flow, entering and leaving, at a faster and faster rate of speed. From birth on, she is inextricably embedded in a throw-away culture.

3   The idea of using a product once or for a brief period and then replacing it, runs counter to the grain of societies or individuals steeped in a heritage of poverty. Not long ago Uriel Rone, a market researcher for the French advertising agency Publicis, told me: "The French housewife is not used to disposable products. She likes to keep things, even old things, rather

than throw them away. We represented one company that wanted to introduce a kind of plastic throw-away curtain. We did a marketing study for them and found the resistance too strong." This resistance, however, is dying all over the developed world.

4   Thus a writer, Edward Maze, has pointed out that many Americans visiting Sweden in the early 1950's were astounded by its cleanliness. "We were almost awed by the fact that there were no beer and soft drink bottles by the roadsides, as, much to our shame, there were in America. But by the 1960's, lo and behold, bottles were suddenly blooming along Swedish highways . . . What happened? Sweden had become a buy, use and throw-away society, following the American pattern." In Japan today throw-away tissues are so universal that cloth handkerchiefs are regarded as old fashioned, not to say unsanitary. In England for sixpence one may buy a "Denta-matic throw-away toothbrush" which comes already coated with toothpaste for its one-time use. And even in France, disposable cigarette lighters are commonplace. From cardboard milk containers to the rockets that power space vehicles, products created for short-term or one-time use are becoming more numerous and crucial to our way of life.

5   We develop a throw-away mentality to match our throw-away products. This mentality produces, among other things, a set of radically altered values with respect to property. But the spread of disposability through the society also implies decreased durations in man-thing relationships. Instead of being linked with a single object over a relatively long span of time, we are linked for brief periods with the succession of objects that supplant it.

Adapted from Alvin Toffler, *Future Shock*

1. What is Toffler's thesis? State his thesis in your own words.

_____

_____

_____

2. What primary supporting example does Toffler use in the first two paragraphs?

_____

3. What are two or three other supporting examples used in these two paragraphs?

_____

_____

_____

4. In the past, how did people in other countries react to this "throw-away" mentality?

_____

_____

Give examples.

_____

_____

_____

Give an example of how this reaction has changed.

_____

_____

_____

_____

5. According to Toffler, what effect does a throw-away society have on its people?

_____

_____

_____

6. The word *transience* is basic to an understanding of this passage. First, try to determine what this word means from clues in the passage. Then look up the word in a dictionary. Finally, using your own words, write a definition below:

_____

Discussion Questions

1. Discuss the idea of transience in class. What objects, feelings, relationships, or conditions in our lives are transient?

2. What effect does a "throw-away society" have on human relationships?

Writing Exercise

Write a
paragraph   3/26/90

Write an essay or paragraph in which you explain our "throw-away society" to a person of your own age who lives in another time. You may choose to write to someone who lived fifty or one hundred years ago, or you may pretend that you are writing for a time capsule to be opened one hundred years in the future.

Limit your paragraph or essay to one specific aspect or example of our throw-away society. You might, for example, want to write about the effects of discarded paper or plastic products on our environment. You might wish to write about how the difference between our society's use of Kleenex tissues and our grandparents' use of linen or lace handkerchiefs reflects the lives of the persons involved. You could contrast past and present ways of life by contrasting two other objects such as paper plates and china plates, disposable containers and returnable bottles, plastic toys and wooden toys, paperback books and leather-bound books, or disposable diapers and cloth diapers. You might even want to consider advantages or disadvantages of living in either the past or the present. What are the advantages or disadvantages, for example, of disposable diapers as compared with cloth diapers? Finally, you could discuss how this changing relationship with things affects human relationships.

Rewriting Exercise

Reread your paper, putting yourself in the place of your audience. Then, using the questions below as a guide, revise your paper.

1. What is your primary purpose?
2. Who is your audience?
3. What is your main idea (topic sentence or thesis)? Is it clearly stated and effectively limited and focused?
4. What method(s) of development have you used?
5. What are your major supporting points? What additional evidence, details, examples, and illustrations can you include?
6. Do all of your details support the main idea? If not, which should be deleted?
7. How have you arranged your supporting points? Is this the most effective arrangement?
8. What types of transition did you use? What additional transitions can you add to improve your composition?
9. What is your conclusion? How can you improve it?
10. Does your composition achieve its purpose and communicate to its audience? Would a person living in a different time and a different society have difficulty understanding your paragraph or essay? Have you assumed that your reader has background information that someone living in another time might not have?

After you have made the major revisions needed in your draft, edit it carefully. As you edit, consider the following questions.

1. Is each sentence a complete sentence with a subject and a verb?
2. Do you have any errors in subject-verb agreement?

3. Do you have any errors in pronoun reference or agreement?

4. What tense have you used? Is your use of tense consistent?

5. What point of view have you used (first person, second person, third person)? Is your point of view consistent?

6. Do you use transitions that indicate appropriate relationships between ideas?

7. Do you have any run-on sentences?

8. Are all of your complex sentences punctuated correctly?
   a. Have you inserted commas after adverb clauses at the beginnings of sentences?
   b. Have you set off nonrestrictive adjective clauses with commas?
   c. Have you incorrectly separated a noun clause from the rest of a sentence with a comma?

9. Have you varied your sentence structure?

10. Is your word choice appropriate? Have you used any unnecessary or repetitious words?

11. Do you have any misspelled words?

12. Do you have any additional errors in capitalization, punctuation, or usage?

After you have edited your composition, write your final draft, and proofread it carefully. Remember that you can improve your proofreading effectiveness by allowing some time to pass between rewriting your paper and proofreading it or by reading your paper aloud.

READING/WRITING ASSIGNMENT 12B

THE GOOD TEACHER
Frank Smith

Pre-Reading/Writing Exercise

Write for five or ten minutes about the topic "teachers." You may employ any one of the prewriting strategies you have used in *Contexts*—freewriting, journal writing, brainstorming, listing and categorizing, mapping, or cubing.

Reading Exercise

In the following passage, Frank Smith defines "the good teacher" and discusses the relationship between good teachers and learners—especially writers.

1   I often ask writers what first made them write. Relatively few people claim to be competent or even keen writers, but there is nothing particularly distinctive about people who regard writing as a worthwhile activity, in their personal lives as well as in their occupations. Writers are not necessarily more intelligent than people who don't write, nor are they inevitably more sensitive, more dedicated or disciplined, more introverted or extroverted, more austere or more self-indulgent. Writers come from large families and from small families, rich families and poor, families where everyone writes and families where no one else ever writes. In other words, the only apparent difference between writers and people who do not write is that writers write. So I am interested in what made them start writing, and what kept them at it. Many writers mentioned school.

2   But none of the writers who mentioned school said anything about programs or tests, about exercises or drills. Not one of them cited inspiring grammar lessons or unforgettable spelling lists. They all mentioned a person; they mentioned a teacher. And the teachers whom the writers mentioned were not necessarily tender and permissive. Some of these teachers were difficult and demanding curmudgeons. But they were all teachers who respected students and who respected the subject that they taught. They thought that writing was worthwhile. They were members of the writers' club.

3   When I question other people with a vocation—artists, artisans, scientists, athletes—they invariably tell me the same story. They were influenced by someone who was already a member of the club they joined, who admitted them as novice members. The influential individuals demonstrated that certain things were worth doing, they collaborated with the novices, and they inspired them to do those things themselves. (It is true that we can sometimes be admitted into clubs through the works of authors, musicians, or artists whom we have never met, but then someone must have earlier initiated us into the club of people who are responsive to books, music, or art.)

4   Good teachers respond instinctively to the way in which children—and adults—learn, without direction from outside authorities. Good teachers never rely on programs or tests, and they resist external control when it is thrust upon them. They do not allow themselves or their "apprentices" to engage in pointless ritualistic activities. Instead, these teachers manifest attitudes and behaviors that learners become interested in manifesting themselves, and then these teachers help learners to manifest such attitudes and behaviors for themselves. Such teachers attract and indenture apprentices without knowing they are doing so; they initiate learners into clubs. The two essential characteristics of all the good teachers I have met is that they are interested in what they teach and they enjoy working with learners. Indeed, they are learners themselves.

Frank Smith, *Insult to Intelligence: The Bureaucratic Invasion of Our Classrooms*

1. Is Smith's thesis stated or implied?

What is his thesis?

_____

_____

    2. According to Smith, what does a learner need most to develop a vocation, or career?

_____

_____

    3. Like most definition essays, this passage includes several methods of development. Which specific paragraph is developed by definition?

_____

    4. What kinds of behavior do good teachers avoid?

_____

_____

What are three characteristics of good teachers?

_____

_____

    5. What are two synonyms for _learner_ used in the passage?

_____

    6. Antonyms have opposite meanings. Smith uses several pairs of antonyms. Write below the antonym for each word listed.
a. introverted

_____

b. self-indulgent

_____

What did you learn about the meanings of the prefixes used in _introverted_ and its antonym?

_____

_____

Discussion Questions

1. You have enrolled in college to "get an education." What is an education? Are teachers necessary for an education?

2. How can teachers contribute to an education? How can they limit an education? Support with personal experiences.

Writing Exercise

Look back at your prewriting about teachers. What ideas for writing did you generate in your prewriting? Did you remember a particular teacher that you could describe or a specific incident about a teacher that you could narrate? Did you compare or contrast two teachers? Did you write about the characteristics of a good teacher or a bad teacher? Or did you write about the effects of good or bad teaching? Decide on your purpose, thesis, and audience. Then, using the most effective method of development for your purpose, write the rough draft of your paragraph or essay.

Alternate Assignment

To an audience of your choice, write the rough draft of a paragraph or essay in which you define *education*. Remember that a formal definition places the term to be defined in a category and then shows how the term is different from other items in the category. Remember, too, that definitions may also employ illustrations, examples, comparisons, classifications, and other methods of development.

Rewriting Exercise

Reread your draft carefully to see that you have achieved your purpose and communicated to your audience. Answer the following questions independently or in a peer review group.

1. What is your primary purpose?

2. Who is your audience?

3. What is your main idea (topic sentence or thesis)? Is it clearly stated and effectively limited and focused?

4. What method(s) of development have you used?

5. What are your major supporting points? What additional evidence, details, examples, and illustrations can you include?

6. Do all of your details support the main idea? If not, which should be deleted?

7. How have you arranged your supporting points? Is this the most effective arrangement?

8. What types of transition did you use? What additional transitions can you add to improve your composition?

9. What is your conclusion? How can you improve it?

10. Does your composition achieve its purpose and communicate to its audience? Why or why not? What revisions do you need to make?

After you have made the major revisions needed in your draft, edit it carefully. As you edit, consider the following questions.

1. Is each sentence a complete sentence with a subject and a verb?
2. Do you have any errors in subject-verb agreement?
3. Do you have any errors in pronoun reference or agreement?
4. What tense have you used? Is your use of tense consistent?
5. What point of view have you used (first person, second person, third person)? Is your point of view consistent?
6. Do you use transitions that indicate appropriate relationships between ideas?
7. Are all of your complex sentences punctuated correctly?
   a. Have you inserted commas after adverb clauses at the beginnings of sentences?
   b. Have you set off nonrestrictive adjective clauses with commas?
   c. Have you incorrectly separated a noun clause from the rest of the sentence with a comma?
8. Have you varied your sentence structure?
9. Is your word choice appropriate? Have you used any unnecessary or repetitious words?
10. Do you have any misspelled words?
11. Do you have any additional errors in capitalization, punctuation, or usage?

After you have edited your composition, write your final draft and proofread it carefully. Remember that to *proofread,* you must not use the predicting process you use when you *read;* that is, you must slow down and look at each word and sentence individually.

Appendix 1

CAPITALIZATION

The following rules illustrate many situations in which capital letters are needed:

1. Capitalize the first word of every sentence. Also capitalize the first word of direct quotations.

> The repairman took the television set with him.
>
> I said, "We'll leave for the game from my house."

2. Capitalize proper nouns. A proper noun is the name of a specific person, place, or thing: Ernest Hemingway, Ronald Reagan, Florida, Greenville, the Washington Monument, Trinity River.

> The Missouri River is the longest river in the United States.

3. Capitalize adjectives and nouns that are derived from proper nouns.

> The Soviet Union was dominated by Stalinism during the 1940s.
>
> She was an expert in Marxist philosophy.

4. Capitalize titles of persons when they precede proper names. When used in place of proper names, titles of officers of high rank should be capitalized. Other titles should not.

> Senator Smith, Admiral Lacy, the Governor, and the Attorney General came to the party for Professor Andrews.
>
> The postmaster of our town appealed to the Postmaster General for help.
>
> Mrs. Murray called Dr. Brinkman for an appointment.

5. Capitalize names of members of the family only when used in place of proper names.

> Today Mother called to tell me about my father's trip.
>
> My mother gave Dad a new fishing rod for his birthday.

6. Capitalize names referring to the people or language of a nation, religion, or race.

> The French and the Spanish were early settlers of Louisiana.
>
> Mary took German and Russian courses to satisfy her foreign language requirements.

7. Capitalize cities, states, and countries.

> On vacation we flew to Paris, France, and then to London, England.
>
> The bus broke down in Denver, Colorado, on its way to Amarillo, Texas.

8. Capitalize organizations such as clubs, churches, corporations, governmental bodies and departments, and political parties.

The members of the Senate passed a resolution praising the American Cancer Society.

The J. P. Stone Insurance Company made large contributions to both the Democratic party and the Republican party.

9. Capitalize geographical areas. Do not capitalize directions.

Mark Twain writes about his boyhood adventures in the South.

Go north when you get to Lee Street.

10. Capitalize brand and commercial names.

I bought a can of Right Guard deodorant spray at the Gibson Discount Center.

The Safeway store received new shipments of aspirin, including Bayer and St. Joseph's.

11. Capitalize days of the week and months.

My birthday, June 9, will fall on a Tuesday this year.

The annual company Christmas party will be held on Friday, December 23.

Notice that seasons are not capitalized.

The first Monday in January was the coldest day of winter.

Last Thursday marked the end of summer and the beginning of autumn.

12. Capitalize abbreviations when the words they stand for would be capitalized.

My brother transferred to U.C.L.A. (University of California, Los Angeles).

The U.S.M.C. (United States Marine Corps) has a long, proud tradition.

13. Capitalize only the official title of a particular course unless the course refers to a nationality or language.

My history class for next semester will be History 122.

I hate math and science, but I enjoy my French class.

14. Capitalize the first word and all nouns, verbs, adjectives, and adverbs in the titles of books, plays, articles, movies, songs, and other literary or artistic works. Do not capitalize words such as articles (*a, an,* and *the*), conjunctions, and prepositions.

To Kill a Mockingbird is a famous novel by Harper Lee.

The professor wrote an article entitled "Too Far from the Shore" about Hemingway's *The Old Man and the Sea.*

15. Capitalize the first word and titles of the person addressed in the greeting of a letter. Capitalize the first word only in the complimentary close.

Dear Madam, Dear President Carter, Dear Sir

Sincerely yours, Yours very truly

16. Capitalize the pronoun "I."

I passed my examination.

Although I worked until 2:00 in the morning, I didn't finish my paper.

Appendix 2

SPELLING

IMPROVING SPELLING SKILLS

Many excellent writers have poor spelling skills but have learned to correct their spelling errors because they know that mispelled words are distracting to a reader. If you have difficulty with spelling, you need to learn how to minimize your spelling errors so that your reader is not unduly distracted by them. Although there is no certain or simple way to become a good speller, there are several approaches that will help you become a *better* speller.

1. *Concentrate on your own particular spelling problems.* You need to keep a careful record of each word you misspell on your writing assignments and to study these words *regularly* until you master them. Next you need to identify and classify the types of spelling errors you are making.

2. *Learn the little words.* Almost everyone misspells a word occasionally, especially difficult words. However, educated people do not misspell common words. Some of these words are difficult in that they frequently look or sound like other words with which they can easily be confused; a glossary of these words is included in this appendix for you to study.

3. *Use the rules that work.* Most spelling rules are so complicated or have so many exceptions that they are not worth learning. However, a few of them work most of the time. These rules are really patterns because they do not always apply but are a general indication of how words are put together in English. Included in this appendix are four of the most useful spelling patterns plus the rules for forming possessives and plurals.

4. *Improve your vocabulary.* Spelling and vocabulary skills are closely related. Each time you learn a new word, be sure that you master its spelling as well as its meaning.

5. *Depend on your dictionary.* Accept the fact that you will always need to check on the spelling of many words in a dictionary or word-list book. However, as you improve your spelling, the number of words you will need to look up should decrease markedly. Learn to use your dictionary rapidly and accurately.

PROBLEM WORDS THAT LOOK AND SOUND ALIKE

a	article used before a consonant sound (*a* book, *a* lamp)
an	article used before a vowel sound (*an* onion, *an* hour)
accept	to receive (I *accept* your apology.)
except	not included (Everyone *except* the teacher laughed.)

advice (noun)	an opinion as to what should or should not be done
advise (verb)	to recommend or suggest; to inform or notify (Please *advise* your employer that his *advice* was appreciated.)
affect (verb)	to have an influence on (The illness *affected* his mind.)
effect (noun)	a result or consequence (What *effect* will the new law have?)
a lot	a large amount, many (two words; not spelled *alot*)
already	previously or by this time; one word (Summer is *already* here.)
all ready	completely prepared; two words (I am *all ready* to go.)
are	present tense form of *to be;* used with *you, we,* and *they* and plural nouns (You and they *are* free to go, but we *are* required to stay.)
our	possessive pronoun (We lost *our* way.)
or	coordinate conjunction (Joe *or* I will stay with you.)
capital (noun)	a city; a sum of money (Legislators in Austin, the *capital* of Texas, control the flow of *capital* in the state.)
capital (adjective)	chief or excellent (What a *capital* suggestion!)
capitol	a building where legislative sessions are held (The state *capitol* has a large dome.)
conscience	knowledge of right and wrong (Your *conscience* should hurt you.)
conscious	aware or alert (Was he *conscious* after the accident?)
complement	to make complete (Her blond hair *complemented* her tan.)
compliment (verb)	to praise (He *complimented* her tan.)
compliment (noun)	an expression of praise (She gave him a *compliment.*)
council	an assembly of persons called together for consultation or deliberation (The student *council* met with the faculty.)
counsel	advice or guidance, especially from a knowledgeable person (She sought her minister's *counsel.*)
coarse	low or common, of inferior quality or lacking in refinement; not fine in texture (That cake has a *coarse* texture.)
course	route or path taken; regular development or orderly succession; a prescribed unit of study (In the *course* of a year, twelve new buildings were built.)
of course	naturally, without doubt (*Of course,* I will.)
dessert	what is eaten at the end of a meal (I like ice cream for *dessert.*)
desert	land area characterized by sand and lack of water (The camel is used for transportation in the *desert.*)
fill	to make full (Please *fill* the dog's water dish.)
feel	to experience; to touch (I didn't *feel* very happy.)
fourth	to be number four in a sequence (We are *fourth* in line.)
forth	onward; in view; forward in place or time (Please step *forth.*)
idea (noun)	a thought; mental image or conception (My *idea* would be helpful.)
ideal (adjective)	perfect; without flaw (The gulf is an *ideal* place to fish.)
ideal (noun)	standard or model of perfection (Her teacher was her *ideal.*)
imply	to suggest; to express indirectly
infer	to conclude, as on the basis of suggestion or implication (A writer *implies;* a reader *infers* from what has been written.)
its	possessive pronoun meaning "belonging to it" (Virtue is *its* own reward.)
it's	contraction meaning "it is" or "it has" (*It's* a shame you are sick.)
knew	past tense of *to know* (He *knew* the name of the song.)
new	not old (She was *new* in town.)

know	to be mentally aware of (Do you *know* the answer?)
no	opposite of yes; not any (That is *no* way to treat a lady.)
lie	to recline (The book *lies* unopened on the table.)
lay	to place (Please *lay* the book on the table.)
	Note: The past tense of *lie* is *lay*; the past tense of *lay* is *laid.*
loose (adjective)	not tight; unfastened (The car has a *loose* wheel.)
lose (verb)	to allow to get away; to misplace (Did you *lose* your umbrella?)
mine (pronoun)	possessive pronoun meaning "belonging to me" (That book is *mine.*)
mind (noun)	mental capacity (Your *mind* can play tricks on you.)
mind (verb)	to obey (You should *mind* your mother.)
passed (verb)	past tense of *to pass* (The train *passed* through the town.)
past (noun)	former times or belonging to former times (It is easy to forget the *past.*)
past (preposition)	beyond in time or position (The burglar slipped *past* the guard.)
peace	opposite of war; tranquillity (The President was determined to keep the *peace.*)
piece	part of (May I have that *piece* of cake?)
personal (adjective)	of or pertaining to a particular person; private (Is this a *personal* call?)
personnel (noun)	those employed by an organization or business (He was referred to the *personnel* department.)
principal (noun)	a governing officer of a school (The *principal* of our high school is Mr. Drake.)
	sum of money on which interest is calculated (I was able to pay the interest on my loan but not the principal.)
principal (adjective)	first in importance (The *principal* actor in the play was ill.)
principle	a fundamental truth, law, or doctrine; a rule of conduct (Mr. Adams is a man of *principle.*)
quiet	not noisy (The library was unusually *quiet.*)
quite	somewhat or rather (The girl was *quite* shocked by the remark.)
rise	to ascend; to move upward (The sun *rises* in the east.)
raise	to lift or cause something to move upward (He wants to *raise* his grades.)
sight	a spectacle; view; scene (The *sight* of the mountains awed him.)
site	a location (They chose a new *site* for the building.)
cite	to quote or use as evidence (He *cited* me as an authority.)
sit	to assume a seated position (Please *sit* in that chair.)
set	to place something (Please *set* the chair by the window.)
than	used in a comparison (Ray is faster *than* George.)
then	at that time (Can you leave *then*?)
there	an adverb of place (*There* is our room.)
their	possessive pronoun meaning "belonging to them" (Where is *their* room?)
they're	contraction of "they are" (*They're* in that room.)
threw	past tense of *to throw* (They *threw* the frisbee across the room.)
through	in one side and out the other; by way of (It went *through* the window.)
though	despite; commonly used at the end of a sentence or with *as* or *even* (He looked as *though* he were exhausted.)
to	used as a preposition (*to* the stars) or with a verb as an infinitive (*to* go)
too	also; to an excessive degree (The car was *too* crowded for him to go *too.*)
two	the number *2* (The child was *two* years old.)

who's	a contraction meaning "who is" or "who has" (*Who's* there?)
whose	a possessive pronoun meaning "belonging to whom" (*Whose* car are we taking?)
your	possessive pronoun meaning "belonging to you" (I like *your* idea.)
you're	contraction meaning "you are" (*You're* wrong about that!)
weather	pertains to the climate (The *weather* is expected to turn cold.)
whether	if it is the case that; in case (I'm not sure *whether* he is going.)

ADDITIONAL PROBLEM WORDS

Although, as a rule, spelling lists are practically useless in improving spelling skills, there are a few words that are so consistently misspelled by students that it might be worth your time to master them. Notice, as you look at this list of problem spelling words, that many of them are misspelled because they are often not pronounced correctly. The words are divided into syllables, with the accented syllables marked so you can check your pronunciation. Say the words aloud as you study them. If you are saying the words incorrectly, try to correct your pronunciation. Pay particular attention to the underlined letters because that is the part of the word that usually causes the spelling error.

athlete (ath′ lete)—two syllables, not three, not athelete

different (dif′ fer ent)—three syllables, not two

environment (en vi′ ron ment)—notice the n

February (Feb′ ru ar y)—notice the r

finally (fi′ nal ly)—three syllables, not two

government (gov′ ern ment)—notice the n

grammar (gram′ mar)—ends in ar not er

interest (in′ ter est)—three syllables, not two

library (li′ brar y)—notice the r

listening (lis′ ten ing)—three syllables, not two

probably (prob′ a bly)—three syllables, not two

quiet (qui′ et)—two syllables, not one; do not confuse with quite

recognize (rec′ og nize)—notice the g

separate (sep′ a rate)—middle vowel is a not e

similar (sim′ i lar)—last syllable is lar not ler or liar

sophomore (soph′ o more)—three syllables, not two

supposed (sup posed′)—don't forget the d if you are using past tense (*He was supposed to call.*)

used (used)—don't forget the d if you are using past tense (*I used to sing.*)

COMPOUND WORDS

Many words are formed in English by a process known as compounding. That is, a new word is made by the combination of two familiar words. *Truck stop,* for example, is a relatively new compound that is still written as two words. The tendency, however, is for compound words to be written (eventually) as one word, as in *hangover, handbook, babysitter,* and *typewriter.* Historically, the compound word was initially written as two words, then as a hyphenated word, and finally as one word. For example, *week end* became *week-end* and then *weekend.* Recently the trend has been for compound words to change from two words to one without going through the hyphenated stage.

Most compound words are easy to spell because they are made up of two familiar words. However, it is sometimes difficult to remember whether the compound is written as one word or two. Occasionally, also, the spelling of the compound word is altered slightly when it becomes one word. Thus, the word *although* is spelled with one *l* in *all* rather than two.

The following categories of compound words will help you remember whether the compounds in them should be written as one word or two. However, you should consult your dictionary if you are in doubt.

1. Compound Words Spelled as Two Words
   a lot, all right (These two words are frequently misspelled as one word rather than two.)

2. Hyphenated Compound Words
   a. *mother-in-law, son-in-law,* etc.
   b. *self-concept, self-image, self-hypnosis* (all compounds beginning with self)
   c. *ex-husband, ex-wife, ex-president,* etc.
   d. *pro-Communist, pro-abortion,* etc.

3. Compound Words Spelled as One Word
   a. *everybody, somebody, anything, everyone, someone, something, anybody, sometime, anyplace, someplace,* etc.
   b. *whenever, wherever, whatever, whichever,* etc.
   c. *although, altogether, always, already, almost* (Note that each of these compound words has only one *l.*)
   d. *moreover, therefore, however, nonetheless,* etc.

FORMING THE PLURAL OF NOUNS

By far the most common way to change a singular noun to a plural noun is to add the inflectional suffix *s* to the word (*car, cars; feeling, feelings; note, notes*). There are, however, several other rules for the formation of plurals you should also know to eliminate distracting spelling errors.

1. To form the plural of words that end with an *s* sound (*s, x, z, ch, sh*), add *es* (*boss, bosses; fox, foxes; buzz, buzzes; ditch, ditches; dish, dishes*).

2. To form the plural of words that end in *y* preceded by a single vowel, add just an *s* (*tray, trays; key, keys; toy, toys; guy, guys*). But to form the plural of words that end in *y* preceded by a consonant, change the *y* to *i* and add *es* (*baby, babies; enemy, enemies*).

3. To form the plural of words that end in *is,* change the *is* to *es* (*basis, bases; analysis, analyses; synopsis, synopses*).

4. To form the plural of some words that end in *f* or *fe,* change the *f* to *v* and add *es* (*leaf, leaves; knife, knives; wife, wives; loaf, loaves; self, selves*).

5. To form the plural of words that end in *o,* add *s* or *es.* The plural of many of these words can be formed either way; with some, however,

there is no choice. The following clues are helpful in determining which ending some words require:

    a. To form the plural of words that end in a vowel plus *o* (*ao, eo, io, oo, uo*), add just an *s* (*stereo, stereos; duo, duos; studio, studios*).

    b. To form the plural of musical terms that end in *o*, add just an *s* (*piano, pianos; solo, solos; combo, combos; cello, cellos*).

    c. To form the plural of *tomato* and *potato*, add *es* (*tomato, tomatoes; potato, potatoes*).

To determine whether other words that end in *o* require an *s* or *es*, check your dictionary.

6. Some words form the plural irregularly by changing internally rather than by the addition of an inflectional suffix (*man, men; woman, women; child, children; mouse, mice; foot, feet*).

7. Some words have the same form in both the singular and the plural (*fish, moose, sheep, deer*).

FORMING POSSESSIVES

Both nouns and pronouns have possessive forms, but the rules for forming possessive nouns and pronouns differ. Learning to form possessives correctly will enable you to eliminate another spelling problem.

Possessive Nouns

Failure to indicate correctly that a noun is possessive causes many needless spelling errors. The rules for forming the possessive are regular and easy to apply.

1. To form the possessive of singular nouns, add an apostrophe and an *s* (*'s*) to the noun.

George's car was in the garage.

My boss's hat is ridiculous.

Today's mail needs to be sorted.

Notice that it does not matter what letter the noun ends in; *all* singular nouns form the possessive by the addition of an apostrophe and an *s* to the noun.

Note: The rule for forming the singular possessive is presently in some dispute. Some authorities now say that if the singular noun ends in an *s*, you may add just an apostrophe after the *s*. Others say that only if the singular noun is a proper noun of one syllable may you omit the *s* and add just the apostrophe. To avoid confusion and controversy, it is better to apply the simple rule given above to all singular nouns, regardless of their final letter or whether they are common or proper.

2. To form the possessive of plural nouns that do not end in an *s*, you also add an apostrophe and an *s* (*'s*) to the noun.

The children's coats were unbuttoned.

He looked into the deer's eyes.

The women's club is meeting in the auditorium.

3. However, to form the possessive of plural nouns that end in *s*, you add just an apostrophe after the *s* ('*s*).

   The cats' tails have all been cut off.

   Dust covered the books' covers.

   The boys' teachers were invited to the meeting.

Now review the steps in forming the possessive of a noun:

1. Determine if the noun is possessive.
2. Determine if the noun is singular or plural.
3. Apply the appropriate rule.

Possessive Pronouns

The possessive pronouns are *my, mine, your, yours, our, ours, his, her, hers, their, theirs,* and *its.*

> *My* dress is torn.
>
> That book is *hers.*
>
> The tree has shed *its* leaves.
>
> Do they want *their* papers returned?

Notice that possessive pronouns *do not* require apostrophes. Rather than adding an inflectional ending (such as an apostrophe and *s* or just an apostrophe) as you do in forming the possessive of nouns, you form the possessive of pronouns by changing the word itself. Thus the pronoun *I* changes to *my* or *mine; we* becomes *our* or *ours; you* becomes *your* or *yours,* and so on.

Note: Three possessive pronouns (*its, your,* and *their*) are pronounced exactly the same as three contractions (*it's, you're,* and *they're*), which do require apostrophes. *It's* is a contraction of *it is; you're* is a contraction of *you are;* and *they're* is a contraction of *they are.* Be careful in your writing not to confuse the contraction with the possessive form. Remember that possessive pronouns *do not* require apostrophes.

FOUR USEFUL SPELLING PATTERNS

There are no simple rules that will eliminate all spelling problems, but the following spelling patterns will help you improve your spelling.

Spelling Pattern for Dropping or Keeping Final *E*

1. To add a suffix beginning with a vowel to a word ending in a final *e*, drop the silent *e* (examples: *usage, safest, caring*).
2. To add a suffix beginning with a consonant to a word ending in a final *e*, keep the silent *e* (examples: *lovely, useless, safety*).

Exceptions:

1. Words ending in *ue* drop the final *e* before a suffix beginning with a consonant (examples: *argument, duly, truly*).
2. Words that have a *c* or *g* before the final *e* keep the *e* before the suffixes *-able* and *-ous* (examples: *noticeable, courageous, changeable, advantageous, peaceable*).
3. awe + ful = awful
4. whole + ly = wholly

Spelling Pattern for Final Y

1. To add a suffix not beginning with an *i* to a word that ends in *y* preceded by a consonant, change the *y* to *i* (examples: *happiness, copier, cried*)
2. To add a suffix to a word that ends in *y* preceded by a vowel (*a, e, i, o, u*), do not change the *y* to *i* (examples: *employer, keys, enjoyment*).
3. To add a suffix beginning with an *i* to a word that ends in *y*, do not change the *y* to *i* (examples: *copying, fortyish, playing*).

Exceptions: daily, gaily, paid, said, laid, shyly, shyness, slyly, slyness, dryly, dryer (the machine), all proper nouns (Kennedy + s = Kennedys; Harry + s = Harrys)

Spelling Pattern for EI/IE Words

1. The *i* comes before the *e* if a *c* does not immediately precede it (examples: *believe, niece, yield*).
2. The *e* comes before the *i* if these letters are immediately preceded by a *c* (examples: *receive, deceit, ceiling*).
3. If the sound of the letters is a long *a*, the *e* comes before the *i* (examples: *vein, weight, neighbor*).

This pattern is most often stated in the form of this familiar rhyme:

Write *i* before *e*
Except after *c*
Or when sounded as *a*
As in *neighbor* and *weigh.*

Exceptions: There are a number of exceptions to this rule. Concentrate on remembering the five most common: *either, neither, seize, weird,* and *leisure.*

Spelling Pattern for Doubling the Final Consonant

Double the final consonant when adding a suffix beginning with a vowel if the word ends in a single consonant preceded by a single vowel and meets either of the following additional criteria:

1. It consists of only one syllable (examples: *bigger, dimmer, stopper*).
2. It is accented on the last syllable (examples: *referred, occurred, beginning*).

Appendix 3

FORMS OF IRREGULAR VERBS

PRESENT TENSE		PRESENT PARTICIPLE	PAST TENSE	PAST PARTICIPLE
First & Second Person Singular	Third Person Singular	(Use with form of *to be*)		(Use *have, has,* or *had*)
1. arise	arises	arising	arose	arisen
2. awake	awakes	awaking	awoke (awaked)	awoke (awaked)
3. bear	bears	bearing	bore	borne (born)
4. beat	beats	beating	beat	beaten
5. begin	begins	beginning	began	begun
6. bend	bends	bending	bent	bent
7. bite	bites	biting	bit	bitten
8. bleed	bleeds	bleeding	bled	bled
9. blow	blows	blowing	blew	blown
10. break	breaks	breaking	broke	broken
11. build	builds	building	built	built
12. burst	bursts	bursting	burst	burst
13. catch	catches	catching	caught	caught
14. choose	chooses	choosing	chose	chosen
15. cling	clings	clinging	clung	clung
16. creep	creeps	creeping	crept	crept
17. deal	deals	dealing	dealt	dealt
18. draw	draws	drawing	drew	drawn
19. dream	dreams	dreaming	dreamed	dreamed
20. drink	drinks	drinking	drank	drunk
21. dwell	dwells	dwelling	dwelt (dwelled)	dwelt (dwelled)
22. eat	eats	eating	ate	eaten
23. fall	falls	falling	fell	fallen
24. feed	feeds	feeding	fed	fed
25. fling	flings	flinging	flung	flung
26. fly	flies	flying	flew	flown
27. forget	forgets	forgetting	forgot	forgotten (forgot)
28. freeze	freezes	freezing	froze	frozen
29. get	gets	getting	got	got (gotten)
30. give	gives	giving	gave	given
31. go	goes	going	went	gone
32. grow	grows	growing	grew	grown

	PRESENT TENSE		PRESENT PARTICIPLE	PAST TENSE	PAST PARTICIPLE
	First & Second Person Singular	**Third Person Singular**	**(Use with form of to be)**		**(Use have, has, or had)**
33.	hang	hangs	hanging	hung (hanged)	hung (hanged)
34.	have	has	having	had	had
35.	hide	hides	hiding	hid	hidden
36.	hit	hits	hitting	hit	hit
37.	keep	keeps	keeping	kept	kept
38.	know	knows	knowing	knew	known
39.	lay	lays	laying	laid	laid
40.	lead	leads	leading	led	led
41.	leave	leaves	leaving	left	left
42.	lend	lends	lending	lent	lent
43.	lie	lies	lying	lay	lain
44.	light	lights	lighting	lighted (lit)	lighted (lit)
45.	lose	loses	losing	lost	lost
46.	mean	means	meaning	meant	meant
47.	pay	pays	paying	paid	paid
48.	ride	rides	riding	rode	ridden
49.	rise	rises	rising	rose	risen
50.	see	sees	seeing	saw	seen
51.	sew	sews	sewing	sewed	sewn (sewed)
52.	shine	shines	shining	shone (shined)	shone (shined)
53.	shrink	shrinks	shrinking	shrank (shrunk)	shrunk (shrunken)
54.	sink	sinks	sinking	sank	sunk
55.	sit	sits	sitting	sat	sat
56.	sleep	sleeps	sleeping	slept	slept
57.	slide	slides	sliding	slid	slid
58.	sling	slings	slinging	slung	slung
59.	speak	speaks	speaking	spoke	spoken
60.	spend	spends	spending	spent	spent
61.	spit	spits	spitting	spit (spat)	spit (spat)
62.	split	splits	splitting	split	split
63.	spoil	spoils	spoiling	spoiled (spoilt)	spoiled (spoilt)
64.	spread	spreads	spreading	spread	spread
65.	spring	springs	springing	sprang	sprung
66.	stand	stands	standing	stood	stood
67.	steal	steals	stealing	stole	stolen
68.	stick	sticks	sticking	stuck	stuck
69.	sting	stings	stinging	stung	stung
70.	stink	stinks	stinking	stank (stunk)	stunk
71.	string	strings	stringing	strung	strung
72.	swear	swears	swearing	swore	sworn
73.	sweat	sweats	sweating	sweat (sweated)	sweat (sweated)

	PRESENT TENSE		PRESENT PARTICIPLE	PAST TENSE	PAST PARTICIPLE
	First & Second Person Singular	**Third Person Singular**	**(Use with form of *to be*)**		**(Use *have, has,* or *had*)**
74.	swell	swells	swelling	swelled	swelled (swollen)
75.	swim	swims	swimming	swam	swum
76.	swing	swings	swinging	swung	swung
77.	teach	teaches	teaching	taught	taught
78.	throw	throws	throwing	threw	thrown
79.	wake	wakes	waking	waked (woke)	waked (waken)
80.	weep	weeps	weeping	wept	wept
81.	wring	wrings	wringing	wrung	wrung
82.	write	writes	writing	wrote	written

Appendix 4

PUNCTUATION

PERIOD

1. Use a period after a declarative sentence.

   A zebra cannot change its stripes.

2. Use a period after an abbreviation (*examples:* Mr., Ms., U.S., S.P.C.A., approx., p.m., a.m.).

QUESTION MARK

Use a question mark after a direct question.

Does this elephant belong to you?

SEMICOLON

1. Use a semicolon in a compound sentence that does not include a coordinating conjunction to join the two independent clauses.

   The elephant belongs to my cousin; the giraffe is mine.

2. Use a semicolon in a compound sentence in which a conjunctive adverb joins the two independent clauses.

The elephant is too wide; however, the giraffe is too tall.

3. Use a semicolon to separate items in a series if the items contain internal commas.

The awards were presented to Big Foot, the elephant; Long Tusk, the walrus; and Long Neck, the giraffe.

APOSTROPHE

1. Use an apostrophe for a possessive noun.

The giraffe's neck is too long.

2. Use an apostrophe for a contraction (*examples:* it's, can't, doesn't, wasn't, couldn't).

QUOTATION MARKS

1. Use quotation marks to enclose a direct quotation.

My cousin asked, "Can my elephant get through the door?"

2. Use quotation marks to enclose the title of a short work (story, essay, song, or poem) to which you are referring.

I like the song "Giraffes Are a Man's Best Friend."

COMMA

1. Use a comma to *separate* the following:

   a. Two independent clauses connected by a coordinating conjunction

   I took my giraffe for a walk, but my cousin stayed at home with his elephant.

   b. Items in a series

   I would like to adopt an aardvark, a walrus, and a crocodile.

   c. Coordinate adjectives that precede a noun

   A neat, courteous rhinoceros would not be a bad pet either.

   d. An introductory modifier from the main clause, especially if it is long or loosely connected to the rest of the sentence

   Wandering through the zoo last week, I saw several animals that I liked.

   However, my wife thinks that we have enough pets.

   Of all the women I have known in my lifetime, she is the most unreasonable.

   e. An introductory adverbial clause from the main clause

   Until we move to a larger house, I guess I'll have to be satisfied with my giraffe and kangaroo.

   f. Items in dates and addresses

   Until then, we'll continue to live at 4321 Animal Crackers Avenue, Beastville, Iowa.

But by January 1, 1999, I hope to move to New York, New York, and rent a large penthouse that will accommodate as many as fifteen new animals.

2. Use commas to *enclose* the following:

   a. A nonrestrictive adjective clause

   My cousin, who also owns a buffalo, lives in a smaller house than ours.

   b. An appositive

   The buffalo, a large male with an impressive hump on its back, stays in the back yard.

   c. A parenthetical expression or interrupter

   My cousin, of course, is not married.

   d. A noun used in direct address

   "Don't worry, Cousin George, you will find a woman some day who loves animals."

   e. Expressions designating the speaker in direct quotations

   "I'm not worried," he said, "just lonely."

COLON

1. Use a colon at the end of a sentence to direct attention to a summary or appositive.

   Eventually, George and I would like to have the following animals: a walrus, a rhinoceros, a crocodile, a sea lion, an aardvark, and a laughing hyena.

2. Use a colon after the salutation of a business letter.

   Dear Ms. Wolf:

3. Use a colon between a title and subtitle, between figures indicating the chapter and verse of a biblical reference, and between the hour and minute of a time reference.

   Adopting Animals: Theory and Practice

   Luke 2:13

   Monday at 4:30 P.M.

DASH

1. Use a dash to mark a sudden break in thought or tone.

   Most animals—notice that I said *most*, not *all*—are friendly and gentle.

2. Use a dash to set off a brief summary or an appositive that is loosely related to the sentence in which it appears.

   My giraffe—the animal I have had longest and that I love best—is named Alfred.

3. Use a dash to set off a parenthetical element or appositive that has commas within it.

   I have never met an ugly animal—an animal that I couldn't love, admire, and enjoy.

Acknowledgments (continued)

"Getting 'em Ready for Darrell" by Larry King is reprinted by permission of the *Texas Observer*. Copyright © 1970, Texas Observer Publishing Company.

From *Dateline America* by Charles Kuralt, copyright © 1979 by CBS Inc. Reprinted by permission of Harcourt Brace Jovanovich, Inc.

Reprinted from *The Mirages of Marriage* by William J. Lederer and Don D. Jackson, by permission of W. W. Norton & Company, Inc. Copyright © 1968 by W. W. Norton & Company, Inc.

From Matthews et al, *Investigating the Earth,* pp. 438, 442. Copyright © 1984. Reprinted by permission of Houghton Mifflin Company.

Reprinted from *The Way to Rainy Mountain* by N. Scott Momaday. Copyright © 1969, the University of New Mexico Press. Reprinted by permission.

From Ashley Montagu, *The American Way of Life* (New York: Putnam's, 1952), pp. 243–44. Reprinted by permission of the author.

From Mary Beth Norton et al., *A People and a Nation: A History of the United States.* Reprinted by permission of Houghton Mifflin Company.

"On Boxing" by Joyce Carol Oates. Copyright © 1985 by The New York Times Company. Reprinted by permission.

Perry: *Unfinished Journey: A World History,* p. 720, is reprinted by permission of Houghton Mifflin Company.

From Chaim Potok: *The Book of Lights.* Reprinted by permission of the author.

From *Aria: A Memoir of a Bilingual Childhood* by Richard Rodriguez. Reprinted by permission of the author. Copyright © 1980 by Richard Rodriguez. First published in *The American Scholar.*

From *Basic Concepts of Chemistry,* 3rd. edition by Sherman, Sherman, and Russikoff. Reprinted by permission of Houghton Mifflin Company.

From *Insult to Intelligence: The Bureaucratic Invasion of Our Classrooms* by Frank Smith. Reprinted by permission of Arbor House.

From Syfers, Judy, "I Want a Wife," originally published in *MS. Magazine,* Spring 1972, p. 56. Copyright © 1971 by Judy Syfers. Reprinted by permission of the author.

From *Future Shock* by Alvin Toffler. Copyright © 1970 by Alvin Toffler. Reprinted by permission of Random House, Inc.

392

Index

Reading process *(continued)*
  purpose in, 7
  questioning in, 6–7, 10, 208
  rate, varying, 7
  reciting in, 10, 14, 208
  responding in, 10–11, 208
  reviewing in, 8, 10, 14, 208
  SQ4R, 9–14, 208
  surveying in, 6, 10, 208
Reading/writing process, 3–9
  preparation for (first stage), 6–7
  processing of (middle stage), 7–8
  review in (last stage), 8–9
  stages of, 3–6
Regular verbs, 240
Relative pronouns, 253–254
Repetition
  of key words and ideas, 144–146
  of structure, 146–149
Reporter's questions, 180–181, 208
Restrictive adjective clause, 347
Revising, 9, 65, 239
Rewriting, 8–9, 65–66, 225, 239–240
  editing, 9, 65–66, 225, 239–240
  proofreading, 9, 66, 240
  revising, 9, 65, 239
  suggestions for, 65–66
Roots, word, 17, 213, 266
Run-on sentences, 329–330

"Scratch" outlines, 94–95
Second-person point of view, 255–257
Semicolon
  in compound sentences, 319–321, 323–324, 329, 389–390
  items in a series, 390
Sensory details, 72–77
  in descriptive paragraphs, 110–111
Sentences, 225, 226
  complex, 342–366
  compound, 316–331
  simple, 226–259
Sentence order, inverted, 249
Sentence patterns, 233–239
  subject-linking verb-complement, 236–238
  subject-verb, 233–234
  subject-verb-object, 235–236
Signal words
  in complex sentences, 343, 347, 351, 357–358
  in compound sentences, 316, 321–322, 324–325
  in narrative paragraphs, 109
  of order of importance, 140–141
  of space order, 140
  of time order, 139
Simple sentences, 226–259
  basic patterns of, 233–239
  editing, 239–259

essential elements of, 226–233
modification of, 269–305
Singular
  indefinite pronouns, 246–247, 252
  subjects and verbs, 240–251
  third person forms, 240–241, 387–389
Sound-alike/look-alike words, 379–382
Space order, 140
Spatial arrangement, 140
  in descriptive paragraphs, 111–112
Specific and general. *See* General and specific.
Specific details, 72–77
  in narrative paragraphs, 109
Spelling, 379–386
  compound words, 382–383
  doubling the final consonant, 386
  ei/ie words, 386
  final *e*, 385–386
  final *y*, 386
  improving spelling skills, 379
  look-alike/sound-alike words, 379–382
  patterns, 385–386
  plural nouns, 383–384
  possessives, 384–385
  problem words, 379–382
SQ4R, 9–14, 208
Statements, general, 25–28, 73–75
  as main ideas, 42–43
Study outlines, 191–193
Subject
  complement, 236–237
  compound, 227, 248–249
  nouns as, 228
  pronouns as, 228–229, 235–236
  of a sentence, 226–230
  in topic sentences, 43, 46–47
  vocabulary for specific subjects, 212–214
  in writing situation, 67–68, 134
Subject forms of pronouns, 235–236, 238
Subject-linking verb-complement pattern, 236–238
Subject-verb agreement, 240–251
  with compound subjects, 248–249
  with indefinite pronoun subjects, 246–247
  with intervening phrases, 248
  with inverted sentence order, 249–250
  special problems with, 246–251
Subject-verb-object pattern, 235–236
Subject-verb pattern, 233–234
Subordinate clause fragments, 364–366
Subordinate clauses, 342–353, 357–366

adjective clauses, 347–350
adverb clauses, 343–347
noun clauses, 351–353
punctuation of, 362–363
subordinate conjunctions, 343, 357–358
Subordination, 342–366
  in complex sentences, 342–366
  and coordination, 80–83
  in outlining, 92–93
  in paragraphs, 79–80
Suffixes, 17
  -ary, 69
  -ate, 69
  -ed, 36, 266
  -ent, 266
  -ly, 36, 64
  -or, 69
  -ous, 266
  -tion, 69, 213, 266
Summarizing, 193–201
  essays and chapters, 198–201
  guidelines for, 194–195
  reading the selection, 194
  writing the summary, 194–195
Supporting main ideas, 72–95
  factual and sensory details, 72–77
  coordination and subordination of details, 77–92
  outlining supporting details, 92–95
Surveying, in reading, 6, 10, 208
Synonyms, 373

Tense, verb, 230–232
  consistency in, 257–259
  irregular, 387–389
  participle forms, past and present, 387–389
  past, 387–389
  present, 240–241, 387–389
  regular, 240
Third-person point of view, 255–257
Third-person singular verbs, 240–241, 387–389
Time order, 139–140
Titles, 46–47
To be, conjugation of, 241
To do, conjugation of, 241
To have, conjugation of, 241
Tone, 134
Topic sentences, 42–58
  main idea, as, 43
  narrowing, 47–50
  subject and focus in, 43, 46–47
Transition, 144–153
  in narrative paragraphs, 109
  order of importance, 140–141
  repetition of key words and ideas, 144–146
  repetition of structure, 146–149
  signal words, 109, 139–141, 149–153

To the Student

We hope that you will take a few minutes to fill out this questionnaire. The comments you make will help us plan future editions of *Contexts*. After you have completed the following questions, please mail this sheet to:

College Marketing
Houghton Mifflin Company
One Beacon Street
Boston, MA 02108

1. Name of college or university _____

2. Which chapters in *Contexts* did you find most helpful?

   _____

   Why? _____

   _____

3. Which chapters did you find least helpful? _____

   Why? _____

   _____

4. Were the exercises in *Contexts* useful? _____

   Were there enough exercises? _____

5. Did you find the reading passages used for the examples and in the chapter exercises interesting? _____

   Which did you enjoy most? _____

   Which did you enjoy least? _____

6. Were the appendixes useful to you? _____

7. Were any reading selections difficult or confusing? Which ones? _____

   _____

   _____

8. Were any chapters too difficult or confusing? Which ones? _____

   _____

9. Please rate the reading passages in the Reading/Writing Assignments.

Reading/Writing Assignments

		Excellent	Good	Fair	Poor	Didn't Read
1A	How to Mark a Book	___	___	___	___	___
1B	The Benefits of Freewriting	___	___	___	___	___
2A	Graduation Day	___	___	___	___	___
2B	College—A New Beginning	___	___	___	___	___
3A	The Language of Clothes	___	___	___	___	___
3B	Bad Students	___	___	___	___	___
4A	A Kiowa Grandmother	___	___	___	___	___
4B	My Native Place	___	___	___	___	___
5A	What is an American?	___	___	___	___	___
5B	Should Men Cry?	___	___	___	___	___
6A	I Want a Wife	___	___	___	___	___
6B	Making Camp	___	___	___	___	___
7A	Teen Privacy	___	___	___	___	___
7B	Getting 'em Ready for Darrell	___	___	___	___	___
8A	The Great Crash and the Great Depression	___	___	___	___	___
8B	Public vs. Private Language	___	___	___	___	___
9A	Elvis Is Dead	___	___	___	___	___
9B	Television Fantasies	___	___	___	___	___
10A	A Lesson in Life	___	___	___	___	___
10B	Aging in the Land of the Young	___	___	___	___	___
11A	The Human Brain and the Computer	___	___	___	___	___
11B	Types of Loneliness	___	___	___	___	___
12A	The Throw-Away Society	___	___	___	___	___
12B	The Good Teacher	___	___	___	___	___

10. Please make any additional comments that you think might be useful. _____

_____

Thank you very much.

Your name (*optional*) _____